Getting Started with

Microsoft®
Excel 4
for Windows™

SECOND EDITION

Getting Started with

Microsoft®
Excel 4
for Windows™

SECOND EDITION

Ralph Soucie

PUBLISHED BY
Microsoft Press
A Division of Microsoft Corporation
One Microsoft Way
Redmond, Washington 98052-6399

Copyright © 1992 by Ralph Soucie

Library of Congress Cataloging-in-Publication Data
Soucie, Ralph, 1952–
    Getting started with Microsoft Excel for Windows / Ralph Soucie.
      p. cm. -- (The Getting started right series)
    Includes index.
    ISBN 1-55615-487-9
    1. Microsoft Excel 3 for Windows (Computer program)   2. Business-
-Computer programs.   3. Electronic spreadsheets.   4. Windows
(Computer programs)   I. Title.   II. Series.
HF5548.4.M523S677   1992
650'.0285'5369--dc20   92-10287
                                                                       CIP

Printed and bound in the United States of America.

2 3 4 5 6 7 8 9 AGAG 7 6 5 4 3 2

Distributed to the book trade in Canada by Macmillan of Canada, a division of Canada Publishing Corporation.

Distributed to the book trade outside the United States and Canada by Penguin Books Ltd.

Penguin Books Ltd., Harmondsworth, Middlesex, England
Penguin Books Australia Ltd., Ringwood, Victoria, Australia
Penguin Books N.Z. Ltd., 182–190 Wairau Road, Auckland 10, New Zealand

British Cataloging-in-Publication Data available.

Acquisitions Editor: Marjorie Schlaikjer
Project Editor: JoAnne Woodcock
Technical Editor: Jerry Joyce

To Jeff and Heidi

Contents

Section I: Worksheets

Section II: Charts and Databases

Section IV: Appendixes

Acknowledgments

I would like to thank the following people at Microsoft Press: JoAnne Woodcock, for her efficiency and pleasant attitude as she edited this book; Jerry Joyce, for his attention to technical details; and Marjorie Schlaikjer, for watching over all of us. Thanks also to Mary DeJong and Lucinda Rowley.

Finally, thanks to the product development team at Microsoft Corporation for their outstanding work on version 4 of Microsoft Excel.

Introduction

Microsoft Excel version 3 was an outstanding product, most experts agree. Version 4 raises the Excel standard to a new level. This version streamlines mundane spreadsheet tasks while greatly enhancing the program's power and flexibility. Whether the task is simple or complex, Microsoft Excel dissolves barriers between mind and data.

WHAT'S NEW WITH VERSION 4

Microsoft Excel version 4 includes nine new toolbars and a drag-and-drop feature for quick moving and copying of data. Charting is more automated thanks to a new ChartWizard. Microsoft has also added hundreds of new functions and a formidable collection of tools for analysis and management of multiple-worksheet models. Printing and reporting are more flexible, and it's easier than ever to migrate from Lotus 1-2-3 to Excel.

SYSTEM REQUIREMENTS

To use Microsoft Excel, you need the following equipment:

- An Industry Standard Architecture (ISA) computer, such as an IBM PC/AT or compatible, or a Micro Channel Architecture (MCA) computer, such as an IBM Personal System/2 or compatible

- At least 2 megabytes of random access memory

- One floppy-disk drive and a hard disk with at least 6 megabytes of space available

- A VGA, Super VGA, EGA, or compatible display; or a Hercules Graphics card or compatible display

Technically, a mouse is optional, but you should consider it a requirement. The examples in this book assume you have a mouse installed. Chapter 1, however, does include keyboard instructions, so if you don't have a mouse, you can still proceed to learn Excel right away.

You must also have installed MS-DOS version 3.1 or higher and Microsoft Windows version 3.0 or higher. Microsoft Windows must be running in Standard or 386 Enhanced mode.

USING THIS BOOK

Getting Started with Microsoft Excel 4 for Windows is a complete introduction to Microsoft Excel for MS-DOS computers running Windows. Its purpose is to get you up and running in the shortest possible time. Working through all the chapters and experimenting on your own is your quickest route to power-user status.

What's in This Book?

This book covers all the basics of Microsoft Excel, plus a good selection of the program's sophisticated features. Although certain advanced topics, such as auditing tools and the Solver, are not covered, the book provides a solid foundation in a short time.

Getting Started with Microsoft Excel 4 for Windows is divided into the four sections described below.

Section I (Chapters 1 through 5) is devoted to worksheets. After a general introduction in Chapter 1, you move on to formulas and functions in Chapter 2. You also learn how to assign names to ranges within a worksheet. Chapter 3 shows you how to revise worksheets by copying and by moving data around, and it shows you how to use data protection. In Chapter 4 you learn how to format worksheets to display data the way you want it to appear, and you learn how to attach informative notes to cells. Chapter 5 covers the topic of printing Microsoft Excel documents.

Section II (Chapters 6 through 8) explains charts and databases. In Chapter 6 you'll run through Microsoft Excel's automated ChartWizard feature for producing quick charts. Chapter 7 covers some of the finer points of formatting charts for maximum impact. In Chapter 8 you'll learn how to create a database in an Excel worksheet, and you'll see how to find and extract data.

Section III prepares you to work on larger projects. Chapter 9 teaches you how to link worksheets and group them together for filing and editing purposes. Chapter 10 explains Excel's customization features. It also covers some heavy-duty analysis tools, such as the Scenario Manager and the Crosstab ReportWizard. Chapter 11 shows you how to use the macro recorder to automate spreadsheet operations.

Section IV contains three appendixes. Appendix A helps you install Microsoft Excel on your hard disk. Appendix B is a reference to the Excel toolbars described in this book. Appendix C gives Lotus 1-2-3 users guidance in migrating to Microsoft Excel.

Getting the Most from This Book

Every chapter in this book refers back to at least one previous chapter, so you will get the best results by working through the chapters in sequence. However, if you are in a hurry to learn some of version 4's power features, skipping topics such as charting won't cause significant problems.

Naturally, you can stop working at any time and pick up later where you left off. Before ending a Microsoft Excel session, however, be sure to save your work first. (See Chapter 1 for instructions on saving files.)

Typographic Conventions

Getting Started with Microsoft Excel 4 for Windows uses certain typographic conventions for clarity. When the text instructs you to enter data, you'll normally see the data printed on a line by itself in special type, as in the following phrase:

    August 1992

When an instruction is embedded in a paragraph, the data to be entered is printed in italic type, as in this example: "Type the heading *Northeast Region* and press Enter."

Keystroke combinations requiring you to hold down one key while pressing another are represented in two ways. In the earlier chapters, the combinations are described in detail: "Hold down the Ctrl key while pressing the Enter key." Later on, the combinations are sometimes abbreviated: "Press Ctrl-Enter."

Special symbols draw your attention to Tips and Cautions throughout the text to alert you to techniques for saving time and avoiding errors.

A FINAL WORD

Learning the many powerful features of Microsoft Excel is quite an enjoyable experience. Simply place *Getting Started with Microsoft Excel 4 for Windows* next to your keyboard, turn to Chapter 1, and have fun!

Section I

Worksheets

Worksheets form the engine that powers Microsoft Excel. In this section, you'll learn how to enter data, create formulas that compute results, and produce attractive, informative reports.

Chapter 1

Getting Acquainted

This chapter introduces Microsoft Excel version 4 and lays the groundwork for the rest of the book. Because you need Microsoft Windows version 3.0 or later to run Excel, the chapter begins with some Windows basics and then moves on to Excel and the components of a worksheet. After starting Excel and learning a few fundamentals, such as how to move around the screen, select cells, choose commands from menus, and work with dialog boxes, you'll pull the pieces together by creating a simple worksheet that summarizes retail sales for a sporting goods store.

 This section assumes that you've already installed Windows with the Windows Setup program. Once Windows is on your computer, you can install Excel. Appendix A, "Installing Microsoft Excel," summarizes the installation procedure. You can also consult the Microsoft Excel documentation.

WINDOWS BASICS

Both Windows and Excel are easier to use with a mouse, so this book assumes that you have installed a mouse and that you know how to move the mouse pointer on the screen. For those of you who have not yet purchased a mouse, this chapter describes how to perform tasks both with the mouse and with the keyboard, but from Chapter 2 on, keyboard methods appear only when they provide handy shortcuts.

TIP *Clicking means moving the mouse pointer to an object and pressing and releasing the left mouse button. Double-clicking means moving the mouse pointer to an object and pressing and releasing the left mouse button twice in succession. Dragging means moving the mouse pointer to an onscreen object, pressing the left mouse button, and moving the mouse while holding down the button.*

Most Windows and Excel mouse operations require you to use the left mouse button, so when you see the phrase "the mouse button," assume the left button. However, certain operations require you to press the right button. In those cases, the text uses the term "right mouse button."

Now for some practice.

■ Start the Windows program by typing *win* at the MS-DOS prompt.

Assuming that you have not customized Windows in any way, the Program Manager window is now displayed on your screen.

CAUTION *This book assumes that your computer is not connected to a network. If you are working on a network, Microsoft Excel will operate exactly as described here, but you'll have to use your customary network procedure for starting Windows.*

STARTING MICROSOFT EXCEL

Windows arranges pictorial representations, called *icons*, of the programs you have installed in Windows into categories, called *groups*. Each group has its own window, which can be fully displayed or shown as an icon. When you install Microsoft Excel, Windows puts the Excel icon in the Microsoft Excel 4.0 group. This group window is probably displayed on your screen as it is in Figure 1-1. If the group appears instead as an icon at the bottom of the Program Manager window, follow these steps:

■ With the mouse, double-click the icon to open the Microsoft Excel 4.0 group window.

■ With the keyboard, hold down Alt and press W to display the Window menu. Type the number to the left of *Microsoft Excel 4.0*.

The Microsoft Excel 4.0 group window also displays icons for the particular Excel-related application programs you chose when you installed Excel on your computer.

Starting Microsoft Excel is easy:

- With the mouse, point to the icon labeled *Microsoft Excel*, and then double-click.

- With the keyboard, press the direction keys to move the highlight to the Excel icon, and then press Enter.

 You can start Microsoft Excel directly from the MS-DOS prompt by typing win excel. *This command first loads Windows and then runs Excel.*

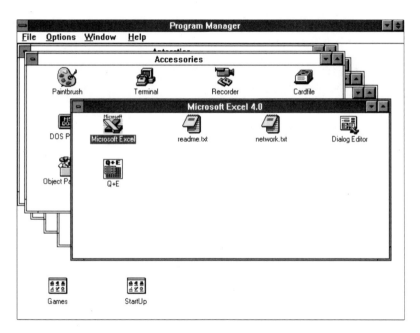

FIGURE 1-1. *The Excel 4.0 group window before you start Excel.*

After a few seconds, you see the screen shown in Figure 1-2.

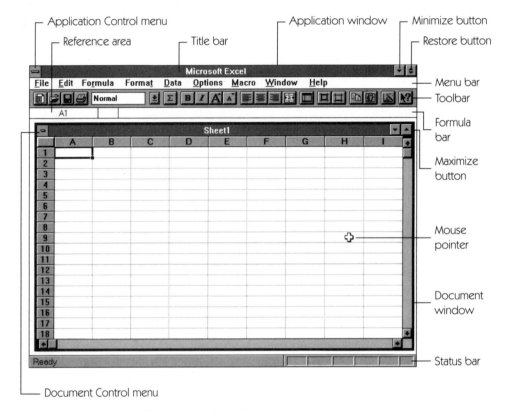

FIGURE 1-2. *The Microsoft Excel window.*

A TOUR OF THE MICROSOFT EXCEL WINDOW

When you first start the Excel program, its window, labeled *Microsoft Excel*, fills the screen. The Microsoft Excel window, known as the *application window,* has many components that you use to size and move the window and to perform Excel operations. You'll see some of these components now and learn about others later in this chapter.

A *title bar* appears at the top of the Microsoft Excel window. At the left end of the title bar is a box labeled with a bar. This box opens the application Control menu (discussed later in this chapter). At the right end of the title bar are two boxes, one labeled with a down arrowhead and the other with stacked up and down arrowheads. These boxes are the Minimize and Restore buttons, which, respectively, allow you to shrink the Microsoft Excel window to an icon and restore a window icon to its former size.

CAUTION *If you are not familiar with the Minimize, Maximize, and Restore buttons, which are standard features of all Windows applications, experiment with them on your own, with a practice document on your screen, so that you know what to expect when you click these buttons. Clicking the Minimize button, for example, "minimizes" the Excel program to an icon at the bottom of the Program Manager screen. To "restore" the program to a window, double-click the icon. If the icon is not visible, hold down the Alt key and press Tab until the message shown below appears, and then release the keys.*

Below the Microsoft Excel window title bar is the *menu bar*, which lists the names of nine menus, each containing commands that you use to give instructions to Excel. Below the menu bar is a *toolbar*. Excel 4 offers nine toolbars; the one you see is the *Standard toolbar*. It contains tool buttons you can click to carry out common program operations. You can use the toolbar only if you have a mouse. You'll learn how to use toolbar tools later in the chapter, and throughout this book, you'll find explanations of specific toolbar operations.

TIP *If you don't have a mouse, Excel does not display the toolbar. With or without a mouse, however, you can turn the toolbar on by pressing Ctrl-7. Press Ctrl-7 again to turn it off.*

Below the toolbar is the *formula bar*, which has three parts. The *reference area* at the left end shows the address of the active cell. (You'll learn about the active cell in a moment.) The middle and right areas of the formula bar should now be blank. You use them when you enter or change data.

A *status bar* appears at the bottom of the Microsoft Excel window. The left part of the bar displays helpful messages. You should now see the message *Ready*, indicating that the program is ready to accept data or to carry out commands. The right part of the status bar displays *keyboard-status indicators*. Right now, this part is probably blank; but if you press the Caps Lock and Num Lock keys, you'll see the indicators shown in Figure 1-3. CAPS tells you that any text you enter will appear in capital letters; NUM indicates that pressing the keys on the numeric keypad will enter numbers in the active cell.

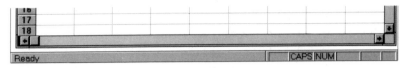

FIGURE 1-3. *The status bar, displaying the Caps Lock and Num Lock indicators.*

A TOUR OF THE DOCUMENT WINDOW

Within the Microsoft Excel window is a *document window*. The document window currently contains Sheet1, a blank *worksheet*. A worksheet is like a gigantic piece of columnar paper on which you organize data by location. Only a small portion of the worksheet, which can potentially contain data in 256 columns and 16,384 rows, is shown in the document window.

A *title bar* at the top of the document window displays the title of the worksheet that appears in the window. (Until you assign a new name—something you will learn later in this chapter—Excel uses a "generic" name, such as Sheet1 in this example.) Like the main Microsoft Excel window title bar, the left end of the document window title bar has a box labeled with a hyphen. This box opens the document Control menu (discussed later in this chapter). At the right end of the document window's title bar is a box labeled with an up arrowhead. You can use this Maximize button to quickly expand the document window to fill as much of the screen as possible. Clicking the Minimize button, located to the left of the Maximize button, shrinks the document to an icon.

 The document Control-menu box also serves as a close box. *Double-clicking the Control-menu box is a quick way of closing the document window.*

The document window is surrounded by a narrow *border*. Down the right side and across the bottom of the window are *scroll bars*. If you create a worksheet too large to be displayed fully in the document window, you use the scroll bars to move different parts of the worksheet into view.

THE MOUSE POINTER

When you move the mouse pointer around the Microsoft Excel window, the pointer changes shape to signal what will happen if you click the mouse in that area of the window. While the mouse pointer is over the worksheet in the document window, the pointer resembles a plus sign. Within the formula bar, the pointer is shaped like an I-beam, which is tailor-made for positioning an insertion point accurately between two characters. Within the toolbar and the menu bar, the pointer is shaped like an arrow. Table 1-1 illustrates the pointer shapes you are most likely to see.

Shape	Location
⊹	Over the worksheet cells
⬐	Over the title bar, toolbar tools, menu bar, and scroll bars, at the left side of the formula bar, and on the borders of selected worksheet cells
I	In the formula bar and in the text box at the left end of the toolbar
↔ ↕	On the boundary of a column or row header (for sizing)
⇔ ⇕	Over window borders
⬉	At the bottom-right and top-left corners of the window border
⬈	At the top-right and bottom-left corners of the window border
⇳	Over the window split bars
+	On the fill handle at the bottom-right corner of the active cell

TABLE 1-1. *The most common shapes of the Microsoft Excel mouse pointer.*

UNDERSTANDING CELLS

As already mentioned, every Microsoft Excel worksheet is divided into a grid of 256 columns and 16,384 rows. Across the top of the worksheet are the *column headers*, labeled A, B, C, and so on. Down the left side are the *row headers*, labeled 1, 2, 4, and so on. The intersection of a column and a row is a *cell*. Right now, each cell is surrounded by light gray lines known as *gridlines*.

Each item of data—text, a number, or a formula—resides in a cell. Each cell has an *address* that consists of the column letter followed by the row number; for example, the address C5 refers to the cell at the intersection of column C and row 5.

Notice that cell A1 in Sheet1 (Figure 1-2) is surrounded by a heavy border. This border indicates that cell A1 is the *active cell*—the cell that will be affected by commands and that will receive any data you enter. Only one cell can be active at a time. As mentioned earlier, the reference area of the formula bar displays the address of the active cell.

Selecting Individual Cells

Many Microsoft Excel commands operate on particular cells within the document. To tell Excel which cells the command should affect, you *select* individual cells or groups of cells before issuing the command.

- To select a cell with the mouse, move the mouse pointer over the cell and click. The heavy border then surrounds the new active cell, indicating that it is selected.

- To select a cell with the keyboard, press a direction key. (If you use the direction keys on the numeric keypad, be sure that Num Lock is turned off; otherwise, you'll enter numbers in the worksheet instead of selecting cells.)

For an example of how this works, try the following:

1. Starting from cell A1, press the Right (→) direction key once to move to cell B1.

2. Hold down the Right direction key to move the active cell steadily to the right. Notice that if you continue pressing the Right direction key after the cell at the far right of the window is active, the window scrolls to the right so that you can select the cell in the next column.

3. Now select cells to the left, below, and above the active cell by pressing the Left (←), Down (↓), and Up (↑) direction keys.

The following table lists some other keys you can use for moving around and selecting individual cells. (Hyphenated key combinations mean you hold down one key, such as Ctrl, while pressing the other, such as Home.)

 If you know the exact address of the cell you want to make active, press the F5 key. Type the cell address in the dialog box that appears, and then press Enter to move to that cell.

Key	Action
Home	Selects the cell in column A of the current row
Ctrl-Home	Selects cell A1 from any location in the worksheet
Home (with Scroll Lock on)	Selects the cell in the top-left corner of the current window (the portion of the worksheet visible on screen)
End (with Scroll Lock on)	Selects the cell in the bottom-right corner of the current window
PgUp or PgDn	Moves up or down one window and selects the cell in the current column, in the row at the top of the window

Selecting Groups of Cells

Often you'll want a command to act on more than one cell, so you need to learn how to select *ranges*. A range is a rectangular block of cells. Figure 1-4 shows some examples of ranges. (The entire worksheet is also a range, albeit a big one.)

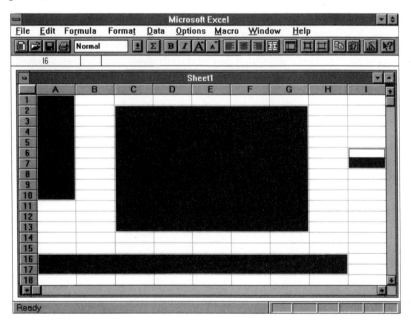

FIGURE 1-4. *Examples of ranges.*

11

To select a range of cells,

- With the mouse, move the mouse pointer to one corner of the range, hold down the mouse button, and drag the pointer to the opposite corner of the range.

- With the keyboard, select the cell in any corner of the range, and then hold down the Shift key while you press the direction keys.

Excel highlights all the cells in the selected range, except the active cell (the one at which you started). For example, if you select cells B4 through C5, Excel highlights cells C4, B5, and C5, and leaves the active cell, B4, unhighlighted but inside the thick border enclosing the four cells.

You can also select entire columns and rows:

- To select an entire column with the mouse, click its column header. To select an entire row, click its row header. To select multiple rows or columns, drag the mouse pointer through their headers. (Be sure that the pointer is cross-shaped when you start dragging.)

- To select an entire column with the keyboard, select any cell in that column, hold down the *Ctrl* key, and press the Spacebar. To select an entire row, select any cell in that row, hold down the *Shift* key, and press the Spacebar.

 To remember which Spacebar combination to use, keep in mind that Ctrl *and* column *both begin with* C. *Simple elimination then associates* Shift *with* row.

To refer to a selected range, you use the addresses of the top-left and bottom-right cells, separated by a colon. For example, you refer to a range consisting of cells B4, B5, C4, and C5 as B4:C5.

MOVING AROUND THE WORKSHEET

If the cell you want to select isn't visible, you can use the scroll bars on the right and bottom sides of the document window to bring the cell into view. Within each bar is a small, plain square called the *scroll box,* shown in Figure 1-5. To move up or down in the worksheet, drag the scroll box in the right scroll bar up or down; to move from side to side in the worksheet, drag the scroll box in the bottom scroll bar to the right or left.

To move an entire window at a time, click the scroll bar. In the vertical scroll bar, clicking above or below the scroll box moves the window up or down one windowful; in the bottom scroll bar, clicking to the left or right of the scroll box moves the window left or right one windowful.

To scroll more gradually, you can click one of the four *scroll arrows*. In the vertical scroll bar, clicking the up or down arrow moves the window up or down one row; in the bottom scroll bar, clicking the left or right arrow moves the window left or right one column.

 When you move around the worksheet with the scroll bars, you don't change the active cell. With the keyboard, however, you can't move around the worksheet without changing the active cell. For example, pressing the PgUp or PgDn key moves the window up or down one windowful but also moves the active cell to the row at the top of the window.

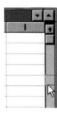

FIGURE 1-5. *Dragging the scroll box.*

WORKING WITH MENUS

As mentioned earlier, you usually tell Microsoft Excel what you want it to do by choosing commands. Excel gives you two ways to choose: the point-and-click toolbar, and the traditional menus—lists of items and actions—that are located on the menu bar.

Using the Toolbar

Often the easiest way to choose a command is to use the toolbar. A single click on a toolbar tool can substitute for several mouse movements, keyboard movements, or both. In many cases, the toolbar is so convenient that you may never need to use the menu. In other cases, however, each method has certain advantages. For those operations, this book will explain both the menu and the toolbar techniques for all operations.

Choosing Commands from Menus

You can choose commands from a menu with the mouse or with the keyboard.

Choosing commands with the mouse

Microsoft Excel, like Windows, uses *drop-down* menus. To use menus with the mouse,

- Display a menu by pointing to the menu name and clicking the mouse button.

- Close a menu by clicking the menu name again, by clicking anywhere outside the menu, or by pressing Esc.

- Choose a command from a drop-down menu by pointing to the command, and then clicking the mouse button.

When you choose a command, the menu disappears, and Microsoft Excel carries out the command. If you hold down the mouse button instead of clicking and releasing, Excel displays the command in light type on a dark background (called *highlighting the command*) and displays a brief explanation of the command's action in the status bar. When you release the mouse button, Excel carries out the command as usual. (If you highlight a command with the mouse and then decide not to carry it out, simply move the pointer off the menu before releasing the mouse button.)

Choosing commands with the keyboard

One letter in each menu name on the menu bar is underlined. To open a menu with the keyboard,

- Hold down the Alt key and press the key that corresponds to the underlined letter in the menu you want.

- Alternatively, press the Alt key to activate the menu bar, use the Right or Left direction key to move to the menu you want, and then press Enter or the Up or Down direction key.

If you select a menu and then decide not to use it, press Esc once to remove the menu from the screen, and a second time to deselect the menu bar.

Each of the commands on the menus also has an underlined letter. After you pull down a menu, you can choose a command by pressing the key that corresponds to its underlined letter. Alternatively, you can use the Up or Down direction key to move to the command name, and then press Enter.

Using Keyboard Shortcuts

Keyboard shortcuts allow you to bypass menus and choose commands by pressing one or more keys simultaneously. After you become familiar with Microsoft Excel, you'll probably find keyboard shortcuts very convenient, even if you usually use a mouse.

To hunt down a shortcut for a specific command, follow these steps:

1. Choose the Search command from the Help menu. A window like the one shown in Figure 1-6 will appear.

2. Type *sho*. Excel skips down the list to the item *shortcut keys*.

3. Click the button labeled Show Topics, or press Enter. A list of related topics appears in the lower half of the window.

4. If necessary, click on the Edit Command Keys topic to select it. Click the button labeled Go To, or press Enter. The Excel Help window now displays the list of shortcuts shown in Figure 1-7.

5. Remove the Help window from the screen by double-clicking the Control-menu box (the box with the hyphen at the left end of the title bar), or use the keyboard shortcut for closing Windows applications: Hold down Alt and press F4.

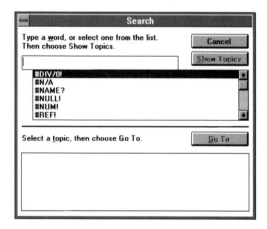

FIGURE 1-6. *The Search window, where you can look for help on specific topics.*

15

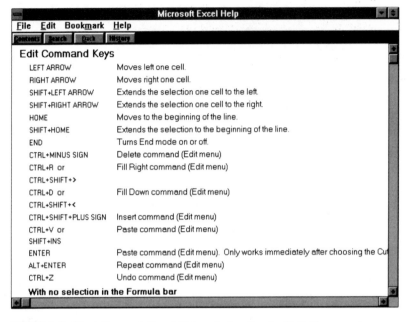

FIGURE 1-7. *The Microsoft Excel Help window for the Edit Command Keys topic.*

 If you have highlighted a command or selected an option in a dialog box, pressing F1 displays a Help screen with information about that particular command or option.

Touring the Menus

To get an idea of the commands at your disposal, take a look at each menu on the menu bar. Some of the command names are self-explanatory; others may seem a bit obscure. Don't worry for now if you can't figure out what all the commands do.

The File menu

Click File in the menu bar (or hold down Alt and press F) to see the File menu, shown in Figure 1-8. You use the commands on the File menu to open, close, save, and delete files. You also use this menu to print worksheets and exit from Microsoft Excel. Notice that some of the commands are followed by three dots (...), meaning that you must give Microsoft Excel more information before it can carry out these commands.

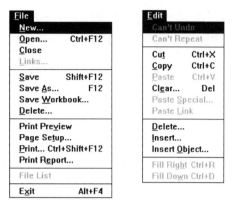

FIGURE 1-8. *The File menu (left) and the Edit menu (right).*

The Edit menu

Click Edit in the menu bar (or hold down Alt and press E) to see the Edit menu, also shown in Figure 1-8. You use the commands on the Edit menu to copy, rearrange, and revise data. Notice that some of the commands are dimmed, indicating that you cannot use them now. Some of the commands have keyboard shortcuts, which are indicated next to the commands. For example, Ctrl+X is shown as the keyboard shortcut for the Cut command.

The Formula menu

Click Formula in the menu bar (or hold down Alt and press R) to see the Formula menu, shown in Figure 1-9. You use the commands on the Formula

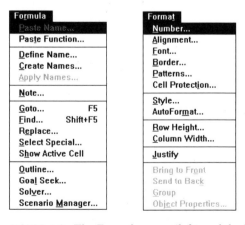

FIGURE 1-9. *The Formula menu (left) and the Format menu (right).*

menu to build and revise formulas and to organize, search, and analyze your worksheets and models. You can also attach names and notes to cells with Formula menu commands.

The Format menu

Click Format in the menu bar (or hold down Alt and press T) to see the Format menu, also shown in Figure 1-9. You use the commands on the Format menu to alter the appearance of your worksheets. For example, you can change font sizes and styles. You also use commands on this menu to protect data from inadvertent changes.

The Data menu

Click Data in the menu bar (or hold down Alt and press D) to see the Data menu, shown in Figure 1-10. You use the commands on this menu to manage Microsoft Excel databases and to summarize data from multiple worksheets. (A database is a convenient way to organize and retrieve information that can be arranged in a table. You'll find information about databases in Chapter 8, "Managing Databases.")

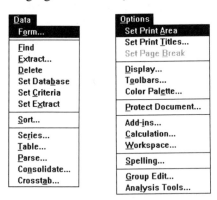

FIGURE 1-10. *The Data menu (left) and the Options menu (right).*

The Options menu

Click Options in the menu bar or hold down Alt and press O to see the Options menu, also shown in Figure 1-10. You use the commands on the Options menu to set display options (to show or hide toolbars or gridlines, for example), and to control a wide variety of global worksheet-management options such as spell-checking, statistical analysis, and calculation.

The Macro menu

Click Macro in the menu bar (or hold down the Alt key and press M) to see the Macro menu, shown in Figure 1-11. You use the commands on the Macro menu to "record" keystrokes and store them as macros (small programs), which you can "play back" later. Most of the commands are dimmed because they aren't available right now. Chapter 11, "Creating Macros," introduces you to this topic.

FIGURE 1-11. *The Macro menu.*

The Window menu

Click Window in the menu bar (or hold down the Alt key and press W) to see the Window menu, shown in Figure 1-12. You use the commands on the Window menu to move quickly between windows and to provide multiple views into a document. You can also use this menu to arrange multiple windows on the screen.

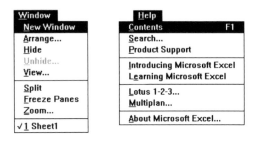

FIGURE 1-12. *The Window menu (left) and the Help menu (right).*

The Help menu

Click Help in the menu bar (or hold down Alt and press H) to see the Help menu, also shown in Figure 1-12. You use the commands on the Help menu to get information about the various features of Microsoft Excel. You can also start the Excel tutorials from this menu.

The Control menus

Microsoft Excel has two menus that are not on the menu bar: the *document* Control menu and the *application* Control menu.

The document Control menu: To see the document Control menu, shown at the left in Figure 1-13, click the box labeled with a hyphen in the top-left corner of the document window, or hold down Alt and press the hyphen (-) key. You use the commands on the document Control menu as an alternative to using the mouse to move, size, or close the document window, and to split the window into subwindows, called *panes*.

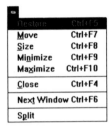

FIGURE 1-13. *The very similar document (left) and application (right) Control menus. Note the difference in size of the bar and hyphen on the menu boxes.*

The application Control menu: To see the application Control menu, shown at the right in Figure 1-13, click the box labeled with a bar in the top-left corner of the screen—the one *above* the document Control icon—or hold down Alt and press the Spacebar. You use the commands on the application Control menu to control the size and position of the Microsoft Excel window and to switch to other currently running Windows applications.

WORKING WITH DIALOG BOXES

As mentioned earlier, before Microsoft Excel can carry out commands followed by three dots (...) on the menu, you need to supply more information. Excel uses *dialog boxes* to prompt you to supply the information it needs.

To display a typical dialog box, choose the Display command from the Options menu. The Display Options dialog box, shown (with annotations) in Figure 1-14, allows you to control the appearance of Microsoft Excel worksheets on the screen by means of buttons, check boxes, and a drop-down list.

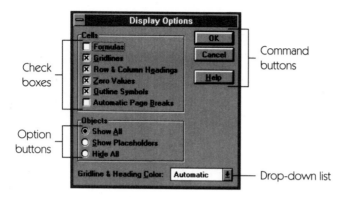

Check boxes

Option buttons

Command buttons

Drop-down list

FIGURE 1-14. *The Display Options dialog box.*

The rectangular buttons, called *command buttons*, in the top-right corner of the dialog box carry out actions. For example, clicking the OK button instructs Excel to carry out the Display command using the options you have specified in the dialog box.

The square buttons, called *check boxes*, that are grouped within the Cells box at the top left of the dialog box offer options that can be selected independently of one another. Simply click the appropriate check box to turn on a desired option (reflected by an X in the box). If an option is already turned on, clicking its check box turns it off (removes the X). For example,

- Click the Gridlines check box to turn off this option, and then click the OK button to carry out the Display command.

The gridlines vanish from the worksheet. To restore the gridlines,

- Choose the Display command from the Options menu again, and click the Gridlines check box to turn the option back on. Leave the Display Options dialog box displayed for now.

The round buttons, called *option buttons*, that are grouped within the Objects box are mutually exclusive; that is, you can select only one of these buttons at a time. For example,

- Click the Hide All button.

Notice that Excel moves the large dot that indicates the selection from the Show All option to the Hide All option. To restore the original selection,

- Click Show All again.

You've finished with the Display Options dialog box, so

■ Click OK or Cancel to close the box. OK tells Excel to make the changes you specified. Cancel closes the box without making any changes.

Table 1-2 summarizes how each dialog-box element operates.

Option	Effect	How to use
Command button	Carries out actions	Click the button. OK instructs Excel to carry out the command using the options you have specified in the dialog box.
Check box	Sets options that can be selected independently of each other	Click the box to turn an option on or off.
Option button	Sets options that are mutually exclusive	Click the button to turn the options on and off.
Text box	Receives text or numeric entries from the keyboard	Type new text; edit or delete existing text.
List box	Presents list of several selections; generally, you can select only one item	Click the item to select it. A list box containing numerous items has a scroll bar on the right. Use the scroll bar to bring other items into view.
Drop-down list box	Presents list of selections when dropped down	Click the arrow box at right, and then click the item to select it. (The box titled Gridline & Heading Color in the Display Options dialog box is a drop-down list box.)

TABLE 1-2. *The components of Excel dialog boxes.*

 If you simply want to change the setting of one option button in a dialog box, you can double-click the button instead of clicking the button and then clicking OK. This shortcut usually carries out the command in one step.

Sometimes different elements work together. In the Font dialog box shown in Figure 1-15, you can type in the text boxes for Font, Font Style, and Size; or, if you select from the list box, the selection appears in the text box.

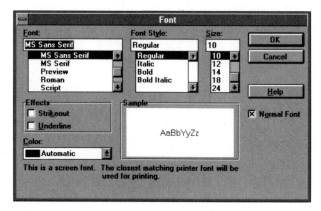

FIGURE 1-15. *The Font dialog box.*

Selecting Options with the Keyboard

You can select a dialog-box option with the keyboard in two ways:

- You can select individual options by holding down Alt and pressing the underlined letter in the name of the option.

- You can press the Tab key to cycle through the options one by one. (Holding down the Shift key while pressing the Tab key moves you backward through the options.) Press the Spacebar to turn the selected option on or off.

Exiting from a Dialog Box

When you're satisfied with all your selections, remember that you can close the dialog box in two ways:

- To tell Microsoft Excel to carry out the command, you can click the OK button or you can make sure the OK button is selected and press Enter.

- To close a dialog box without carrying out the command, you can click the Cancel button or press Esc.

UNDOING ACTIONS

One of the most important Microsoft Excel commands is Undo on the Edit menu—it reverses your last action. Even experienced users slip up occasionally, and it's nice to be able to undo the mistake and start over.

You can undo any change you've made in the formula bar, even after you've entered the change. To see how Undo works, follow these steps:

1. Select cell A1.

2. Type your first name and press Enter.

3. Select the Edit menu. The first menu command is now Undo Entry. (Excel changes the name of this command to let you know exactly what action it will reverse when you choose Undo.)

4. Click Undo Entry. (Alternatively, you can press Enter, because Undo Entry is highlighted.) Excel removes the cell entry.

5. Hold down Ctrl while pressing Z. This is the shortcut for the Undo key. Excel "undoes" the Undo command you carried out a moment ago.

Excel can undo most worksheet commands. If a command cannot be undone, a dimmed Can't Undo appears on the Edit menu where Undo usually appears. Note that the Undo command can undo only the most recent action.

USING TOOLBARS

It's time to introduce Excel's varied selection of toolbars. The Standard toolbar (now on your screen) includes tools (buttons) for the most commonly used commands.

Although the number of tools might seem a little bewildering at first, you'll soon get used to the sight, and if you have a mouse, at least some of the tools will become invaluable. You'll learn more about toolbars as you work through this book, but you're probably curious right now about the tools you see. The pictures and brief descriptions in Table 1-3 should be enough to help you get your bearings. Later chapters give you the details.

But Excel 4 also contains eight other special-purpose toolbars. All of the toolbars, including the Standard bar, are optional, so you can display or suppress any of them.

Follow these steps to display the Utility toolbar:

1. Move the mouse pointer to any place on the toolbar.

Tool	Description
	Opens a new worksheet
	Opens a previously created worksheet or other document
	Saves the active (current) worksheet
	Prints the active worksheet
Normal	Applies or creates a style (look) for selected cells
Σ	Totals cell contents
B *I*	Applies boldfacing or italics
	Makes characters larger or smaller
	Aligns cell contents to the left, center, or right
	Centers text across selected columns
	Refines the appearance of a table by applying any of several predefined formats including boldfacing, italics, and so on
	Creates a border around one or more selected cells
	Creates or deletes bottom border of selected cells
	Copies contents of selected cells to Clipboard
	Pastes only formats from copied cell
	Starts a special program that helps create or modify a chart
	Provides help on whatever command or screen region you point to

TABLE 1-3. *A brief introduction to the tools on the Standard toolbar.*

2. Click the *right* mouse button to display the toolbar shortcut menu (shown below):

3. Point to Utility and click either button to display the Utility toolbar.

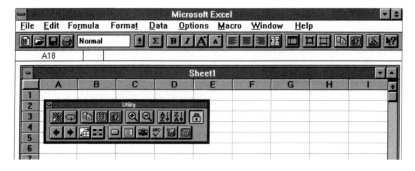

4. To move the Utility toolbar to the *toolbar dock* (where the Standard toolbar is currently displayed), drag its outline to the toolbar dock area. When you release the mouse button, the Utility toolbar stretches out and settles in below the Standard toolbar.

You'll learn more about how to use toolbars later in this book.

To remove the Utility toolbar,

1. Choose the Toolbars command from the Options menu.

2. If necessary, highlight Utility in the dialog box that appears:

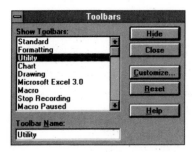

3. Click the button labeled Hide, and the Utility toolbar disappears.

 If a toolbar is displayed as a floating toolbar, you can close it quickly by clicking the Control-menu box in the upper-left corner of the toolbar window.

CREATING A WORKSHEET

It's time to put Microsoft Excel to work by entering some meaningful data into Sheet1.

Entering Text

Suppose you've been asked to analyze some sales figures for a chain of sporting goods stores and you want to use an Excel worksheet to do the job. To begin, give the worksheet a title:

1. Select cell A1, and type the store's complete name:

   `Allen's Sporting Goods Emporium`

   Notice that the characters you type appear in the formula bar. A blinking vertical line, called the *insertion point*, moves to the right of the characters as you type them. Also notice that two symbols in boxes are now displayed to the left of the entry; you'll learn about these symbols later in the chapter.

2. Press Enter. Excel displays the name of the store in cell A1, and the insertion point disappears, indicating that the formula bar is no longer active.

Suppose you realize you've made an error; the name should be *Alan's* instead of *Allen's*. To correct the entry, follow these steps:

1. Reactivate the formula bar by moving the mouse pointer over the bar. Click to "anchor" the insertion point in the formula bar. Alternatively, you can press F2, the Edit key. Use this key when you want to edit the contents of the active cell. Pressing F2 causes the insertion point to appear at the end of the entry in the formula bar.

2. Move the insertion point between the two *l*'s in *Allen's*, either by positioning the mouse pointer and clicking or by pressing the Left or Right direction key.

3. Press the Del key twice to remove *le*. (If you use the numeric keypad, be sure Num Lock is off.)

4. Type *a*.

5. Press Enter to complete the correction in the worksheet.

Now try making the same correction in a different way. Undo the edit you just made by choosing the Undo Entry command from the Edit menu. Then follow these steps:

1. Position the pointer between the *e* and the *n*, and click to activate the insertion point.

2. Press the Backspace key twice.

3. Type *a*.

4. Press Enter to complete the correction in the worksheet.

As you can see, the Backspace key removes characters to the left of the insertion point; the Del key removes characters to the right of the insertion point.

You can use other keys to move quickly through an entry you are editing. To move to the beginning of the entry, press Home after activating the formula bar. To move to the end of the line, press End after activating the formula bar. To move to the next or previous word, hold down Ctrl and press the Right (next) or Left (previous) direction key.

Try making changes and reversing them with the Undo command. You can reverse an Undo command by choosing Redo, which appears in place of Undo on the Edit menu after you perform an Undo.

The leftmost button (labeled with a pencil eraser) on the Utility toolbar introduced earlier is an Undo tool. If you display the toolbar, you can click the Undo tool once to undo your last action and click a second time to undo the undo.

The Enter and Cancel Boxes

The two boxes that appear to the left of your entry when you work in the formula bar represent the *enter box* (the checkmark) and the *cancel box* (the X). As an alternative to pressing Enter, you can click the enter box to enter data from the formula bar into the worksheet. If you have not yet entered the data by pressing Enter or clicking the enter box, you can click the cancel box to cancel either a new entry or an edit you decide you don't want.

Entering Numbers

Numeric data in Microsoft Excel can take one of two forms: It can be a *constant* or a *formula*. Constants are simply numeric values, such as 1,253 or $10.57. You enter them in the same way you enter text. Formulas are *numeric expressions* or *logical expressions* that result in different values depending on the values of their components. Don't worry about formulas for now; you'll learn more about them in Chapter 2, "Using Formulas and Functions."

Excel treats numbers differently from text, so it must have a way of distinguishing between the two. Excel treats an entry as a number if the entry consists only of numeric characters (the numbers 0 through 9) and any of these special characters:

+ − ( ) , / $ % . E e

You must use these special characters in certain ways for Excel to recognize an entry as a constant. Excel ignores a plus sign (+) at the beginning of a numeric constant, as well as embedded commas. When you enter a negative value, you can precede the value with a minus sign (−). Excel treats a single period (.) in a numeric constant as a decimal point. A capital or lowercase *E* embedded in a series of numeric characters denotes scientific notation. If you use a dollar sign ($) in front of a number or a percent sign (%) after a number, Excel interprets the number as a dollar amount or a percentage.

If an entry contains anything other than numbers and the special characters, Excel treats the entry as text. For example, the address *1000 Wilshire Boulevard* is a text entry. If you want to enter a number but have Microsoft Excel treat it as text, precede the number with a single quotation mark, as in this example:

'306

Again, let's use the worksheet for Alan's Sporting Goods Emporium to demonstrate entering data. Suppose you need to enter sales results for July 1992, broken out by department. You've been given the sales figures shown at the top of the next page.

Dept.	Sales
Skiing	15600
Hunting	27280
Camping	13750
Apparel	15920
Other	22600

To enter this information in the worksheet, you could select cell A3 and type *Dept.*, select cell B3 and type *Sales*, and so on. But there's a faster way to accomplish this task.

Entering data the quick way

You can save time by selecting the data-entry area before you type the data. To enter the data this way, follow these steps:

1. Point to cell A3, hold down the mouse button, and then drag down and to the right to select the range A3 through B8. (With the keyboard, select cell A3, and hold down the Shift key while pressing the Down and then the Right direction keys.) The selected cells look like those in the following illustration:

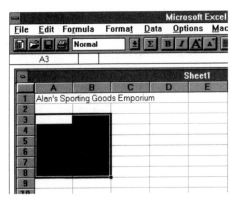

2. Type the first heading, *Dept.*, and press the Tab key. Notice that the range you selected remains highlighted, but the active cell is now cell B3.

3. Type the second heading, *Sales*, and press the Tab key. Cell A4 is now the active cell.

4. Continue entering the department names and the July sales data from the table, pressing the Tab key after each entry. Each time you press the Tab key, the active cell moves right one cell or down one row to the next cell in the selected range. (To move backward, hold down the Shift key while you press Tab.) Press a direction key when you finish.

 To enter data into a selected range column by column instead of row by row, press Enter after each entry. For example, if cell A3 is active when you press Enter, cell A4 becomes the active cell. If the active cell is the last selected cell in that column, the first selected cell in the next column becomes the active cell.

Correcting Errors

Now that you know how to make entries in a worksheet, you can try a few tricks for formula-bar editing.

Suppose the sporting goods company shortens its name to *Alan's Sports*. To correct the title of the worksheet, you could use the Del key or the Backspace key to revise the entry, but there's an easier way. You can select a group of characters and delete them all at one time:

1. Start by selecting cell A1, which contains the entry *Alan's Sporting Goods Emporium.*

2. With the mouse, drag through the characters in the formula bar to select them. In this case, position the I-beam pointer after the *t* in *Sporting*, and drag just past the *d* in *Goods*. Be sure you've selected only the characters you want to remove, and then release the mouse button.

   With the keyboard, press F2 and then use the direction keys to place the insertion point between the *t* and the *i*. Hold down the Shift key and then press the Right direction key until all the characters from *i* through the *d* in *Goods* are highlighted.

Whether you use the mouse or the keyboard, your worksheet should look like the one at the top of the next page.

31

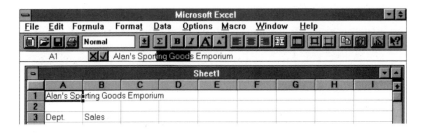

3. Press the Del key. The name becomes *Alan's Sports Emporium.* Don't press Enter yet.

Now use a different method to delete the word *Emporium.*

1. With the mouse, position the I-beam pointer anywhere in the word *Emporium*, and double-click. This selects the entire word.

    With the keyboard, position the insertion point before the *E* in *Emporium*, hold down both Shift and Ctrl, and then press the Right direction key. Don't be concerned if the highlight extends far to the right of *Emporium.* No matter how your screen looks right now, just remember that the Shift-Ctrl-Right direction key combination extends the selection one word at a time.

2. Press the Del key to remove the selected word.

3. Examine the entry for errors, and make any necessary corrections before pressing the Enter key to enter the change in the worksheet.

MANAGING DISK FILES

You'll come back to the Alan's Sports worksheet in the next chapter. Now, however, it's time to learn how to save and retrieve worksheets, delete obsolete worksheets, create new worksheets, and close worksheets.

Saving Your Work

If you want to exit from Microsoft Excel and pick up later where you left off, you must save your work on a disk. Even while you're working in Excel, you should save your work at least once every 10 minutes or so, to avoid losing data if a power failure or other problem requires you to restart the computer.

Saving a worksheet for the first time

When you create a new worksheet, Excel assigns it a generic name. The Alan's Sports worksheet, for example, is currently named Sheet1. Because Sheet1 isn't

32

very meaningful, you will want to change it. To save the worksheet and, at the same time, to give it the name *ALSPORTS*, follow these steps:

1. Press F12 (or Alt-F2), the keyboard shortcut for the Save As command, or choose Save As from the File menu. Excel displays this dialog box:

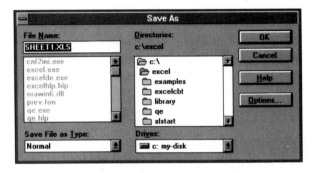

2. Type *ALSPORTS* (uppercase or lowercase doesn't matter) in the File Name text box. (Excel adds the XLS extension to all worksheet names unless you specify a different extension in the File Name box.) If you make a mistake, edit the name in the File Name text box just as you would edit an entry in the formula bar.

3. Click OK or press Enter to save the file.

CAUTION *If you choose the Save As command and type the name of an existing worksheet in the File Name text box, Microsoft Excel displays a message asking whether you want to replace the existing worksheet with the current one (the one you're saving). If you click OK or press Enter in this situation, Excel overwrites, and thus destroys, the existing file. Be sure this is what you want to do.*

Where did it go?

When you clicked OK to save your *ALSPORTS* worksheet, Excel stored it in a directory named EXCEL on your hard disk. Why there? Because EXCEL is the *default* directory—the one Excel uses unless you specify a different drive or directory. Although you won't hurt anything by saving a few sample files in the EXCEL directory, you won't want to do so on a regular basis, especially when you start creating and saving many Excel files. To keep your work organized and easy to find, you should form the habit of saving files in task-related or work-related directories of their own.

To save a file in a different directory, or on a disk in a different drive, you once again use the Save As command. To see how this works,

■ Press F12 or choose Save As again.

This time, notice the Directories and Drives list boxes in the middle of the Save As dialog box.

To save a file in a different directory with the mouse, you double-click the directory name in the Directories list box. For example,

■ Double-click *library.*

With the keyboard, you press the Tab key twice to move to the Directories list box, press the Down direction key to highlight *library,* and then press Enter.

Excel changes to the LIBRARY directory and displays the names of the files it contains in the list box to the left. If you wanted to save *ALSPORTS* in this directory, you would now simply click OK or press Enter.

Suppose, however, that you wanted to save *ALSPORTS* on a disk in drive A. To turn Excel's attention to drive A with the mouse:

1. Place a formatted floppy disk in drive A. (Any disk will do, because you'll just try changing drives here.)

2. Click the down arrow to open the Drives drop-down list box.

3. Click *a:* to switch to drive A. To actually save *ALSPORTS* on drive A, you would click OK. Because you're simply seeing how to use the Save As dialog box, however, click Cancel to cancel the Save As command.

To save the file on a disk using the keyboard,

1. Place a formatted disk in drive A.

2. Hold down Alt and press V to move to the Drives drop-down list box.

3. Press the Down direction key to open the list box.

4. Use the Up direction key to highlight *a:.*

5. Press Enter to switch to drive A. To save the file you would press Enter, but press the Esc key now to cancel the Save As command.

Saving a named worksheet

After you name and save a worksheet for the first time, you can easily update the file to save any changes you want to keep. You have three ways to save a named worksheet:

- The traditional method is to choose the Save command from the File menu.

- A faster way is to press Shift-F12 (or Alt-Shift-F2), the keyboard shortcut for the Save command.

- Fastest of all, if you have a mouse, is to click the Save File tool, the third from the left on the Standard toolbar:

Even though you have not made any changes to *ALSPORTS* since saving it a few minutes ago, try one of the preceding methods to save the file again.

CAUTION *The Save command overwrites the old version of a file with the new version you save. The command does* not *display a message asking whether you want to replace the existing worksheet with the current one. If you want to make changes to an existing worksheet but still retain the original version, use the Save As command to change the worksheet's name immediately after opening it.*

Although the preceding examples saved your *ALSPORTS* file in the EXCEL directory, the remainder of this book will assume all examples, including *ALSPORTS*, are saved in a SAMPLES directory on drive C. If you want to keep your EXCEL directory uncluttered, create such a directory on your hard disk using Windows File Manager. Alternatively, save your sample files on a floppy disk in drive A.

Saving a worksheet in a "foreign" format

If you want to save your worksheet in a format that can be read by other applications (for example, by Lotus 1-2-3 or Microsoft Word for Windows), choose the Save As command, and with the mouse click the down arrow, or with the keyboard press Alt-T and then the Down direction key to open the Save File As Type drop-down list box. Select the file format you want from the list that appears, and then click the OK button or press Enter.

Table 1-4 explains the available format options.

Option	Format
Normal	Microsoft Excel standard format
Template	Microsoft Excel template (explained in Chapter 4, "Formatting Worksheets")
Excel 3.0	Microsoft Excel version 3.0 standard format
Excel 2.1	Microsoft Excel version 2.0/2.1 standard format
SYLK	Format used to transfer spreadsheet data to different Microsoft applications, such as Multiplan
Text	Tab-separated ASCII format, useful for moving Microsoft Excel data into word processing programs
CSV	Comma-separated format, useful for moving Microsoft Excel data to other applications
WKS, WK1, and WK3	Formats for Lotus 1-2-3 Release 1A, Release 2, and Release 3, respectively
DIF	Data Interchange Format for VisiCalc
DBF 2, DBF 3, and DBF 4	Formats for dBASE II, III, and IV, respectively
Text (Macintosh) and Text (OS/2 or MS-DOS)	Tab-separated format, useful for moving Microsoft Excel data to other applications
CSV (Macintosh) and CSV (OS/2 or MS-DOS)	Comma-separated format, useful for moving Microsoft Excel data to other applications

TABLE 1-4. *The formats in which you can save Microsoft Excel worksheets.*

Creating a New Worksheet

You can begin work on a new worksheet without closing other open Excel files. To open a new, blank worksheet,

- Click the New Worksheet tool shown below:

Microsoft Excel gives the new worksheet the title Sheet2 and displays it in a new document window in front of the *ALSPORTS* worksheet. You'll need the new worksheet in a minute, so save it now with the name Sheet2:

■ Click the Save File tool or choose the Save command from the File menu.

Notice that Excel displays the Save As dialog box, as if you had chosen Save As instead of Save. Excel is anticipating that you want to change the name. In this case, though, simply click the OK button to save the worksheet as Sheet2.

You can also open a new worksheet by choosing New from the File menu. Try this now. The dialog box shown in Figure 1-16 appears, asking what type of file you want to open. (You'll learn how to create chart, macro, and workbook files later.) The Worksheet option is already selected, so click the OK button, or press Enter, to open a new worksheet.

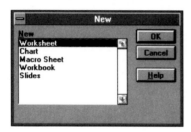

FIGURE 1-16. *The New dialog box.*

Closing a Worksheet

You close the current worksheet by choosing the Close command from the File menu:

■ Close the Sheet3 worksheet now.

If, as here, you haven't made any changes to a new or previously saved worksheet, the program closes the file without first asking whether you want to save it.

If you make changes to a worksheet without saving them, and then you choose Close, the dialog box shown in Figure 1-17 appears, asking whether you want to save the revised worksheet before closing it.

■ To save the worksheet, click the Yes button or press Y or Enter.

■ To close the file without saving the changes, click the No button or press N.

■ To cancel the Close command, click the Cancel button or press Esc.

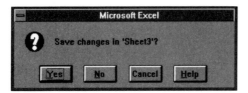

FIGURE 1-17. *The message that appears when you try to close a worksheet without saving changes.*

After you close the Sheet3 worksheet, its document window disappears from the screen, uncovering *SHEET2* and then, beneath it, the *ALSPORTS* worksheet:

■ Use the Close command to close both *SHEET2* and *ALSPORTS*.

Most of the Microsoft Excel window is now blank. With no worksheets open, only the File and Help menus are available. To bring back the full menu bar, create a new worksheet, or open one that you have previously saved.

 Remember, you can also close a worksheet with the mouse by double-clicking the document Control-menu box.

Opening an Existing Worksheet

The method you use to open an existing worksheet depends on how recently you used the worksheet.

Opening a recently used worksheet with the File menu

Microsoft Excel "remembers" the last four worksheets you worked with and displays their names on the File menu. To open the *ALSPORTS* worksheet, follow these steps:

1. Open the File menu. Near the bottom, you'll see the filenames *SHEET2.XLS* and *ALSPORTS.XLS*—the files for the two worksheets you have worked with so far.

2. Click *ALSPORTS*, or use the Down direction key to highlight the filename and then press Enter to tell Excel to open the worksheet.

Now close the worksheet so that you can see how to open it another way.

Opening a worksheet with the Open command

Whether the worksheet you want appears on the File menu or not, you can choose the Open command from the File menu to open an existing file. When you choose this command, Excel displays a dialog box similar to the one shown in Figure 1-18. To open the *ALSPORTS* worksheet again,

1. Press Ctrl-F12 or choose Open from the File menu.

2. Double-click on the worksheet name in the list of files.

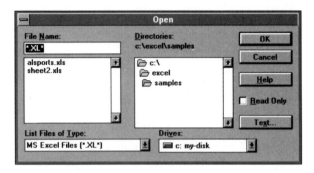

FIGURE 1-18. *The Open dialog box.*

Opening a worksheet stored in another directory

When you choose Open from the File menu, Excel displays the names of the worksheets stored in the current directory. If the worksheet you want to open is not in the current directory, display the worksheets stored in other directories on the current disk by selecting from the list of directory names shown in the Directories list box. To display worksheets on a disk in a different drive, choose the drive from the Drives box.

Deleting Worksheets

After a while, you'll have created many files, some of which are no longer useful. You can clean up your disk from within Microsoft Excel by choosing the Delete command from the File menu.

Let's delete *SHEET2* now. Follow these steps:

1. Choose the Delete command from the File menu. The Delete Document dialog box appears. This dialog box is similar to the Open dialog box, except that the specification in the File Name text box is *.*, and all the files in the current directory are listed in the Files list box.

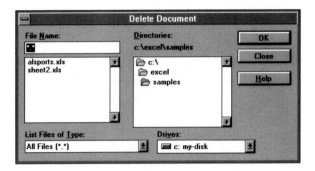

If the current directory contains files of many types, you can list specific files by choosing the type you want from the List Files of Type box. If *SHEET2* is in your Excel directory, open the List Files Of Type box and choose *Worksheets*.

2. Select *sheet2.xls*.

3. Click the OK button, or press Enter. Because you normally can't undo the Delete command, Excel always displays a dialog box asking you to confirm the deletion.

4. Click the Yes button, press Y, or press Enter to delete the file.

5. Click the Close button or press Esc to close the dialog box.

EXITING FROM MICROSOFT EXCEL

To exit from Microsoft Excel, do one of the following:

- Double-click the Control-menu box in the Excel (not document) window.

- Hold down Alt and press F4.

- Choose the Exit command from the File menu.

If any open worksheet has unsaved changes, Excel displays a dialog box asking whether to save the changes. (Click Yes or press Y when Excel asks whether you want to save the changes, or click No or press N to exit Excel without saving the changes.

After you respond to this dialog box for each worksheet that has unsaved changes, Excel quits and you return to the Windows screen.

CONCLUSION

You've covered a lot of territory in this first chapter. You now know how to select cells and make entries in them, and you know the basics of saving and retrieving files. The next chapter introduces formulas and functions so that you can start doing useful work with Microsoft Excel.

Chapter 2

Using Formulas and Functions

By now, you should be comfortable entering text and numbers in worksheets and making corrections to your entries. But if this were all you could do with Microsoft Excel, you could just as easily use a word-processing application. The power of Microsoft Excel lies in its ability to work with the information you enter—to calculate, to analyze, and to predict. In this chapter, you will begin harnessing this power by learning how to use Microsoft Excel formulas and functions.

UNDERSTANDING MICROSOFT EXCEL FORMULAS

You enter a formula in a cell in the same way you enter text—through the formula bar. Excel calculates the result (value) of the formula and displays (returns) that result in the cell containing the formula.

To try a simple formula, enter the following in a blank worksheet:

1. If you quit the Microsoft Excel program at the end of Chapter 1, start Excel again by double-clicking the Excel icon. If Windows is not running, start both Windows and Excel by typing *win excel* at the DOS prompt. If Excel is already running, go to step 2.

2. Open a new worksheet by clicking the New Worksheet tool on the toolbar. As mentioned in Chapter 1, in a new worksheet, cell A1 is the active cell.

3. Now type

   =40+27

As you type, notice that your keystrokes appear both in the formula bar and in cell A1. Press Enter. The formula you typed is still displayed in the formula bar, but the result of the formula, 67, is displayed in cell A1.

Every formula must begin with an equal sign (=). If you omit the equal sign, Excel interprets the entry as text and displays the "text" in cell A1, instead of calculating its value.

For some additional practice before you move on,

1. Select each of the cells listed in the first column of the following table, one by one.

2. Enter the corresponding formula shown in the second column. The result of each formula is shown in the third column of the table.

Cell	Formula	Value
A2	=3 *16	48
A3	=53/20	2.65
A4	=100−36.83	63.17

Using Numeric Operators in Formulas

The formulas you just typed included *numeric operators*: plus (+) for addition, minus (−) for subtraction, asterisk (*) for multiplication, and slash (/) for division. Other kinds of numeric operators include percent (%), which divides the preceding value by 100, and caret (^), which multiplies the preceding value by itself the number of times specified by the following value (exponentiation).

By way of example, try the following:

1. Select cell A5, type

=23^3

2. Press Enter.

Excel multiplies 23 by itself three times and displays the result: 12167.

Using more than one operator

Each cell in a worksheet can contain as many as 255 characters. As long as you don't exceed this limit, you can create long formulas that include as many operators as you need. The longer the formula, however, the greater the risk of error. Consider the following formula:

```
=84*0.7^2/24*3.26-29
```

Excel has to make five different computations—one for each operator—to calculate this formula. The result, however, depends on the sequence in which Microsoft Excel performs the computations.

Excel follows a rigid set of rules, known as the *order of evaluation*, when performing multiple computations in a single formula. For formulas to work the way you want them to, you must be familiar with these rules. Table 2-1 lists the Microsoft Excel numeric operators in order of evaluation, from first to last. When two operators have equal precedence (for example, division and multiplication), Excel performs the computations from left to right.

Operator	Action
−	Negation
%	Percentage
^	Exponentiation
/, *	Division, multiplication
+, −	Addition, subtraction

TABLE 2-1. *Microsoft Excel's order of evaluation of numeric operators.*

Order of evaluation is best shown by example, so let's look again at the previous formula:

```
=84*0.7^2/24*3.26-29
```

The following table shows, step by step, the procedure Microsoft Excel goes through as it calculates the formula. In the third column, the computation made at each step appears in boldface.

Step	Operation	Formula
1	Exponentiation	=84***0.7^2**/24*3.26−29
2	Multiplication	=**84*0.49**/24*3.26−29
3	Division	=**41.16/24***3.26−29
4	Multiplication	=**1.715*3.26**−29
5	Subtraction	=**5.5909−29**
6	Result	−23.4091

You can override Excel's order of evaluation by enclosing parts of the formula in parentheses. Excel then performs the enclosed computations before proceeding with the usual order of evaluation. So, if you enter the formula

    =84*0.7^2/24*(3.26-29)

Excel performs the subtraction operation as the first step instead of the fifth step. The result is −44.1441.

Be careful: If you don't consider the order of evaluation when you create complex formulas, the formulas might yield unexpected results.

Using Cell Addresses in Formulas

So far, the formulas you've seen have consisted solely of values and operators. But formulas can also refer to other cells. For example, the formula =C3+C4+C5 returns the sum of the values in cells C3, C4, and C5.

Try using a formula that uses cell addresses in the *ALSPORTS* worksheet you created in Chapter 1. Because the *ALSPORTS* worksheet is probably one of the last four Excel files you saved, the filename should appear in the bottom section of the File menu.

1. Click on the filename to open the worksheet. If the *ALSPORTS* file does not appear on the menu, choose the Open command from the File menu, use the Directories and Drives list boxes, if necessary, to find the file, and double-click *ALSPORTS.XLS* in the list of files.

2. Cells B4 through B8 of the worksheet contain sales amounts. To total these amounts, select cell B10, type

    =B4+B5+B6+B7+B8

and then press Enter.

Your screen looks like the one in Figure 2-1. Cell B10 displays the value 95150, the sum of all the departments' sales. (If your result is different, look for typographical errors in your formula or in the sales amounts.)

Typing cell addresses can be tedious. Fortunately, you can enter a cell address in a formula simply by clicking the cell you want the formula to reference. For example, you can enter the formula

    =B4+B5+B6+B7+B8

by selecting cell B10, typing =, clicking cell B4, typing +, clicking cell B5, typing +, clicking cell B6, typing +, clicking cell B7, typing +, and finally clicking cell B8. When you click the enter box (the check mark in the formula bar) or press Enter, Excel enters the result, 95150, in cell B10.

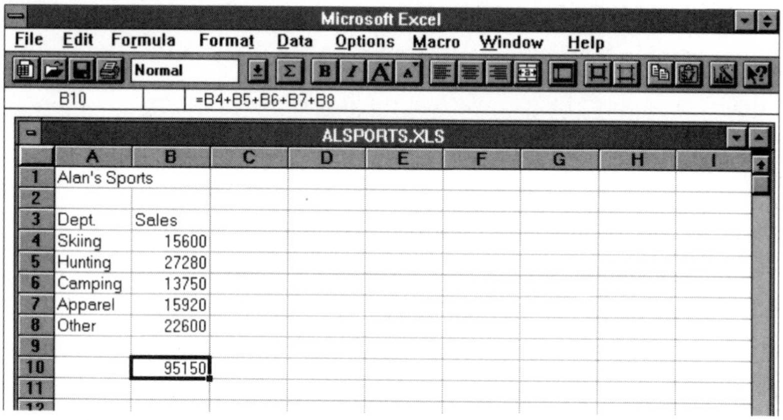

FIGURE 2-1. *A simple addition formula using cell addresses.*

UNDERSTANDING MICROSOFT EXCEL FUNCTIONS

Some formulas—for example, those for calculating financial transactions involving compound interest and variable payments over long periods of time—can be extremely complex. Microsoft Excel offers a battery of *functions* that take a lot of the hard work out of creating and entering formulas. For example, to calculate the monthly payment necessary to amortize a five-year loan of $15,000 at an interest rate of 10 percent, you can tell Excel that you want to use the PMT function with a principal of 15000, an interest rate of 0.8333% (the monthly equivalent of 10% annual interest), and a term of 60 months. Behind the scenes, Excel calculates the correct formula and gives you the result: $318.70 per month.

Providing a shorthand method of entering complex formulas, functions save keystrokes and are easier to read than long formulas. Excel has functions for common mathematical, financial, and statistical calculations. Every Excel function consists of a *name* followed by opening and closing parentheses. Within the parentheses, most functions have at least one *argument*. Arguments are values that you supply. For example, in the function

```
=SUM(B4,B5,B6,B7,B8)
```

SUM is the function name and B4, B5, B6, B7, and B8 are the arguments. As you might have guessed, the SUM function totals the values of all the cells listed within the parentheses, so this particular SUM function performs the same calculation as the formula

    =B4+B5+B6+B7+B8

which you entered earlier in cell B10 of the worksheet.

 Although all function names are shown in capital letters in this book, you don't have to type them in capitals; Microsoft Excel converts them for you, so if you enter =sum(A1+A2), you'll see =SUM(A1+A2) in the formula bar when you press Enter.

Using Ranges in Functions

Entering the function =SUM(B4,B5,B6,B7,B8) in cell B10 is actually quite laborious: It requires more keystrokes than the addition formula you started out with. The AutoSum tool is much more efficient. Follow these steps:

1. Select cell B10 of the *ALSPORTS* worksheet.

2. Click the AutoSum tool (the one labeled with a Greek Σ, the summation symbol):

   Excel enters the formula =SUM(B4:B9) in the formula bar.

Notice that Excel is guessing at the range you want to sum and has surrounded the cells in the range with a moving border, the *marquee*. Excel's guess is based on the contents of the cells above or to the left of the formula and is usually a good starting point. If the guess is correct, you can click the AutoSum tool a second time or press Enter to accept the formula. If the guess is incorrect, you can edit the formula.

In this case, Excel's guess includes cell B9, an empty cell, so edit the formula to adjust the proposed range as follows:

1. Move the mouse pointer to cell B9.

2. Hold down the Shift key and drag the pointer up into cell B8. Release the mouse button when the marquee moves up to exclude cell B9 and the formula in the formula bar reads =SUM(B4:B8).

3. The formula is correct now, so click the AutoSum tool again or press Enter to accept the formula.

In the example you have been using, all the cells in the range are in one column, B, of the worksheet. However, you can also specify rectangular ranges. For example, the function

```
=SUM(F6:K10)
```

returns the sum of all the values in a rectangular block of cells beginning with cell F6 in the top-left corner and ending at cell K10 in the bottom-right corner.

You learned earlier that you can enter individual cell addresses in formulas by clicking the cells with the mouse, and modify a range by holding down the Shift key and dragging. You can also enter an entire cell range in a function with the mouse.

To enter a cell range in a function,

1. Select cell B10.

2. Type the first part of the function:

   ```
   =SUM(
   ```

   The formula in the formula bar is deleted as soon as you start typing the new function.

3. Drag through the range B4:B8 to select it. The range appears in the formula bar and is surrounded by a marquee in the worksheet.

4. Press Enter to complete the function.

Cell B10 again displays the total of all department sales. Note that Excel automatically entered the required right parenthesis to complete the entry.

 To use the keyboard to enter a range in a function, select a cell in one corner of the range with the direction keys. Hold down the Shift key and press the direction keys until the entire range is surrounded by the marquee.

You can include more than one range as arguments in a SUM function by separating the ranges with commas, and you can mix single cells and ranges, as in the following example:

```
=SUM(F6:K10,K12,L6:M10)
```

You can include as many as 30 arguments in a Microsoft Excel function, but because Excel treats a range as one argument, you can actually include the addresses of many more than 30 cells.

Using Functions in Formulas

You can also use functions as part of formulas. For example, suppose the management at Alan's Sports wants to compare the performance of individual departments against the average performance of all departments. Although you could simply divide the total in cell B10 by 5 (the number of departments), try the following to see how a function fits into a formula:

- Enter the following formula in cell B12 of the *ALSPORTS* worksheet:

      =SUM(B4:B8)/5

This formula first determines the total of all department sales and then divides the total by 5, to give the average sales per department (19030).

To try another example,

- Enter the following formula in cell C4:

      =B4/SUM(B4:B8)

This formula results in a decimal fraction that represents the portion of total sales made by the Skiing department.

 You enter only one equal sign at the beginning of each formula; you don't enter an equal sign before a function that is embedded in a formula.

Pasting Functions in Cells

Excel provides another shortcut for entering functions: pasting them from a list. Pasting functions can reduce the chance of error in your worksheets.

As shown in Figure 2-2, the Paste Function command on the Formula menu displays lists of Excel functions. By default, the Paste Function list box displays a list of all Excel functions in alphabetic order, but you can narrow the list by selecting a category from the Function Category list. If you select Financial, for instance, the Paste Function list will display Excel's financial functions.

You can select a function from the Paste Function list, paste it into the formula bar, and then fill in the function's arguments. If you leave the Paste Arguments option (at the bottom of the dialog box) turned on, Excel puts *placeholders* for the arguments between the parentheses that follow the name of the pasted function. (Placeholders for the function highlighted in the Paste

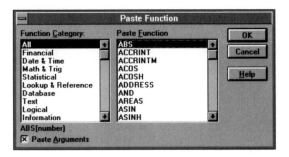

FIGURE 2-2. *The Paste Function dialog box.*

function list box are displayed below the Function Category box—ABS (*number*) in Figure 2-2.)

To use the Paste Function command on the Function menu to enter a SUM function, follow these steps:

1. Select cell B10 in the *ALSPORTS* worksheet.

2. Choose the Paste Function command from the Formula menu. Make sure the Paste Arguments check box is checked.

3. Select the Math & Trig category from the Function Category list.

4. Scroll to the functions beginning with the letter S. You can do this by pointing to the down scroll arrow and holding down the mouse button, or you can save time by clicking on the first function in the Paste Function list box and then pressing the S key to move directly to the first function beginning with S.

5. Select the SUM function either by clicking on it or by pressing S repeatedly to move through the functions beginnning with S. Click OK or press Enter to paste the function into the formula bar. Your formula bar should look like this:

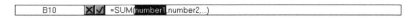

Now to replace the placeholders with actual values.

6. In the Formula bar, drag through the entire SUM argument (everything inside the parentheses) to highlight it.

7. Select the range B4:B8, and click the enter box or press Enter.

If you have entered everything correctly, the formula results in the usual value: 95150.

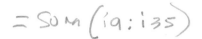

> **TIP** *You can quickly select any given placeholder by moving the I-beam pointer over the placeholder and double-clicking. Excel highlights the entire placeholder. Also, bear in mind that some functions have optional arguments. If you don't replace the placeholders for these arguments with values, Excel displays a #NAME? error value in the cell containing the formula. (Error values are discussed later in this chapter.) If you don't use a particular optional argument, delete the corresponding placeholder.*

Entering a Formula in a Cell Range

Let's put some more functions and formulas into the *ALSPORTS* worksheet, and at the same time try out a shortcut for entering variations of a single formula into a range of cells.

Suppose you want to create a report that shows how the various departments are performing. Assume that it's now September 1992, and you need to add more data to update the *ALSPORTS* worksheet. Follow these steps to set up the worksheet:

1. Change the label in cell B3 from *Sales* to *July*, and enter *August* in cell C3.

2. In column C, select cells C4:C8, and enter the following sales figures for August 1992, pressing Enter to move from cell to cell:

Dept.	Cell	August
Skiing	C4	21270
Hunting	C5	25900
Camping	C6	11085
Apparel	C7	23540
Other	C8	23635

3. Select cell C10. Click the AutoSum tool and adjust the range being summed to C4:C8. Press Enter to enter the total into cell C10.

In your analysis, you want to display the percentage gain in sales for each department from July to August. So, for example, to calculate the percentage gain for the Skiing department, you need to subtract the July figure (B4) from the August figure (C4) and divide by the July figure (B4). Proceed as follows:

1. Select cell D3, and enter the label *Gain(%)*.

2. Select the range D4:D8, starting with cell D4 so that it is the active cell within the range.

3. Enter the following formula, but don't press Enter:

   `=(C4-B4)/B4`

4. Hold down Ctrl and now press Enter. You now see the following screen.

Microsoft Excel has entered a formula into each of the cells in the range you selected. Using the direction keys or the mouse, select each cell in the range D4:D8. As you move from cell to cell, look at the formulas in the formula bar. Notice that they're not identical. The formula in cell D4 refers to cells B4 and C4, the formula in cell D5 refers to cells B5 and C5, and so on. By entering one formula into a range of cells, you have entered formulas for the entire range, leaving Excel to adjust the cell references as needed.

Right now, the gains and losses in column D appear as decimal fractions rather than as percentages. You'll learn how to change the values to percentages in Chapter 4, "Formatting Worksheets."

UNDERSTANDING MICROSOFT EXCEL MESSAGES

As you're learning Microsoft Excel, you're bound to make mistakes from time to time when entering formulas. When this happens, Excel gives you a clue about where you went astray, by displaying an *error value* in a cell or an *alert message* in a dialog box.

Error Values

An error value is one of a set of "codes" that Microsoft Excel uses when it cannot make sense of a formula. An error value in a cell, however, doesn't necessarily mean the entry in that particular cell is causing the problem. The problem may lie somewhere else in the worksheet. When the formula in one cell refers to a value in another, which is itself the result of a formula that refers to yet another cell, errors tend to ripple through the worksheet and produce multiple error values.

Table 2-2 shows all the Excel error values you might encounter and gives brief explanations of probable causes of the errors.

Error value	Cause
#DIV/0!	You've entered a formula that asks Excel to divide a value by 0. You might have done this indirectly by entering a reference to a cell that is currently blank.
#N/A	You've probably omitted one or more arguments from a function, although other errors also produce this value.
#NAME?	You've entered a formula containing text that Excel does not recognize. You've made a typographical error, forgotten to delete a placeholder from a pasted function, or used a name that hasn't yet been defined. (You'll learn about names later in the chapter.)
#NULL!	You've specified an intersection between two ranges that don't intersect. (This error value occurs only with certain advanced Excel features, which are beyond the scope of this book.)
#NUM!	You've used an inappropriate argument in a mathematical function. (For example, you've asked Excel to calculate the square root of a negative number.)
#REF!	You've probably deleted from the worksheet a cell that is referenced by another cell.
#VALUE!	You've entered text where a number or logical value is expected, or you've entered a range as an argument where a single value is required. (Logical values are discussed later in this chapter.)

TABLE 2-2. *Error values and their probable causes.*

The absence of error values doesn't guarantee that a work-sheet contains no errors. It simply means that nothing in the worksheet prevents Excel from computing a result.

Alert Messages

Some types of errors cause Microsoft Excel to display the alert message shown in Figure 2-3 immediately after you enter a formula. Excel also highlights the part of the formula that is causing the problem and will not accept the formula until you correct the error.

FIGURE 2-3. *The alert message displayed for certain types of formula errors.*

Excel displays other alert messages in response to procedural errors. If you've included too many arguments in a function, for instance, the alert message will tell you so.

Click OK or press Enter to close an alert message dialog box. You can also click the Help button in the alert window, or press F1, to display a Help screen that provides an explanation of that particular message.

To close the Help screen and return to your worksheet, double-click the Control-menu box in the Help window or choose Exit from the Help Window's File menu. When the alert message reappears, click OK, or press Enter.

EXPLORING MICROSOFT EXCEL'S FUNCTIONS

As mentioned earlier, Microsoft Excel offers functions for most common formulas and also for many not-so-common ones. This section takes a look at a few functions you might use frequently.

The ROUND function

Microsoft Excel computes all fractional values to 15 digits. You might not want to calculate your values that precisely, however. In calculating prices, for example, tracking fractions of pennies is sometimes more trouble than it's worth. To round off a value, you can simply use the value as the first argument of the ROUND function.

The ROUND function has the following form:

=ROUND(*number,num_digits*)

The *num_digits* argument indicates the number of decimal places you want to appear in the result.

To experiment with rounding,

1. Move to a blank cell in your worksheet.

2. Enter the following function:

   =ROUND(6123.77889,2)

   The result, 6123.78, is rounded to two decimal places.

3. Now edit the function in the formula bar to replace the second argument (2) with 0:

   =ROUND(6123.77889,0)

   to round the value to the nearest whole number.

To round the value to the *left* of the decimal point, you use a negative number for the second argument. For example, to round the value in the cell to the nearest thousand, you would change the 0 to −3.

The IF Function

The IF function is the most important of Microsoft Excel's *logical functions* — functions that return one value if a condition is true and another if it is false. The IF function has the following form:

=IF(*logical_test,value_if_true,value_if_false*)

The *logical_test* argument is usually a comparison of two items. The items can be values, cell references, formulas, functions, or text. You indicate the kind of comparison you want by using one of the *comparison operators* listed in Table 2-3.

Operator	Meaning	Operator	Meaning
<	Less than	<>	Not equal to
>	Greater than	<=	Less than or equal to
=	Equal to	>=	Greater than or equal to

TABLE 2-3. *Comparison operators for use in logical tests.*

Let's look at an example. Suppose that cell K6 contains the function

```
=IF(J6="APPROVED",50,"N/A")
```

The *logical_test* argument specifies that if cell J6 contains the text *AP-PROVED*, the result in cell K6 will be the value 50 (the *value_if_true* argument). If cell J6 doesn't contain *APPROVED*, the result in cell K6 will be the text *N/A* (the *value_if_false* argument).

Now let's see how to put the IF function to work at Alan's Sports. Suppose that, in an effort to boost sales, Alan's Sports has decided to allocate money for bonuses based on total sales for July and August. The total amount made available for bonuses is to be 25 percent of the amount by which sales for each month exceeded $100,000.

To compute the bonus totals,

■ Enter the following functions in the cells indicated (if necessary, replace any practice entries you may have made):

Cell	Function
B12	=IF(B10>100000,25%*(B10−100000),0)
C12	=IF(C10>100000,25%*(C10−100000),0)

Because total sales in August (the value in cell C10) exceed $100,000, the logical test of the function in cell C12 is true, and Excel thus enters the *value_if_true* argument, 1357.5, in cell C12. Because July sales were less than $100,000, the function in cell B12 returns the *value_if_false* argument, 0.

The arguments of the IF function can themselves be IF functions. In fact, you can nest IF functions up to seven levels deep. Here's a formula with three nested IF functions (entered as one long formula, but broken into two lines here for readability). See if you can figure out what the function does:

```
=IF(A1=100,"Bravo",IF(A1>=85,"Well done",
IF(A1>=70,"You can do better","See me after class")))
```

Excel's Financial Functions

If you frequently perform financial calculations, Microsoft Excel's financial functions can save you more calculation time than any other type of worksheet function. The financial functions are perfect for computing compound interest, and they're also convenient for determining the wisdom of an investment. In this section, you'll see a few examples showing ways you might use these functions.

As you read about the Microsoft Excel financial functions in this section, remember that a plus or minus sign attached to an argument indicates the direction *in which the money flows. For the arguments you enter, a negative (−) number means a payment (money that you must spend) and a positive (+) number means money that you receive. In the values Excel returns, negative amounts (payments) are enclosed in parentheses.*

The FV function

The FV function determines the future value of an investment. It answers the question, "How much money will I accumulate if I put away a given amount regularly for a given time at a given interest rate?" The FV function has the following form:

=FV(*rate,nper,pmt,pv,type*)

The *rate* argument is the annual interest rate. If you make periodic payments during the year, divide this rate by the number of payments per year to get the periodic interest rate. Include the percent sign (%) after this number when you enter it in the formula. The *nper* (number of periods) argument is the number of actual payments you will make over the term of the investment. The *pmt* (payment) argument is the periodic payment you will make. The *pv* (present value) argument and the *type* argument, both of which are optional, specify whether the investment has an initial value and whether the payments will be made at the beginning (0) or at the end (1) of each period.

Suppose you're interested in saving money to send your child to college 10 years from now. You estimate that you will be able to put away $100 per month for this purpose at a 5 percent after-tax rate of return. You want to know if this will be enough. To find out,

1. Open a blank worksheet by clicking on the New Worksheet tool on the toolbar or by choosing New from the File menu and clicking OK or pressing Enter.

2. To accommodate the large numbers you are about to calculate, increase the width of column B by selecting any cell in column B, choosing the Column Width command from the Format menu, and typing *10* in the Column Width text box. Click OK or press Enter. (You'll learn more about this command in Chapter 4, "Formatting Worksheets.")

3. Now enter the following information in the cells indicated:

Cell	Entry
A1	Rate
B1	5%
A2	Years
B2	10
A3	Amount
B3	100
A1	Rate
A5	Total

4. Now enter the following function in cell B5:

```
=FV(B1/12,B2*12,-B3)
```

(The minus sign in front of the third argument, B3, is necessary because the savings amount represents money that you pay out.) Excel returns the value $15,528.23. (Notice that Excel automatically displays the result as currency, to two decimal points.) Now all you have to do is figure out how much four years of college will cost 10 years from now. If it's more than $15,528.23, you'll need to save more than $100 per month.

Notice that cell B1 gives the annual *rate of return and that the period in cell B2 is also expressed in years. The amount of savings in cell B3, however, is a monthly amount. To adjust for the different time periods, you must divide cell B1 by 12 and multiply cell B2 by 12. Failure to coordinate the rate of return with the time period is a common error in this type of function.*

The PV function

The PV function determines the present value of an investment. It answers the question, "How much is it worth to me to receive a given amount at regular intervals for a given time at a given rate of return?" The PV function has the following form:

=PV(*rate,nper,pmt,fv,type*)

The arguments for this function are the same as those for the FV function, except that you use the *fv* (future value) argument instead of the *pv* (present value) argument when you want to calculate the present value of a series of lump-sum payments that will be made in the future.

For example, suppose your retired parents have decided to sell their home. They will realize $100,000 from the sale. They've been told that the $100,000 can purchase an annuity that will pay them $600 per month for 20 years, and they want to know whether you think the annuity is a good investment. You estimate that they could earn 5 percent annually after taxes on the money in conservative investments. To evaluate the annuity,

1. Enter the following values in the cells indicated, overwriting the values you entered for the FV calculation:

Cell	Entry
B1	5%
B2	20
B3	600

2. Now edit the function in cell B5 as follows:

```
=PV(B1/12,B2*12,B3)
```

Microsoft Excel returns the negative value ($90,915.19). This means your parents could achieve the same $600 monthly income by simply investing about $91,000, leaving them more than $9,000 to spend or to save as they pleased. Assuming they're willing to bear whatever risks are involved in alternative investments, purchasing the annuity is not advisable.

The PMT function

The PMT function determines the periodic payment needed to amortize a loan. It answers the question, "What periodic payment must I make to pay off a loan of a given amount over a given number of periods at a given interest rate?" The PMT function has the following form:

=PMT(*rate,nper,pv,fv,type*)

where the arguments are the same as those described for the FV and PV functions. The *pv* argument is the principal amount of the loan.

Suppose you're considering buying a house with a 30-year mortgage loan of $72,000 and an annual mortgage interest rate of 8.5 percent. To calculate your monthly payments,

■ Enter the following function in an empty cell:

```
=PMT(8.5%/12,360,72000)
```

The result is ($553.62), meaning your monthly payment would be $553.62.

Be sure to include the percent sign in the interest rate. If you omit it, the payment returned will be alarming! For example, omitting the percent sign in the previous formula produces a monthly payment of $51,000!

Now suppose a 15-year loan is available at the lower interest rate of 8 percent. To find the monthly payments on that loan:

■ Enter the following function in another cell of your worksheet:

```
=PMT(8%/12,180,72000)
```

The payment for this loan would be $688.07 a month. You can now decide whether the larger monthly payments (approximately $134 more) are acceptable in return for a mortgage that will be fully paid after 15 years, saving you tens of thousands of dollars in interest.

DEALING WITH CIRCULAR REFERENCES

Sooner or later, you'll encounter the Microsoft Excel circular-reference alert message shown in Figure 2-4. Excel displays this message when you enter a formula that refers to its own cell, as cell A2 in Figure 2-5 does. The circular

FIGURE 2-4. *The circular-reference alert message.*

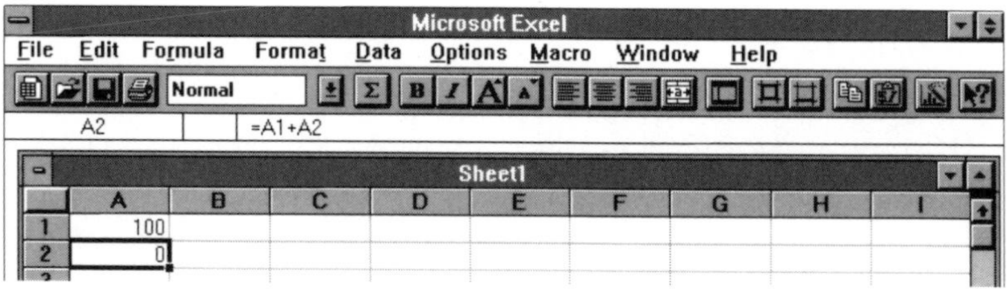

FIGURE 2-5. *A worksheet with a circular reference in cell A2.*

61

reference can also be indirect, as when cell A3 refers to cell B5, cell B5 refers to cell B10, and cell B10 refers back to cell A3.

The circular-reference alert message means that Excel can't calculate a result because the computation depends on the value of the formula itself. Generally, a circular reference results from a data-entry error or from a flaw in the logical structure of your worksheet. You can usually track down data-entry errors quickly. Look first in the cell listed in the message area of the status bar at the bottom of the screen. Then, if you see no mistake there, look in each of the cells referred to by the formula. If you still can't find the error, the problem might require a thorough, methodical examination of the inter-relationships in the worksheet.

At times, you can intentionally create a circular reference to calculate a value. For example, suppose you want to make a contribution equal to 25 per-cent of your net income to a retirement plan. By "net income," you mean in-come after all expenses, *including* the retirement-plan contribution. This computation is expressed algebraically for a net income of $60,000 as follows:

$C = .25 * N$
$N = 60000 - C$

where C is the amount of the contribution, N is net income, and net income before the contribution is deducted is $60,000.

To solve this type of equation in Excel, follow these steps:

1. First, unclutter your worksheet: Drag through a range of cells that covers all the entries in your practice worksheet, and then choose the Clear command from the Edit menu. Click OK, or press Enter in the dialog box that appears. This will clear all the entries. (You'll learn more about the Clear command in Chapter 3, "Revising and Reviewing Worksheets.")

2. Now enter the following formula in cell A1:

   `=60000-A2`

3. Enter the following formula in cell A2:

   `=A1*25%`

After you enter the formulas, Excel beeps, displays the alert message shown in Figure 2-4, and waits for your response without performing any calcula-tions. The problem is that to compute the value of cell A1, Excel first has to compute the value of cell A2. But the value of cell A2 is dependent on the value of cell A1. To solve the equations, Excel must temporarily overlook the circular reference. To proceed, follow these steps:

1. Click the OK button, or press Enter, to remove the alert message from your screen.

2. Choose Calculation from the Options menu. The following dialog box appears.

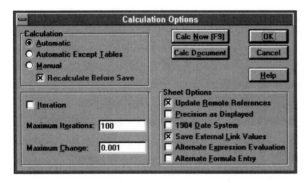

3. Click the Iteration check box to tell Excel you want it to try to resolve the circular reference, and change the entry in the Maximum Iterations box to 1.

4. Click the OK button, or press Enter.

When the dialog box disappears, the value of cell A2 changes to 15000 (25 percent of 60000). Excel has set the initial value of cell A2 to 0 for the purpose of calculating a value for cell A1. After Excel has a value for cell A1 (60000), it uses that value in the formula in cell A2.

Now follow these steps:

1. Press F9, the shortcut key for choosing the Calc Now button in the Calculation Options dialog box. Excel recalculates the formulas based on the current values of cells A1 and A2. The value of cell A1 changes to 45000, and the value of cell A2 changes to 11250.

2. Continue pressing F9. The values of cells A1 and A2 continue changing, but by ever-decreasing amounts.

Each time you press F9, Excel calculates new values for the two cells, using their current values. Each round of calculations is called an *iteration*. Eventually, the values in the cells change little, if at all, with each iteration. At that point, your problem is solved.

Normally you'll want the program to run through as many iterations as are necessary to find correct values for the formulas, without your having to press F9 for each iteration.

1. Choose the Calculation command from the Options menu again.

2. Change the value in the Maximum Iterations box back to 100. This setting, combined with the Maximum Change setting, tells Excel to perform up to 100 iterations, but to stop when the maximum change in the computed values is less than or equal to 0.001. (These default iteration entries allow Microsoft Excel to return correct values in most cases.)

3. To close the dialog box, click the OK button, or press Enter.

To see the default iteration settings in action,

1. Select cell A2 in the worksheet.

2. Change the formula to

```
=A1*20%
```

When you press Enter, the value in cell A1 becomes 50000, and the value in cell A2 becomes 10000. Excel has almost instantaneously iterated its way to the correct values.

When the Iteration option is selected in the Calculation dialog box, you won't see a message if you accidentally create a circular reference, so,

1. Choose the Calculation command from the Options menu again, and turn off the Iteration option.

2. Click OK or press Enter when Excel displays its circular-reference message.

Remember, turn on iteration only when you've consciously decided to use a circular reference.

Don't forget that when Excel displays the circular-reference alert message, it also displays a status-bar message that tells you which cell contains the circular reference.

WORKING WITH DATES AND TIMES

With Microsoft Excel, you can use dates and times in formulas. For example, suppose you will receive payments on a loan, and the exact amount to be allocated to interest depends on the time that has elapsed since the previous payment. Excel represents time intervals as decimal numbers, making short work of this type of calculation.

Entering Dates and Times

You can type dates and times in Microsoft Excel worksheets in a number of formats. For example, all of the following are valid ways to enter *April 15, 1995, at 5:00 PM*:

    4/15/95 5:00 PM
    15 Apr 95 17:00
    April 15, 1995 5 PM
    17:00:00 4-15-1995

To see how Microsoft Excel handles these different formats,

1. Select an empty column in your worksheet.

2. Enter each of the dates and times from the preceding list.

As you do so, watch the formula bar after you press Enter. The date value always appears there in the following format:

    4/15/1995 5:00:00 PM

However, Excel fills the cells with pound signs (#) because the cells aren't wide enough to display the date and time. Widen the cells now:

1. Point to the right border of the header of the column in which you made the entries.

2. Drag the border to the right.

As you can now see, Excel displays these date/time entries in m/d/yy h:mm format (4/15/1995 17:00) unless you specify a different format.

Excel selects different formats depending on how you enter the dates. In this example, Excel uses one format when a month, day, year, and time are all included. But a date such as 15 April 1995 would be displayed in a different format: *15-Apr-95*. If you enter only the day and month, Excel supplies the current year from your computer's system clock. Only the day and month are displayed on the worksheet, but you can see that the year is included in the formula bar.

Take a minute to enter a variety of dates in different formats to become familiar with how Excel handles them. You'll learn how to change the format in Chapter 4, ''Formatting Worksheets.''

Microsoft Excel can use dates and times in formulas and functions because it holds all dates and times as serial numbers in your computer's memory. The numbers from 1 through 65380 represent the dates January 1, 1900, through December 31, 2078. If you try to enter a date outside this range, Excel treats the entry as a number, but not as a date. Internally, Excel expresses any date within this span as a number equal to the number of days elapsed between December 31, 1899, and the given date. Thus, *April 15, 1995*, is represented as 34804, the number of days since December 31, 1899.

Excel expresses time as a decimal fraction of a whole day. For example, the time 5:00 PM is represented as the value 0.708333333333333 (that is, 17 divided by 24). Thus, the complete serial number for *April 15, 1995, at 5:00 PM* is the day number plus the time fraction: 34804.7083333333.

Using Dates and Times in Formulas

Suppose that on March 1, 1992, you purchased a new home and in the process took out a second mortgage for $20,000. You're required to make payments on this second mortgage once a year, and the interest rate is 11 percent. It is now August 10, 1992, and interest rates have dropped. You realize that because of the high interest rate, you should pay off this loan as quickly as possible. You would like to know how much interest has accumulated to date.

To calculate the interest,

- Enter the following data in the cells indicated (overwriting any existing entries):

Cell	Entry
A1	3/1/92
A2	8/10/92
A3	=ROUND(20000*(A2−A1)/366*11%,2)

The formula in cell A3 returns 973.77, the amount of interest that has accumulated on the $20,000 balance as of August 10, 1992. To pay off the loan, then, you'll need to come up with a total of $20,973.77.

Using Date and Time Functions

Thanks to some useful Microsoft Excel functions, you have considerable flexibility in using dates and times in worksheets. Let's take a look at a few of these functions.

The NOW function is one of the few Excel functions that do not require any arguments.

1. Open a blank worksheet, and widen column A by dragging to the right as you did earlier.

2. Type the following function in cell A1:

```
=NOW( )
```

The NOW function obtains the current date and time from your computer's internal clock and displays the information in the cell. You'll use this worksheet again in a moment, so keep it on your screen now.

The date and time displayed in the cell aren't continuously updated. They change only when the worksheet is opened or recalculated.

Table 2-4 lists functions that extract parts of a date or time from the serial number. You can use these functions to determine, for example, what day of the week a particular date falls on. Each of these functions returns an integer. The ranges of possible values are shown in the third column of the table.

Function	Value returned	Range
YEAR()	Year	1900 through 2078
MONTH()	Month of the year	1 through 12
DAY()	Day of the month	1 through 31
WEEKDAY()	Day of the week	1 through 7 (1 equals Sunday)
HOUR()	Hour of the day	0 through 23
MINUTE()	Minute of the hour	0 through 59
SECOND()	Second of the minute	0 through 59
DAYS360()	Number of days between two dates based on a 360-day year	1 through 64440 (for example, =DAYS360("11/1/89","11/1/90") produces 360)

TABLE 2-4. *Date and time functions.*

Experiment with these functions using the value returned by the NOW function you entered in cell A1 of your worksheet. To get you started, an example is shown at the top of the next page.

■ To display the year, select cell A2 and enter the function

=YEAR(A1).

Close all worksheets except *ALSPORTS* when you're done. (You don't need to save them.)

USING NAMES

Microsoft Excel allows you to assign names to individual cells and ranges so that you can refer to the cell or range by name instead of by reference. This capability means that you don't have to worry about remembering the precise locations of the cells you want to use in your formulas, and you don't have to spend time scrolling around the worksheet looking for them.

Naming Individual Cells

To assign a name to a single cell (for example, cell B5 in the *ALSPORTS* worksheet), follow these steps:

1. Select cell B5.

2. Choose the Define Name command from the Formula menu. The following dialog box appears:

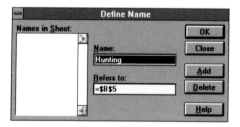

When you select the Define Name command, Microsoft Excel searches adjacent cells for text entries that might provide an appropriate name. Having found the word *Hunting* in cell A5, Excel suggests that name for cell B5. Excel also displays the reference of the active cell. (The reference is displayed in fixed-reference format, which you'll learn about in Chapter 3, ''Revising and Reviewing Worksheets.'')

3. Now edit the name. Type *JulyHunting* (no spaces) in the text box. The name Excel suggested disappears as you start typing.

4. Click the Add button. At this point you could add more names to your worksheet if you wanted.

5. For now, though, click the Close button.

6. Now select a blank cell in the worksheet, and enter the formula:

   =JulyHunting

7. Press Enter, and Microsoft Excel displays the value from cell B5 in the active cell, just as if you had entered the formula =B5.

After you define a name, it appears in the Name list box whenever you choose the Define Name command from the Formula menu.

Microsoft Excel names can contain numeric characters, but names must begin with a letter. The letters R (for row) and C (for column) are valid first letters only if they are immediately followed by an additional letter, not a number.

Naming Ranges

You can assign a name to a range of cells in the same way you assign a name to a single cell. Simply select the range, and then choose the Define Name command from the Formula menu. In the Define Name dialog box, type the name you want to assign, and then click OK.

Allowing Excel to Assign Names

You can define multiple names with one command. To define multiple names in the *ALSPORTS* worksheet, follow these steps:

1. Select the range A3:C8.

2. Choose the Create Names command from the Formula menu. The following dialog box appears:

   Microsoft Excel goes to the edge of the specified range to find text entries to use as names.

3. Because you have entered text labels in column A and row 3, accept the default options (Top Row and Left Column) by clicking OK or pressing Enter.

You can now use any of the words in the top row and left column of the selected range as names for the corresponding cells. For example, to reference a cell in the *ALSPORTS* worksheet by name, all you need to do is enter the department name and month, in any order, separated by a space. To try this for yourself,

1. Move to a remote part of the worksheet, and press F5 (the shortcut key for the Goto command).

2. Type *August Camping* (note the space) in the dialog box that appears.

3. Click OK or press Enter, and the highlight jumps to cell C6, which is the intersection of the *August* column and the *Camping* row.

Using Names in Formulas

You can use names as arguments in formulas. To see how this works, follow these steps:

1. Select a blank cell and enter the following formula:

```
=SUM(Hunting:Other)
```

2. Select another blank cell, and enter the following formula:

```
=SUM(B5:C8)
```

Both formulas return the same value (163710).

Deleting Names

When you select a rectangular range and choose the Create Names command from the Formula menu, Microsoft Excel assigns the label in the top-left corner to *every* cell in the range. The word *Dept.* has therefore been assigned to every cell in the range A3:C8. However, in the *ALSPORTS* worksheet, only the specific departments and the months are useful as names, so you can delete the name *Dept.* and any other names you no longer need.

To delete *Dept.* and *JulyHunting*, follow these steps:

1. Choose the Define Name command from the Formula menu.

2. Select *Dept.* from the list box.

3. Click the Delete button to delete the name.

4. Select *JulyHunting* from the list box.

5. Click the Delete button again, then click OK or press Enter.

Clean up the worksheet now by deleting the entries you made in blank cells while learning to use cell names. Then click on the Save tool to save the *ALSPORTS* worksheet for use in the next chapter.

CONCLUSION

This chapter has introduced formulas, briefly explained some of the most important Microsoft Excel functions, and explained the concept of cell and range names. We will cover more Microsoft Excel functions later on. Many functions, however, such as the functions that manipulate text, are not covered in this introductory book. For detailed information on these functions, use the Help command, or refer to the Microsoft Excel documentation.

Chapter 3

Revising and Reviewing Worksheets

The real beauty of Microsoft Excel worksheets lies in the ease with which you can make revisions. In this chapter, you'll learn how to revise worksheets, and you'll see how Excel keeps track of your data changes and recalculates the worksheet. You'll also learn how to use Excel's document protection to prevent unwanted revisions to your worksheets.

COPYING AND MOVING DATA

The ability to copy and move data and formulas is important when you are constructing large, sophisticated worksheets. In this section, you'll look at the tools Microsoft Excel provides for copying, cutting, and pasting.

 You can display more of your worksheet on the screen by enlarging (maximizing) both the Microsoft Excel window and the document window if they are not already maximized. Simply click the Maximize button (with the up arrowhead) in the top-right corner of each window.

Copying Data with Drag and Drop

Copying cell contents with Microsoft Excel is a snap thanks to the mouse and a feature called *drag and drop*. To demonstrate, let's calculate, in cell D10, the July-to-August sales gain for all departments combined in the *ALSPORTS* worksheet. To prepare for the example,

■ Start Excel, if necessary, and open the *ALSPORTS* worksheet.

To make this calculation, you could select cell D10 and enter the appropriate formula, but it's much easier to copy the formula in cell D8 by dragging it to cell D10. To drag the formula, follow these steps:

1. First, verify that the drag-and-drop feature is turned on by selecting the Workspace command from the Options menu. The check box next to Cell Drag and Drop should contain an X. If it does not, click the box. Click OK or press Enter.

2. Now, select cell D8.

3. Hold down the Ctrl key and move the mouse pointer to the border of cell D8. Stop when the pointer takes the shape of an arrow next to a plus sign:

4. Hold down the left mouse button and drag toward cell D10. As you drag, a pale gray rectangle shadows the movement of the mouse pointer.

5. When the rectangle surrounds cell D10, release the mouse button and the Ctrl key.

Cell D10 now displays the value 0.10804. As you can see in the formula bar, Excel copied the formula in cell D8 to show you the increase in sales from July to August.

Copying Data with Copy and Paste

Microsoft Excel often gives you more than one way to carry out an action. To copy, for example, you can not only use the drag-and-drop method, you can also use the Copy tool on the Standard toolbar or the Copy command, as described next, or you can use keyboard shortcuts.

Suppose you have just received the September sales figures for Alan's Sports. You want to add another section to your worksheet to show the increase in sales, for each department, from August to September. To create the new section, begin by copying the department names, as follows:

1. Select the range A4:A8.

2. Click the Copy tool on the Standard toolbar:

or choose the Copy command from the Edit menu. A moving dotted line, the *marquee,* surrounds the selected cells.

3. Select cell A13.

4. Press Enter.

Cells A13 through A17 now display the department names you copied from cells A4:A8.

Although it might seem that you carried out only one command, you actually carried out two. Copying in Microsoft Excel requires choosing two successive commands: the Copy command and the Paste command. Because you began this operation with the Copy command, Excel interpreted the Enter key as a shortcut for using the Paste command. It also canceled the marquee to prevent further pasting of the data.

As you can see, Microsoft Excel copies data to a *paste range* the same size and shape as the *copy range,* with the top-left cell as the active cell.

 The data you copy or move into a given cell replaces any data currently occupying that cell. Remember, though, that if you mistakenly overwrite data with the Paste command, you can recover it with the Undo command from the Edit menu (if you haven't yet carried out any other command).

When you use the Copy and Paste commands, you don't have to visit the Edit menu repeatedly. You can use keyboard shortcuts for both the Copy and Paste commands:

■ To copy data: Hold down Ctrl and press C.

■ To paste data: Hold down Ctrl and press V.

If you need to copy a given range to multiple locations in a worksheet, choose the Paste command or hold down Ctrl and press V instead of Enter to complete the copy operation. The marquee remains active, signaling that you can paste the selected data in as many locations as you want, as long as you paste with Ctrl-V. To complete the command, press Enter when you paste the data for the last time, or press Esc to remove the marquee.

Now that you know how to copy cells from one location in the worksheet to another, use the method of your choice to add to the new section of your worksheet. Do the following:

1. Copy cell D3 to cell D12.

2. Copy the range C3:C10 to B12:B19. Click OK or press Enter if Excel asks for confirmation before it overwrites existing data.

Your worksheet should now look like the one in Figure 3-1.

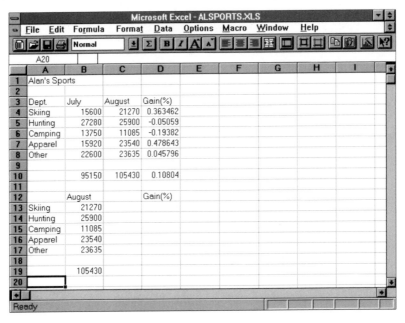

FIGURE 3-1. *The* ALSPORTS *worksheet with Gain(%) and the August sales figures copied.*

Moving Data with Drag and Drop

Like the copy operation, the move operation consists of two commands. You must use both the Cut and the Paste commands from the Edit menu.

Moving cell data with the drag-and-drop method is very straightforward. It's identical to copying, except that you don't hold down the Ctrl key while dragging. To learn how to move cell data from one part of a worksheet to another, start by entering the September sales figures. Enter *September* in cell E3, and then enter the following sales figures in the range E4:E8:

Cell	Value
E4	36560
E5	28710
E6	7250
E7	27800
E8	30840

Now suppose you decide to move the September data to the lower portion of the worksheet. Follow these steps:

1. Select the range E3:E8.

2. Move the pointer to the border surrounding the selected range. Stop when the pointer takes the shape of an arrow.

3. Press the mouse button, drag the gray outline to the range C12:C17, and release the mouse button. Click OK or press Enter if Excel asks for confirmation before it overwrites existing data.

The range C12:C17 now displays the September data, leaving the original cells E3:E8 blank.

Moving Data with Cut and Paste

Cutting and pasting with commands is much like copying and pasting with a twist: You use the Cut command instead of the Copy command, and you move data rather than duplicate it. To move the contents of cell D12 to cell E12, follow these steps:

1. Select cell D12.

2. Hold down Ctrl and press X (the keyboard shortcut for the Cut command on the Edit menu). The marquee surrounds cell D12.

3. Select cell E12 and press Enter to move the data.

4. The move you just made was not a necessary one, so undo the move by choosing Undo Paste from the Edit menu and pressing Esc.

When you undo a copy or move operation, you are actually undoing only the Paste command because that was the most recent command. As a result, the cut range remains active, and you must press Esc to cancel the Cut command.

The Fastest Way to Copy

You might have noticed that a small black square appears in the bottom-right corner of the border around the selected range. It's called the *fill handle,* and it's a great timesaver when you need to fill a range of cells with similar formulas. The following practice uses the fill handle to enter formulas in cells D13:D17. Although you could achieve the same result by simply copying the formulas from cells D4:D8, follow the steps outlined below to see how easily you can fill a range of cells with similar data or formulas.

When you fill cells, you must have something to fill them with, so start as follows:

1. Select the formula in cell D4.

2. Copy the formula to cell D13.

Now follow these steps:

1. If necessary, select cell D13.

2. Move the pointer to the fill handle. The pointer takes the shape of a plus sign as shown here:

3. Press the mouse button and drag the fill handle down until the gray outline covers cells D14 through D17.

4. Release the mouse button.

Like copying, fill operations overwrite any existing data in the destination portion of the selected range.

Using the Fill Commands on the Edit Menu

Generally, the fill handles are the best way to replicate formulas in adjacent cells. But you can also use the Fill Down and Fill Right commands from the Edit menu. Copy the formula in cell B19 to cell C19 by following these steps:

1. Select the cell range you want to fill, including the cell(s) containing the formula(s) you want to copy. In this case, select cells B19 and C19.

2. Select the desired command (Fill Down or Fill Right) from the Edit menu. In this case, choose Fill Right.

To perform a Fill Left or a Fill Up, select the area to fill, hold down the Shift key, and open the Edit menu. The Edit menu will show Fill Left in place of Fill Right and Fill Up in place of Fill Down.

You've nearly completed the August-September portion of your worksheet. As a final step,

1. Select cell D10.

2. Use the method of your choice to copy the formula from cell D10 to cell D19.

Your screen should now look like Figure 3-2.

	A	B	C	D	E	F	G	H	I
1	Alan's Sports								
2									
3	Dept.	July	August	Gain(%)					
4	Skiing	15600	21270	0.363462					
5	Hunting	27280	25900	-0.05059					
6	Camping	13750	11085	-0.19382					
7	Apparel	15920	23540	0.478643					
8	Other	22600	23635	0.045796					
9									
10		95150	105430	0.10804					
11									
12		August	Septembe	Gain(%)					
13	Skiing	21270	36560	0.718853					
14	Hunting	25900	28710	0.108494					
15	Camping	11085	7250	-0.34596					
16	Apparel	23540	27800	0.180969					
17	Other	23635	30840	0.304845					
18									
19		105430	131160	0.244048					
20									

FIGURE 3-2. *The* ALSPORTS *worksheet with the August-September sales comparison.*

INSERTING AND DELETING

Unlike paper worksheets, Microsoft Excel worksheets give you the ability to insert blank rows or columns to hold information that might have slipped your mind when you were creating the original worksheet layout.

Inserting Rows and Columns

Suppose you want to add a descriptive title to your worksheet, but you still want to retain the blank row above the sales data. To do so, you must insert a new row. To insert a new row above row 3 and add a title, follow these steps:

1. Select the entire row 3 by clicking its header.

2. Choose the Insert command from the Edit menu. The rows from 3 on move down, leaving a new, blank row 3. (If Excel displays a dialog box, you selected a cell or a range instead of the entire row. Press Esc, select row 3, and choose the Insert command again.)

3. In cell A2, enter *Month-to-Month Sales*.

Now suppose Alan's Sports has decided to break the Other category into two parts: Team Sports and Golf. To make this change, follow these steps:

1. Insert a new row above row 9.

2. Enter *Team Sports* in cell A9.

3. Replace Other by entering *Golf* in cell A10.

4. Enter the following sales figures in columns B and C of rows 9 and 10 for the newly created departments.

Department	July Sales ·	August Sales
Team Sports	12500	13930
Golf	10100	9705

5. Copy cell D8 to cell D9 (using the fill handle if you want) to compute the percentage gain for the Team Sports department.

Now you'll use a different method to add another new row immediately above row 19:

1. Select the entire row 9.

2. Choose Copy from the Edit menu.

3. Select cell A19.

4. Choose the Insert Paste command from the Edit menu.
    Excel copies the data in row 9 to row 19, and in the process, moves everything below row 19 down a row to make room.

5. Press Esc to cancel the Copy command.

To finish up,

1. Copy the August sales figures for the Team Sports and Golf departments from cells C9:C10 to cells B19:B20.

2. In cells C19 and C20, enter *22570* and *8270* (the September sales figures for Team Sports and Golf).

3. Replace *Other* in cell A20 with *Golf.*

Your worksheet should now look like the one in Figure 3-3.

	A	B	C	D	E	F	G	H	I
1	Alan's Sports								
2	Month-to-Month Sales								
3									
4	Dept.	July	August	Gain(%)					
5	Skiing	15600	21270	0.363462					
6	Hunting	27280	25900	-0.05059					
7	Camping	13750	11085	-0.19382					
8	Apparel	15920	23540	0.478643					
9	Team Spc	12500	13930	0.1144					
10	Golf	10100	9705	-0.03911					
11									
12		95150	105430	0.10804					
13									
14		August	Septembe	Gain(%)					
15	Skiing	21270	36560	0.718853					
16	Hunting	25900	28710	0.108494					
17	Camping	11085	7250	-0.34596					
18	Apparel	23540	27800	0.180969					
19	Team Spc	13930	22570	0.620244					
20	Golf	9705	8270	-0.14786					

FIGURE 3-3. *The* ALSPORTS *worksheet with Other replaced by the Team Sports and Golf departments.*

Excel makes it as easy to insert new columns as it is to insert new rows in your worksheets. Practice inserting a new column in front of the current column D, as follows:

1. Select all of column D by clicking its header. (When you insert columns, select the column to the right of the location where you need the new column.)

2. Choose the Insert command from the Edit menu.

Deleting Rows and Columns

Deleting rows and columns is as straightforward as inserting them. To delete the blank column you just inserted in the *ALSPORTS* worksheet:

1. Select column D (if it is not already selected).

2. Choose the Delete command from the Edit menu.

 If you enter data in a remote area of the worksheet, you might forget that it's there. It's a good policy always to scroll through the worksheet before deleting rows or columns, to ensure that you don't inadvertently delete important data.

Inserting Cells

You don't always have to insert entire rows or columns in a worksheet. When you want to insert only a few cells, simply select the same number of cells below or to the right of the location where you need the new cells, and choose the Insert command from the Edit menu. Microsoft Excel shifts other cells in the worksheet to make room for the new cells. However, you must first choose between shifting the selected cells and all cells located to the right of them to the *right* and shifting the selected cells and all cells located below them *down*. To see how this works, follow these steps:

1. Select the range A4:A12.

2. Choose the Insert command from the Edit menu. The following dialog box appears:

3. Confirm that Shift Cells Right is selected.

4. Click OK, or press Enter.

The labels in these cells move one column to the right.

Deleting Cells

The Delete command on the Edit menu works in much the same manner as the Insert command. To delete some cells, follow these steps:

1. If the cells are not selected, select the range A4:A12.

2. Choose the Delete command from the Edit menu.

3. Confirm that Shift Cells Left is selected.

4. Click OK, or press Enter.

The labels move left to column A, again without changing anything above or below the selection.

 Note that the Insert and Delete commands on the Edit menu work only with single, rectangular selections. You cannot insert or delete multiple, noncontiguous ranges (or multiple rows or columns) with one command.

USING THE SHORTCUT MENU

Microsoft Excel offers *shortcut menus* that include the most frequently used editing commands related to the current selection. These handy little menus are often the quickest means of accomplishing a task, such as inserting or deleting cell ranges. To see a shortcut menu, you select the cell or cells you want to affect, and then click the *right* mouse button. To see how it works, follow these steps:

1. Select column C by clicking the column header.

2. Click the right mouse button. The shortcut menu shown below appears.

3. Click the Delete command (using the left mouse button).

You've deleted a column with three clicks and minimal wrist movement. Before you proceed, choose the Undo Delete comand from the Edit menu to restore column C.

CLEARING DATA

One way to clear cells is to use the Backspace key for deleting characters and the Enter key for making the deletions permanent. This isn't practical when you have several cells to clear. To remove data from ranges of cells, it's better to use the Clear command on the Edit menu. Although you can choose Clear from the menu, the fastest way to clear unwanted data from a range of cells is to simply press the Del key. For example:

1. Select D14:D17 and press the Del key. This dialog box appears:

2. Click OK or press Enter. Excel erases the entries from the selected range.

3. To avoid permanent loss, restore the cleared fields by selecting the Undo Clear command from the Edit menu.

As you saw, the Clear dialog box lets you choose the kinds of data you want to delete. Usually, you will accept the default response (Formulas), which, as you've just seen, clears the contents of the selected cells. Any formatting, such as boldfacing, that you have applied remains, however, so any new entries you make in the cells will be displayed with that formatting. (Chapter 4, "Formatting Worksheets," discusses formatting in detail.) You can erase the formatting but not the contents by selecting the Formats option in the Clear dialog box, and you can erase both the contents and the formatting by selecting the All option.

The Clear dialog box allows you to clear cell notes as well as formulas and formats. You'll learn more about cell notes, which are Microsoft Excel's onscreen version of sticky tags, in the next chapter.

CAUTION *The distinction between the Clear command and the Delete command is important. Clear erases data from a cell but leaves the cell in place; clearing data has no effect on surrounding cells. Delete removes the cell itself from the worksheet and moves adjacent cells up or to the left into the position formerly occupied by the deleted cell.*

RELATIVE VS. FIXED CELL ADDRESSES

Revising worksheets can become an exercise in error-trapping if you don't understand the difference between Microsoft Excel's two types of cell addresses: *relative* and *fixed*. Relative addresses identify cells by their positions in relation to the active cell; these are the type of addresses you've used so far. Fixed cell addresses, on the other hand, refer to the fixed, or *absolute*, positions of cells. Fixed addresses use dollar signs ($) to indicate the absolute portions of the cell address. To see an example of relative addressing,

1. Select cell D10, which contains a formula you copied from cell D8 earlier in this chapter. Notice that the formula bar shows relative addresses (no dollar signs) in the cell references. By default, Microsoft Excel uses relative references unless you specify otherwise, as described below. Notice, too, that the formula in cell D10 references cells (B10 and C10) in the same row.

2. Now select cell D8, the cell from which you copied the formula. Look at the formula bar. The addresses, though different, refer to cells that are in the same position *relative to* the cell containing the formula.

To see the difference between using relative and fixed cell addresses, try converting a relative reference to a fixed reference and then copying a cell using a fixed address:

1. First, save the *ALSPORTS* worksheet in case you make an error and want to get back to where you were.

2. Select cell B12.

3. In the formula bar (not on the worksheet), select the range reference B5:B10. When all characters are highlighted, press F4. This key changes cell references from relative to absolute, and vice versa. (You'll learn more about F4 shortly.) Press Enter to complete the edit of the formula. Now the formula should read

```
=SUM($B$5:$B$10)
```

4. Copy the revised formula to cell C12.

Your worksheet now looks like the one in Figure 3-4. Because the formula in cell B12 contains fixed cell references, the formula in cell C12 is exactly the same as the formula in cell B12. However, the formula now in cell C12 doesn't produce the result you want because it totals cells B5 through B10, rather than cells C5 through C10. Because the formula uses a fixed cell reference, copying it to cell C12 yielded unintended (and erroneous) results.

	A	B	C	D	E	F	G	H	I
1	Alan's Sports								
2	Month-to-Month Sales								
3									
4	Dept.	July	August	Gain(%)					
5	Skiing	15600	21270	0.363462					
6	Hunting	27280	25900	-0.05059					
7	Camping	13750	11085	-0.19382					
8	Apparel	15920	23540	0.478643					
9	Team Spc	12500	13930	0.1144					
10	Golf	10100	9705	-0.03911					
11									
12		95150	95150	0					

FIGURE 3-4. *The* ALSPORTS *worksheet after a formula with fixed cell referencing is copied from cell B12 to cell C12.*

To restore the original formula, choose the Undo command from the Edit menu. Press Esc if a marquee surrounds cell B12.

You still have to change the referencing mode in cell B12. First, though, let's investigate mixed cell referencing, in which part of the address is relative and part is fixed. You create a mixed reference by inserting a single dollar sign in front of either the column letter or the row number. The following example shows what happens when you do this. Follow these steps:

1. Select the range F1:F10.

2. Type *10*, hold down Ctrl, and press Enter.

3. Select the range G1:G10.

4. Type the formula

   ```
   =SUM(F$1:F1)
   ```

5. Hold down Ctrl, and press Enter.

Now look at the formulas in cells G2 through G10. The cell address to the left of the colon is F$1 in each formula; the cell address following the colon always reflects the active row in column F. The result is a series of formulas in column G that return cumulative totals of the amounts in column F from row 1 through the current row. The dollar sign, in effect, "anchors" the row number of the first half of the range argument.

The entries you made in columns F and G are not pertinent to the rest of your *ALSPORTS* worksheet, so clear cells F1:G10.

Now change cell B12 back to relative referencing. Use the F4 key again:

1. Select cell B12 and select the entire range reference ($B$5:$B$10) in the formula bar.

2. Press F4. This time, the reference changes from fixed to mixed, with the dollar signs in front of the row numbers.

3. Press F4 again. Now Excel moves the dollar signs in front of the column letters.

4. Press F4 again. The reference changes to relative.

   As you can see, pressing F4 lets you cycle through the possible addressing modes. Pressing F4 a fourth time would change the formula back to fixed.

5. Press Enter to complete the edit of the formula.

UPDATING CELL REFERENCES

When you relocate data referenced by formulas in other cells, Microsoft Excel updates all the formulas that reference the relocated data so that they reflect its new address. This updating happens whether you relocate the data by cutting and pasting or by inserting or deleting cells.

To see how Microsoft Excel updates cell references, follow these steps:

1. Select the entire column C in the *ALSPORTS* worksheet. Take note of the values in the *Gain(%)* column.

2. Choose the Insert command from the Edit menu.

The August sales values now appear in column D, but the values shown in the *Gain(%)* column didn't change. Select any cell in rows 5 through 10 of that column, and you'll see that the gain formulas now refer to cells in column D instead of those in column C. When you're finished, undo the Insert command to return the worksheet to its previous state.

Excel adjusts cell formulas whether the references to the relocated cells are relative, fixed, or mixed.

Updating SUM Functions

In general, deleting a cell referenced by another cell produces a #REF! error value in the worksheet. However, when you insert or delete cells from a range referenced by a SUM function, Microsoft Excel adjusts the range argument to account for the revision.

To see how this adjusting works,

1. Select cell B22 of the *ALSPORTS* worksheet. The formula currently reads as follows:

```
=SUM(B15:B20)
```

2. Now select the entire row 17, and choose the Insert command from the Edit menu.

3. Look again at the SUM formula (now located in cell B23). The formula now reads

```
=SUM(B15:B21)
```

Microsoft Excel has stretched the range argument to include the newly inserted row.

4. Choose the Undo command to undo the row insertion.

 Of course, if you delete the entire range referenced by a SUM function—rows 15 through 20, for example—you will get a #REF! error.

FINDING DATA

Microsoft Excel allows you to move from one cell to another by using either cell references or cell names. It also allows you to search the cells in the worksheet for specific data within the cells.

Finding a Specific Cell

Some worksheets are too big to be entirely displayed on the screen, and size can make it difficult to move from a cell that is currently displayed to a cell that is not on screen. To move to a cell remote from the active cell, you can use the Goto command on the Formula menu. To see how this works, follow these steps:

1. Press F5 (the keyboard shortcut for the Goto command). Excel displays the following dialog box:

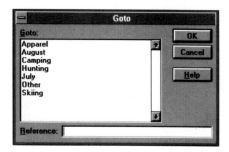

2. Type *D200* in the Reference box and click OK, or press Enter. Microsoft Excel scrolls down and selects cell D200.

3. Press F5 again. This time, the Goto list box and the Reference text box display the address of the worksheet location from which you moved to cell D200.

4. To move back to where you started, click OK or press Enter.

The Goto list box can display the addresses of the last four selected cells to help you move through a large worksheet. As you can see, it also displays all cell and range names for the current worksheet.

Finding Data Within Cells

At times you might want to find cells in the worksheet that contain specific data: a formula, a value, a character sequence, or a format. To find specific data within cells, Microsoft Excel provides the Find command on the Formula menu.

To illustrate, let's use the Find command to locate cells in the *ALSPORTS* worksheet containing numbers divisible by 100. Follow these steps:

1. Select cell A1.

2. Hold down Shift and press F5. This is the keyboard shortcut for the Find command.

3. Type *00* in the Find What box, and click OK or press Enter. The active cell is now B5.

4. Press F7, the repeat Find key. The active cell is now C6—the next cell (going left to right, row by row) containing the characters 00.

Pressing F7 repeatedly selects other cells containing the characters 00, from top to bottom of the worksheet. Pressing Shift-F7 does the same thing, but it searches the worksheet from right to left, bottom to top.

CONTROLLING WORKSHEET CALCULATION

By default, Microsoft Excel recalculates the formulas in a worksheet whenever you make any kind of change. Excel does not, however, automatically recalculate every cell in the worksheet. To save time, it determines which cells are affected by your change and recalculates only those cells. Even so, automatic recalculation can slow you down when you're working with large documents. Luckily, Excel provides a way to turn off recalculation:

■ Choose the Calculation command from the Options menu to display the dialog box shown in Figure 3-5.

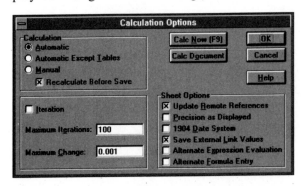

FIGURE 3-5. *The Calculation Options dialog box.*

The Calculation option group offers you three selections: Automatic, Automatic Except Tables, and Manual. The Automatic option turns automatic recalculation back on after you have turned it off. The Automatic Except Tables option turns automatic recalculation on except for cells in data tables. (The subject of data tables is beyond the scope of this book. For more information on this topic, see the Microsoft Excel documentation.) The Manual option postpones recalculation until you specifically ask Microsoft Excel to recalculate the worksheet.

To see how manual recalculation works, follow these steps:

1. Select the Manual option in the Calculation Options dialog box.

2. Click OK, or press Enter.

3. Select cell B9 and change the value in the cell to *10000*. Before you press Enter, look at cell B12.

4. Press Enter. Notice that the total value in cell B12 doesn't change to reflect the lower amount you entered in cell B9.

5. Keeping your eye on cell B12, press F9, the keyboard shortcut for the Calculate Now command, which recalculates the values in a worksheet that is set to Manual recalculation. The value of cell B12 decreases from 95150 to 92650.

Before you continue, reenter 12500 in cell B9. Then choose the Calculation command from the Options menu again, select the Automatic option, and click OK, or press Enter.

PROTECTING DATA FROM CHANGE

You might eventually create worksheets that will be used primarily by people who are less familiar with Microsoft Excel than you are. Or you might want to hide certain private areas of your worksheet to prevent other people from changing or viewing certain vital parts of the worksheet. (For example, you might not mind a little editing of the department names or column headings in the *ALSPORTS* worksheet, but you probably wouldn't want anyone to change the monthly figures or the formulas.) Microsoft Excel lets you protect such important data. Let's look at the protection process in detail.

If you are working on a network, consult the Microsoft Excel documentation or your network system manager for information about document-protection procedures.

Locking and Unlocking Cells

By default, all cells in a worksheet are given a *locked* status. This alone, however, does not protect your formulas or data. So far, for example, the locked status hasn't affected your work on the *ALSPORTS* worksheet. Why not? Because you haven't activated Microsoft Excel's *document-protection* system.

If you intend never to activate document protection, you can leave the status of all cells locked in every worksheet you create. At the opposite extreme, you can also leave all cells locked if you intend to protect every cell in a worksheet.

If, however, you want to protect some cells but not others, you must follow a three-stage procedure: You must unlock the entire worksheet, lock the desired cells, and then activate document protection. To see how this works, follow these steps:

1. Select the entire worksheet by clicking the small, empty rectangle to the left of column header A and above row header 1 (the circled area shown here):

2. Choose the Cell Protection command from the Format menu. The following dialog box appears:

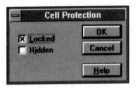

3. Turn off the Locked option and click OK, or press Enter.

The second step in protecting specific cells is to change the appropriate cells back to locked status. To lock certain cells, follow these steps:

1. Select the portions of the worksheet you want to protect. For this example, use the ranges B5:D12 and B15:D22. First, select cells B5:D12. To select the second range, hold down the Ctrl key and drag from cell B15 through cell D22.

2. Choose Cell Protection from the Format menu again. This time, the Locked option in the dialog box is turned off.

3. Turn on the Locked option and click OK, or press Enter.

Now only the cells you want to protect are locked. However, the cell contents can still be changed, because you haven't yet activated the Microsoft Excel document-protection system—the final step in protecting your worksheet's cells. To turn on document protection, follow these steps:

1. Choose the Protect Document command from the Options menu. The following dialog box appears:

2. Type a password in the text box. (For this example, use your initials.) Notice that asterisks appear instead of the characters you type so that no one can read your password as you type it.

3. Click OK, or press Enter.

4. Reenter the password when a dialog box prompts for confirmation. Click OK, or press Enter.

For this example, you used your initials as a password—a relatively easy code to crack. For important data, you will want something more obscure. But be warned: After you protect a document with a password, you cannot change the data without removing that protection, and you cannot remove protection without supplying the password. Record your passwords, but store the records in a secure place.

Now try to enter data in one of the protected cells. You won't be able to do so; instead, you'll hear beeps and see a message telling you that *Locked cells cannot be changed.* Click OK, or press Enter, to remove the error message.

To remove protection, you simply choose the Unprotect Document command from the Options menu. To practice, follow these steps:

1. Choose Unprotect Document from the Options menu.

2. Deliberately enter the wrong password. Microsoft Excel displays an error message and refuses to act. Click OK, or press Enter, to remove the message.

3. Choose the Unprotect Document command again.

4. Type the correct password in the Password text box. Click OK, or press Enter.

Now you can make changes to any cell in the worksheet.

If you don't provide a password in the Password text box when you turn on document protection, Microsoft Excel doesn't require a password before allowing you to turn off protection. Anyone can then remove document protection. If you forget your password and you haven't written it down, all is not lost. Select the entire worksheet, copy it, and then paste it into a blank new worksheet. Because protection status is not copied, you will be able to select cells and change data in the new worksheet.

Using Various Types of Protection

Unless you specify otherwise, Microsoft Excel protects both cell contents and screen objects, such as charts, illustrations, and text boxes you create and add to a worksheet (more about this in Chapters 4 and 6). By choosing the Windows option in the Protect Document dialog box, you can also prevent windows from being moved or resized.

On another level, you can use the Save As command to keep users who don't have the password from opening a document in the first place. To see how this works, follow these steps:

1. Choose the Save As command from the File menu.

2. Click the Options button. The following dialog box appears:

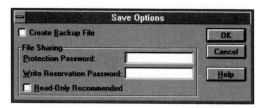

3. Type your initials in the Protection Password text box, and then click OK, or press Enter.

4. Reenter the password as requested. Click OK, or press Enter.

5. Click OK, or press Enter, in the Save As dialog box.

6. Click OK when Microsoft Excel displays a message asking you to confirm that you want the revised file to replace the current one on disk.

7. Close the *ALSPORTS* worksheet, and then reopen it. The following dialog box appears:

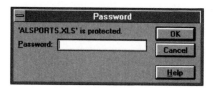

8. Microsoft Excel will open the file only if you enter the correct password. Type the correct password to open the file.

To remove the password protection, follow these steps:

1. Choose the Save As command from the File menu and click the Options button.

2. Delete the password from the Protection Password text box, and then click OK, or press Enter.

3. Click OK, or press Enter, to carry out the Save As command.

4. When Microsoft Excel displays a message asking you to confirm that you want to replace the old version of the file with the new (unprotected) version, click OK, or press Enter.

Finally, suppose you want to protect a file that others must have access to. Once again, you use the Save As command, as follows:

1. Choose Save As from the File menu and click Options to open the Save Options dialog box.

2. Type a password in the Write Reservation Password box instead of in the Protection Password box. Click OK, or press Enter, to close the dialog box. Reenter the password when requested and click OK or press Enter. Click OK, or press Enter, to close the Save As command and, finally, click OK, or press Enter, one last time to confirm replacing the existing file.

After you've closed the file, this type of protection enables anyone to open the file for viewing. To change the file, however, the user must enter the correct password. Otherwise, Microsoft Excel refuses to save the file under its current name.

CONCLUSION

In this chapter, you've learned the basics of revising and protecting worksheets. Next you'll cover worksheet formatting techniques.

Chapter 4

Formatting Worksheets

So far, you've covered the basics of entering, calculating, saving, and revising data in your worksheets. This chapter shows you ways to format data to make it easier to interpret or to give it more impact. First, you'll learn ways to change the width of columns, format numeric data, and align the data within cells. Then you'll find out how to change the appearance of either numbers or text. Finally, you'll look at ways to annotate a worksheet and to add design elements, such as borders and colors, that guide a reader's eye to specific parts of a worksheet.

CHANGING COLUMN WIDTH

When you create a worksheet, all cells have the same width, and all the text and numbers you type appear in the same general size and style. By formatting cells, you can enhance the information in your worksheets, making them more comprehensible and easy to read. To start taking a look at formatting:

1. Open the *ALSPORTS* worksheet if it isn't already open.

2. Maximize the worksheet by clicking the Maximize button in the upper-right corner of the document window.

Notice that all the entries are displayed in a simple, unembellished way known as the General format. Basically, General format aligns text at the left of the cell and numbers at the right. If you don't enter a number as a currency value or a percent, General format displays the number as an integer, a decimal fraction, or (if a whole number is too long for the cell) in scientific notation.

Now you're ready to change this format to accommodate more information and to clarify the information in the worksheet.

Some cell entries are too long to fit into the Microsoft Excel standard columns, which hold eight numeric characters in the default display font. Sometimes an entry fits in the cell in the General format, but becomes too long to fit when you apply a different format. Text entries that are too long appear truncated, or partially hidden, and decimal values are rounded, but the entire entry is still stored in the column.

You can see some examples of long text in the *ALSPORTS* worksheet, shown for reference in Figure 4-1. In Chapter 3, "Revising and Reviewing Worksheets," you replaced the Other department with the Team Sports and Golf departments. The *Team Sports* label is too long to fit in column A of the worksheet, and because the adjacent cell in column B contains an entry, Excel has truncated the *Team Sports* label. Similarly, the word *September* is too long to fit in cell C14. To see again how Excel truncates a label,

■ Replace the entry in cell A4 with the longer word *Department*.

If cell B4 were blank, *Department* would overlap into it, just as the company name (*Alan's Sports*) in cell A1 overlaps into cell B1. Because cell B4 contains

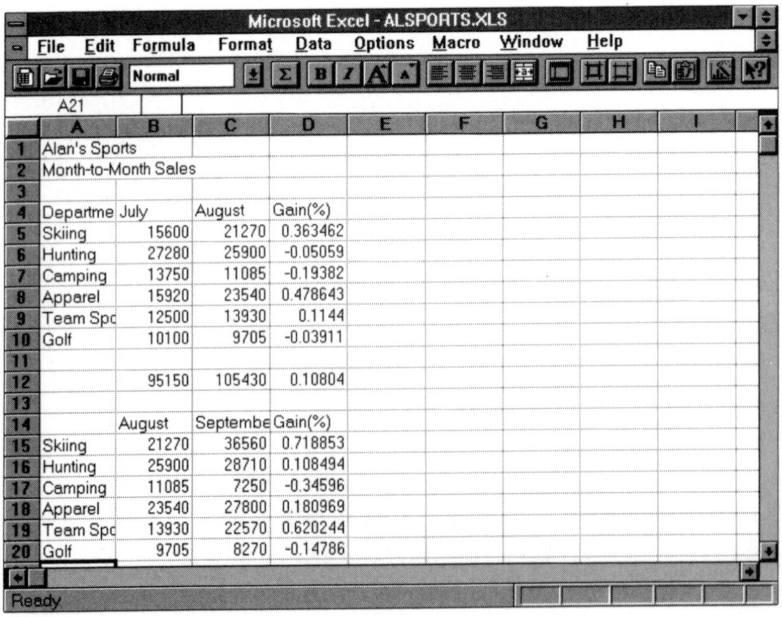

FIGURE 4-1. *The truncated text entries in cells A4, A9, A19, and C14 are too long to be fully displayed.*

a label, however, Microsoft Excel truncates *Department* at the boundary between cells A4 and B4.

Adjusting Columns with the Mouse

When an entry is too long to be fully displayed, you can remedy the situation by widening the column. To widen column A, follow these steps:

1. Point to the right edge of the column A header. Notice that when the pointer is over the vertical line, called a *border*, between the column headers, it changes into the shape shown here:

2. To widen the column, drag the border to the right. As you move the pointer, a shaded vertical line moves with it. The shaded line shows where the new column border will appear if you release the mouse button at that moment.

3. When the column is wide enough to accommodate the words *Department* and *Team Sports*, release the mouse button. Column A expands to the position of the shaded vertical line, as shown below. (You might have to adjust the width again to get it just right.)

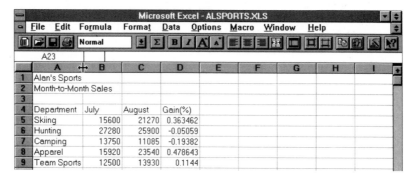

Using the Column Width Command

Another way to change the width of columns is to use the Column Width command on the Format menu. Follow these steps:

1. Select any cell in column C.

2. Choose the Column Width command from the Format menu. Excel opens the dialog box shown at the top of the next page.

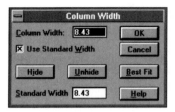

3. Type a new column width in number of characters in the Column Width text box. For this example, *10* or *11* should do. Click OK, or press Enter.

You probably noticed that Microsoft Excel displayed the standard column width as a decimal value, 8.43, in the Column Width dialog box. This measurement refers to fixed-width numeric characters. Because text characters vary in width, you could find yourself using trial-and-error to get the column width you need. A much easier way is to click the Best Fit button in the Column Width dialog box. Best Fit tells Microsoft Excel to adjust the column to fit the longest entry currently selected. (That means you must select either the entire column or the cell containing the longest entry in that column to display all values fully.) If you use the Best Fit button, however, remember that you must use it again, or specify a particular column width, to accommodate subsequent edits or additions.

To reset a column to the standard width, you would follow these steps:

1. Select any cell in the column you want to reset.

2. Choose Column Width from the Format menu.

3. Click the Use Standard Width check box and click OK, or press Enter, to carry out the command.

The Effect of Column Width on Numeric Entries

Microsoft Excel treats a long numeric entry differently from a text entry. Instead of truncating them, Excel rounds decimal numbers and displays very large and very small numbers in scientific notation, which expresses the number in exponential form to fit the number within the current cell width.

To see this change,

1. Select any standard-width cell in the worksheet.

2. Enter the 10-digit decimal number *0.123456789*.

Because the cell can hold only eight digits and the number is in General format, Excel rounds the number to 0.123457 in the cell, but note that the full number is displayed in the formula bar. Excel has rounded, but not modified, the value of the number.

3. Replace the decimal number with *7777777777*. Now Excel displays the number in scientific notation (7.78E+09). Excel would also display a very small number, such as 0.0000000007, in scientific notation (7E–10).

Now follow these steps:

1. Reduce the width of the column containing the 10-digit number to about half the standard width by dragging the right border to the left. Because there's no longer sufficient room to display the number even in exponential format, Excel fills the cell with pound signs (#) to indicate that the cell contains an entry that cannot be displayed. (You might recall seeing these pound signs earlier when you worked with date and time values in Chapter 2, "Using Formulas and Functions.")

2. Finally, drag the right column border to the right until the column is wide enough to display the entire number.

Changing the Width of Several Columns

With Microsoft Excel, you can change the width of several columns at a time. Try the following example:

1. Select columns D through F.

2. Drag the right border of any selected column to the right. When you release the mouse button, Excel widens all three columns.

You can also widen multiple columns by selecting them, choosing the Column Width command from the Format menu, entering a new width in the Column Width text box, and pressing Enter.

Before continuing,

1. Delete the 10-digit numeric entry.

2. Restore any columns you have widened, except columns A and C, to standard width.

CHANGING ROW HEIGHT

Because you inserted rows into the *ALSPORTS* worksheet in Chapter 3, "Revising and Reviewing Worksheets," the data in the worksheet no longer fits on one screen. To see all the data at once, and improve the look of the worksheet, you can reduce the height of blank rows.

Adjusting Rows with the Mouse

To reduce the row heights in your *ALSPORTS* worksheet, follow these steps:

1. Select rows 3, 11, and 21 by clicking the row 3 header, and then holding down the Ctrl key while clicking the row 11 and row 21 headers. (To select row 21 and, at the same time, keep rows 3 and 11 on screen, click the Down scroll button in the vertical scroll bar.)

2. Point to the row 3 header's bottom border. The pointer changes to the following shape:

3. Drag the border up until the row height is about one-third the height of the other rows and release the mouse button to complete the operation.

All three selected rows are now about one-third normal height.

Using the Row Height Command

Here's an alternative method of changing row height:

1. Scroll up if necessary and click the row 1 header to select the entire row.

2. Choose the Row Height command from the Format menu. This dialog box appears:

3. Type *24* in the Row Height box, and press Enter. Excel increases the height of row 1.

This was only an experiment, so before continuing, return row 1 to its original height by choosing Undo Row Height from the Edit menu.

HIDING CELLS

On occasion, you might want to hide some of the data in a worksheet. Perhaps you simply want to reduce clutter. Or you might want to protect certain parts of your worksheet from being changed.

When you hide a row or column of cells, you reduce the row height or the column width to 0. You can hide (or unhide) either columns or rows by clicking the Hide and Unhide buttons in the Column Width and Row Height dialog boxes. You can also use the mouse. The following steps affect row 13 of your worksheet, but you can use the same basic procedure to hide and unhide columns. To hide and unhide row 13, do the following:

1. Point to the bottom edge of the row header and drag it up until the bottom edge is even with the top edge. (Don't drift into row 12, or you'll wind up making row 12 shorter.)

2. Release the mouse button, and row 13 disappears from view.

3. To unhide row 13, drag through the row headers surrounding the hidden row. Doing this will select them all. Choose the Row Height command and click the Unhide button.

 If the hidden row still doesn't appear, the row height probably is not 0. Choose the Row Height command again, click the Standard Height box, and click OK or press Enter.

USING NUMBER FORMATS

As you use Microsoft Excel in your day-to-day work, you'll want to display numeric values in different ways—currency, percentages, and so on. As mentioned earlier, Excel lets you determine how numbers are displayed.

Excel's General number format (the default) does not automatically insert special characters, such as dollar signs, embedded commas, and percent signs. As a result, the numbers in the Alan's Sports sales analysis worksheet are not immediately identifiable as dollar amounts and percentages. A few simple improvements—dollar signs, for instance, or parentheses around negative numbers—would make a big difference. Making the improvements will be simple, thanks to the Formatting toolbar.

Using the Formatting Toolbar

The Formatting toolbar contains tools for performing the most common formatting operations. Follow these steps to display the Formatting toolbar:

1. Choose the Toolbars command from the Options menu.

2. Double-click Formatting in the Show Toolbars list. The Formatting toolbar (shown below) appears on the screen.

3. Drag the toolbar up to the toolbar dock.

 Although the Toolbar command on the Options menu is easy to remember, don't forget that you can also open a new toolbar by pointing to a toolbar, clicking the right *mouse button, and clicking the name of the toolbar you want in the shortcut menu that appears.*

To format the sales figures in the *ALSPORTS* worksheet, follow these steps:

1. Select the range B5:C22.

2. Click the Currency Style tool (shown below) on the Formatting toolbar.

This adds preceding dollar signs, commas, and cents to the numbers on the screen. However, column B is now too narrow to display the figures. The numbers will fit, however, if you remove the decimal places:

1. Point to the left end of the Formatting toolbar and click the down arrow to the right of the Style box (displaying the word *Currency*). The following list drops down:

2. Click the item *Currency (0)*, which means "currency, no decimals." Your worksheet now looks like the one in Figure 4-2.

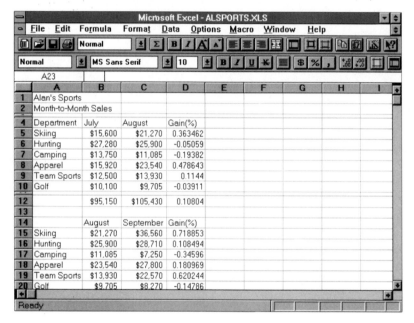

FIGURE 4-2. *The* ALSPORTS *worksheet with the sales figures in Currency format.*

Excel's Built-in Number Formats

Formatting numbers as dollar values told Microsoft Excel to add not only the correct currency symbol but any needed commas, a decimal point, and two digits for cents. How did Excel "know" what to do? It used one of its built-in number formats, some of which were described in the toolbar list box from which you picked Currency (0). The built-in formats tell Excel exactly how to display and print numeric values. If you want, you can choose from, and apply, any of numerous formats by using the Number command on the Format menu. To see some number formats,

1. Select cells B5:C22 if they are no longer highlighted.

2. Choose the Number command from the Format menu. The following dialog box appears:

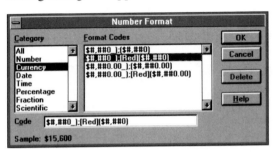

Here, the highlighted entries tell you at a glance both the type (category) and style (format code) Excel is currently applying to the selected cells. To apply a different number format, you would choose the category you wanted from the list in the Category box, and you would choose the code representing that style from the list in the Format Code box. The Code list box toward the bottom of the dialog box shows the code highlighted in the Format Codes list box; it is where, as you'll see later, you can edit a built-in format. The Sample line at the bottom shows how the number in the active cell will look if formatted with that code.

Of all the parts of the dialog box, the codes in the Format Code box are potentially the most confusing, if only because they take a little more explanation. Notice that some of the format codes use zero (0) as a placeholder and others use the pound sign (#). Here's the difference: Choosing a format with 0 in any digit position causes Microsoft Excel to display that digit even if it is a zero. Choosing a format with # causes Excel to suppress the display of nonsignificant zeros. For example, when you display dollar-and-cents amounts, you will generally prefer a format like $#,##0.00, which would display 50 cents as *$0.50* because it suppresses all but one leading zero to the left of the decimal point but always displays the two digits to the right of the decimal point.

Table 4-1 illustrates the effects of the Microsoft Excel built-in formats on cell entries of various types.

Format	Entry	Displayed As
General	1648.2357	1648.2357
0	1648.2357	1648
0.00	1648.2357	1648.24
#,##0	1648.2357	1,648
#,##0.00	1648.2357	1,648.24
#,##0_);(#,##0)	−2345.12	(2,345)
#,##0_);[Red](#,##0)	2345.12	2,345
#,##0.00_);(#,##0.00)	−1456.789	(1,456.79)
#,##0.00_); [Red](#,##0.00)	1456.789	1,456.79
$#,##0_);($#,##0)	2374.1	$2,374
$#,##0_);[Red]($#,##0)	−2374.1	($2,374)
$#,##0.00_);($#,##0.00)	−2374.1	($2,374.10)
$#,##0.00_); [Red]($#,##0.00)	2374.1	$2,374.10
0%	1.179	118%
0.00%	1.179	117.90%
0.00E+00	34586792.51	3.46E+07
# ?/?	3.9375	4
# ??/??	3.9375	3 15/16

TABLE 4-1. *Excel's built-in number formats and their effects. (The column headed* Displayed As *does not show how the numbers are aligned within a cell.)*

Notice that several of the format codes in Table 4-1 actually contain two formats separated by a semicolon (;). In these cases, Excel applies the format on the left of the semicolon to positive values and the format on the right to negative values. The formats that include the word *Red* in brackets display negative numbers in red on a color monitor.

Some of the formats include an underscore (_) followed by a right parenthesis. The underscore tells Excel to skip the width of the character that follows it, so _) creates a space the width of a right parenthesis. This format is used to make positive numbers line up with negative numbers that are enclosed in parentheses.

Entering Data with Built-in Formats

When you start a new spreadsheet, all the blank cells have the General built-in format, but when you enter a number Excel tries to match the number to one of its other built-in formats. For example, if you enter the number 5,280 and include the comma in the number, Excel will assign the #,##0 built-in format. Table 4-2 illustrates the types of entries that Excel will match to one of its built-in formats.

You can change the built-in format assigned to any of the numbers by using the Format Numbers command.

Entry	Format
123.456	General
1,234	#,##0
1,234.23	#,##0.00
$100	$#,##0_);($#,##0)
$1,234.50	$#,##0.00_);($#,##0.00)
20%	0%
22.2%	0.00%
6.02E+23	00E+00
3 3/4	# ?/?
1 11/16	# ??/??

TABLE 4-2. *Types of entries Excel matches to built-in formats.*

Using the Built-in Date Formats

To help you format dates, Microsoft Excel also offers a number of date formats, all accessible through the Numbers command on the Format menu. Table 4-3 illustrates how various built-in date formats affect the appearance of the date July 4, 1995, in a worksheet.

To see how date formats work,

■ Enter *7/31/92* in cell B4 and *8/31/92* in cell C4 of the *ALSPORTS* worksheet.

Although it might appear that Excel treats your entries as text, the program actually assigns them a built-in date format.

Format	Display
m/d/yy	7/4/95
d-mmm-yy	4-Jul-95
d-mmm	4-Jul
mmm-yy	Jul-95
m/d/yy h:mm	7/4/95 0:00

TABLE 4-3. *Excel's built-in date formats and their effects.*

Suppose you don't like the date format used in the worksheet. You'd rather show the month's three-letter abbreviation and the year. To apply the new format (mmm-yy), follow these steps:

1. Select cells B4 and C4.

2. Choose the Number command from the Format menu. Because dates are selected, Microsoft Excel automatically displays the format codes for dates:

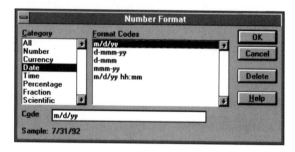

3. Double-click the *mmm-yy* format in the Format Codes list.

The month names now read *Jul-92* and *Aug-92*, respectively.

Changing Formats

Suppose you've looked at your worksheet again and realize you don't want dollar signs in every row. They're easy to remove:

1. Select the ranges B6:C10 and B15:C20. (Remember, hold down Ctrl while dragging to select the second range.)

2. Click the down arrow next to the Style box at the left-hand end of the Formatting toolbar. When the list opens, notice that Excel offers both comma and currency formats with no decimals.

3. The only real difference between the two is the presence of a dollar sign in the currency format, so click *Comma (0)*. The dollar signs disappear from the selected cells, yet the numbers still contain comma separators and maintain the same alignment down the column.

Often, changing from one number format to another can be as simple as you've just seen. At other times, however, Excel might not offer a built-in format that is exactly what you need. When that happens, you can build your own.

Creating Custom Formats

For percentages, Excel offers two basic built-in formats: 0% and 0.00%. Suppose, however, that you want a different format for the percentages in column D of your *ALSPORTS* worksheet: You want percentages displayed with one decimal place, and with negative values enclosed in parentheses to make them stand out more clearly. You can do it all by building a custom format. Follow these steps:

1. Select the ranges D5:D12 and D15:D22.

2. Click the Percent Style tool shown below:

3. Choose the Number command from the Format menu. When the Number Format dialog box opens, Excel highlights its 0% built-in format and displays the same item in the Code text box below.

4. To build your custom format, click in the Code text box and edit the 0% entry to look like this:

0.0%–);(0.0%)

(The underscore and single closing parenthesis in the first part of the format are needed to make positive values line up properly with negative values.)

5. Click OK or press Enter. When your worksheet reappears, it looks like the one in Figure 4-3.

Microsoft Excel - ALSPORTS.XLS

File   Edit   Formula   Format   Data   Options   Macro   Window   Help

Normal

Normal   MS Sans Serif   10

A24

	A	B	C	D	E	F	G	H	I
4	Department	Jul-92	Aug-92	Gain(%)					
5	Skiing	$15,600	$21,270	36.3%					
6	Hunting	27,280	25,900	(5.1%)					
7	Camping	13,750	11,085	(19.4%)					
8	Apparel	15,920	23,540	47.9%					
9	Team Sports	12,500	13,930	11.4%					
10	Golf	10,100	9,705	(3.9%)					
12		$95,150	$105,430	10.8%					
13									
14		August	September	Gain(%)					
15	Skiing	21,270	36,560	71.9%					
16	Hunting	25,900	28,710	10.8%					
17	Camping	11,085	7,250	(34.6%)					
18	Apparel	23,540	27,800	18.1%					
19	Team Sports	13,930	22,570	62.0%					
20	Golf	9,705	8,270	(14.8%)					
22		$105,430	$131,160	24.4%					

Ready

FIGURE 4-3. *The* ALSPORTS *worksheet with currency and percent formats applied.*

Not only have you created a custom format for this occasion, you've created one for as long as you need it. To see it,

1. Choose the Number command again.

2. When the Number Format dialog box opens, your custom format appears at the end of the percentage category list:

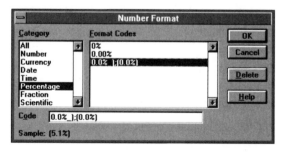

Notice that Excel automatically adds custom formats to the most appropriate category for them. You should keep this new format, at least until you finish the examples in this book. If you later want to delete it or any other formats you've created, simply choose the Number command, highlight the

111

format you want to remove, click the Delete button in the Number Format dialog box, and click OK to complete the command.

Table 4-4 lists a series of custom formats and the resulting worksheet displays. These formats may give you some ideas for putting Excel to work in your own worksheets. The 00000-0000 and (000) 000-0000 formats can be particularly useful in entering 9-digit ZIP codes and 10-digit telephone numbers, respectively. They streamline data entry by inserting the non-numeric characters for you.

Format	Entry	Displayed As
$#,###.00_C_R;$#,###.00CR	−437.59	$437.59CR
#,###_);(#,###)	−437.59	(438)
0.####%	0.918	91.8%
0.##%	0.918369	91.84%
00000-0000	487063034	48706-3034
(000) 000-0000	2137645555	(213) 764-5555
d mmmm yyyy	11/9/92	9 November 1992
mm-dd-yy	11/9/92	11-09-92

TABLE 4-4. *Custom number formats and their effects, excluding alignment in the cell.*

Let's look more closely at the date-format symbols. Table 4-5 shows the format symbols for each of the elements of a date (month, day, and year) and their effects on the date July 4, 1995. You can use any of these symbols in your custom date formats.

Format	Display	Format	Display
m	7	dd	04
mm	07	ddd	Tue
mmm	Jul	dddd	Tuesday
mmmm	July	yy	95
d	4	yyyy	1995

TABLE 4-5. *Excel's date-format symbols and their effects, excluding alignment in the cell.*

POSITIONING DATA WITHIN CELLS

Unless you specify otherwise, Microsoft Excel uses General alignment in which it left-aligns text and right-aligns numbers. That is, text fills cell space from left to right, and numbers fill cell space from right to left. You can change this alignment in either of two ways:

- With the Left, Center, and Right Align tools on the Standard toolbar:

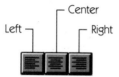

- With the Alignment command on the Format menu, which displays the dialog box shown in Figure 4-4.

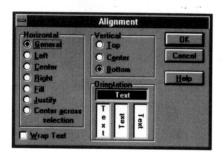

FIGURE 4-4. *The Alignment dialog box.*

Although the Alignment dialog box offers more than side-to-side alignment, this book does not have room enough to cover all of the options. You can, however, easily and enjoyably experiment with them on your own.

Aligning and Centering Entries

Right, Left, and Center alignments are self-explanatory. You can use any of these alignment settings with either numeric or text entries. Figure 4-5 on the next page shows how these alignments (column A) affect text entries (column B) and numeric entries (column C).

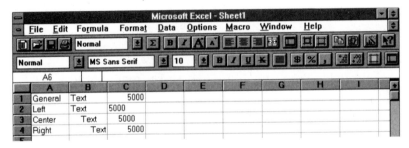

FIGURE 4-5. *The four primary alignments available for Excel worksheets.*

To see the effects of these alignment settings in the *ALSPORTS* worksheet, follow these steps:

1. Select cell A5.

2. Click the Right Align tool on the Standard toolbar. Alternatively, choose the Alignment command from the Format menu, select the Right option, and click OK, or press Enter.

To see other alignment options,

1. Select cell A6.

2. Click the Center Align tool on the toolbar or choose the Center option in the dialog box produced by the Alignment command.

To return alignment to ''normal,''

3. Select cells A5:A6.

4. Click the Left Alignment button or choose Left in the Alignment dialog box.

If a left-aligned cell entry is too long and the adjacent cell to the right is empty, the excess spills over to the right. If a right-aligned cell entry is too long and the adjacent cell to the left is empty, the excess spills over to the left. If a centered entry is too long and both adjacent cells are empty, the overflow is evenly divided between the right and left edges of the cell, as shown in Figure 4-6.

Wrapping Text

Sometimes you may want to keep a long text entry within a single cell. In such cases, you can choose the Wrap Text option in the Alignment dialog box.

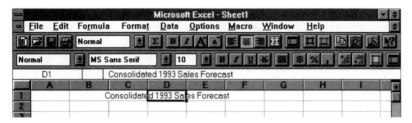

FIGURE 4-6. *A centered entry too long for the cell containing it.*

To see how this works, do the following:

1. Open a blank worksheet.

2. In cell A1, type the following entry. As you type, notice that the formula bar expands to display the entire entry.

   These figures have not been audited. Please do not release any of this information outside the company.

3. Press Enter. The entry doesn't entirely fit on the screen:

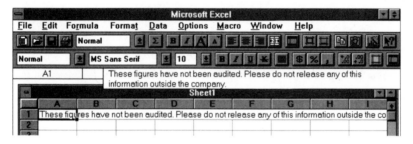

4. Widen column A to 40 characters.

5. Choose the Alignment command from the Format menu.

6. Click the Wrap Text option, and click OK or press Enter.

Your worksheet now looks like Figure 4-7 on the next page.

Justifying Text over Several Cells

Sometimes you might need to fit some lengthy text into a specific range of cells in a worksheet by breaking the text into several lines. You do this by using the Justify command on the Format menu. Follow the steps listed on the next page.

115

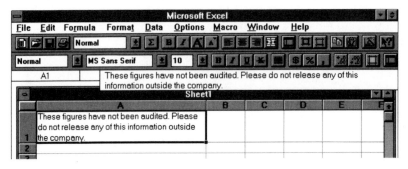

FIGURE 4-7. *A wrapped text entry.*

1. Choose Undo Alignment from the Edit menu to undo the formatting in cell A1.

2. Select the range A1:A3.

3. Choose the Justify command from the Format menu.

The text is now split among cells A1 through A3.

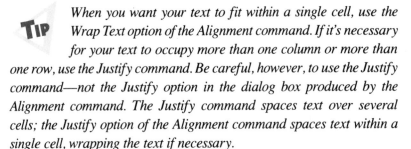

When you want your text to fit within a single cell, use the Wrap Text option of the Alignment command. If it's necessary for your text to occupy more than one column or more than one row, use the Justify command. Be careful, however, to use the Justify command—not the Justify option in the dialog box produced by the Alignment command. The Justify command spaces text over several cells; the Justify option of the Alignment command spaces text within a single cell, wrapping the text if necessary.

CHANGING THE APPEARANCE OF CHARACTERS

The word *font* is commonly used in two ways. Sometimes it refers to a specific typeface, such as Helvetica, Script, or Roman. More commonly, the word *font* refers to the aggregate of all the attributes—size, style (such as bold or italic), typeface, and color—that determine how a character looks on the Microsoft Excel screen and when printed.

By using tools on the Standard and Formatting toolbars, or by using the Font command on the Format menu, you can control the appearance of onscreen and printed characters. Altering the typeface, the size, or the style is the easiest way to spruce up your worksheet. To experiment with this type of formatting,

1. Close (without saving) the worksheet you used for practicing with alignments.

2. Make *ALSPORTS* the active worksheet.

Using the Bold and Italic Cell Styles

You'll start by changing the appearance of the worksheet title. First,

1. Select the range A1:A2 in the *ALSPORTS* worksheet.

2. Point to one of the borders and drag to move the title and subtitle of the worksheet one column to the right.

3. Now, click the Italic tool shown below. (If you're still displaying both the Standard and Formatting toolbars, note that both have an Italic tool; it doesn't matter which one you use.)

4. Now add bold formatting by clicking the Bold tool shown below.

The titles *Alan's Sports* and *Month-to-Month Sales* are now bold and italicized.

The Bold and Italic tools can be used as *toggle switches*, meaning that you click them once to turn on their attributes and click them again to turn off their attributes. For example, if the current selection is bold, clicking the Bold tool removes the bold formatting. To see how this works,

1. Click the Bold and Italic tools a few times.

2. When you finish experimenting, make the title bold, but not italic, and the subtitle both bold and italic.

Selecting Fonts

In addition to adding bold or italic formatting, you can also change the font used in your worksheet. You might want to use a different font for titles to make them distinct from numeric values. Or you might want to use different fonts for totals to make summary information stand out.

To add a more distinctive font to your worksheet title, follow these steps:

1. Select cell B1.

2. Click the arrow next to the Font Name box on the Formatting toolbar. Doing this opens a list of available fonts.

3. Scroll to the end of the list and select Times New Roman. (If you don't have this font, pick another you like, such as Courier.)

4. Click the Increase Font tool three times. This tool, located on the Standard toolbar, is pictured below at left (next to its neighbor and opposite number, the Decrease Font tool).

Your worksheet now looks like the one in Figure 4-8. Notice that Excel automatically increased the row height to make room for the larger characters. If you've previously changed the row height, however, Excel does not adjust the height.

	Microsoft Excel - ALSPORTS.XLS							
File Edit Formula Format Data Options Macro Window Help								

	A	B	C	D	E	F	G	H	I
1		**Alan's Sports**							
2		*Month-to-Month Sales*							
4	Department	Jul-92	Aug-92	Gain(%)					
5	Skiing	$15,600	$21,270	36.3%					
6	Hunting	27,280	25,900	(5.1%)					
7	Camping	13,750	11,085	(19.4%)					
8	Apparel	15,920	23,540	47.9%					
9	Team Sports	12,500	13,930	11.4%					
10	Golf	10,100	9,705	(3.9%)					
12		$95,150	$105,430	10.8%					
13									
14		August	September	Gain(%)					
15	Skiing	21,270	36,560	71.9%					
16	Hunting	25,900	28,710	10.8%					
17	Camping	11,085	7,250	(34.6%)					
18	Apparel	23,540	27,800	18.1%					
19	Team Sports	13,930	22,570	62.0%					

FIGURE 4-8. *The ALSPORTS worksheet with a new font for the title.*

The Increase and Decrease Font tools are convenient for incremental adjustments in font size. For more dramatic resizing, open the Font Size box (pictured below) and select the desired size.

 Bold fonts sometimes make entries too wide to display in their entirety. If this happens, increase the width of the column or columns by dragging the column-header border or by choosing the Column Width command from the Format menu.

Fonts You See and Fonts You Can Print

In addition to using the Standard and Formatting toolbars, you can work with fonts through the Font command on the Edit menu. To see what it does,

■ Choose the Font command from the Format menu.

A large dialog box like the one in Figure 4-9 appears on your screen. Except for color, all the options in this dialog box are available on the toolbars. The dialog box does, however, include two additional elements: the box labeled Sample and the small symbols to the left of some of the names in the Font list box.

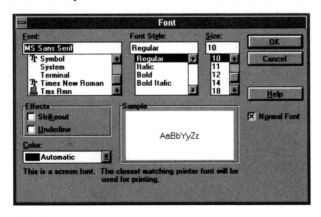

FIGURE 4-9. *The dialog box produced by the Font command.*

The Sample box shows representative characters for the font, font style, font size, effects, and color you highlight in the remainder of the dialog box. The symbol to the left of a font name tells you what type of font it is:

- A picture of a printer represents a *printer* font. This is a font that is "native" to your printer. If you choose a printer font, Windows matches it as closely as possible on screen.

- The overlapping letters TT (with Windows version 3.1 only) represent a *TrueType* font. TrueType fonts give exact matches, so what you see on screen is exactly what you get on paper.

- A font without a symbol is one of two types of display-related fonts. It is either a *screen* font, such as System, that is a bitmapped, or raster font and that Windows matches as closely as possible to fonts available on your printer, or it is a *vector* font, such as Script, that Windows creates on screen and also reproduces on your printer, even though it is not an actual printer font.

To familiarize yourself with the Font dialog box,

1. Click on different fonts in the Font list box. As you do, notice that Excel displays a message below the Sample box that tells you about the font you've highlighted.

2. Click on different combinations of style, size, effect, and color. The characters in the Sample box change to match the font characteristics you choose.

3. When you finish, click Cancel to close the Font dialog box without applying any of your choices to the *ALSPORTS* worksheet.

HIGHLIGHTING DATA WITH LINES AND BOXES

Lines and boxes can emphasize important information in a worksheet. Before you add some of these elements to the sales analysis, save the *ALSPORTS* worksheet so that you can return to it in its present state after you've finished experimenting.

Underlining Cells

Underlining can be useful for formatting certain kinds of reports. To add underlining to the *ALSPORTS* worksheet, follow these steps:

1. Select the ranges B10:D10 and B20:D20.

2. Click the Bottom Border tool on the Standard toolbar. It looks like this:

Move the highlight to a different cell so you can see that the previously selected cells now have a single underline.

Now suppose you want to double-underline the totals in the worksheet. Follow these steps:

1. Select the ranges B12:D12 and B22:D22.

2. Choose the Border command from the Format menu. This brings up the Border dialog box.

3. Select the double-underline style in the Style box, as shown here:

4. Select the Bottom option, and click OK or press Enter.

Enclosing Cells in Boxes

Suppose you want to draw attention to the percentage differences shown in column D, including the total percentage gain for all departments. Follow these steps:

1. Select the ranges D4:D12 and D14:D22.

2. Click the Outline Border tool on the Standard toolbar:

Your worksheet now looks like the one in Figure 4-10 on the next page.

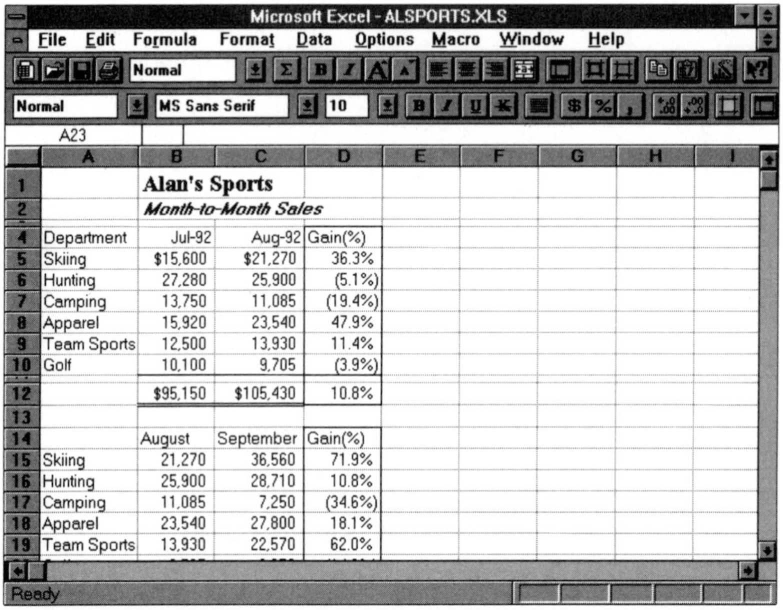

FIGURE 4-10. *The* ALSPORTS *worksheet with underlining and boxes.*

Do you notice anything wrong with the worksheet? When you applied the Outline format, you lost the double-underline format in column D. To reinstate this format:

1. Select cells D12 and D22.

2. Add double-underlining to the cells with the Border command.

Save the document for later reference, and let's take a few minutes to experiment some more.

ATTACHING NOTES TO CELLS

Sometimes, you might need to submit a preliminary report before you have collected all the information you need. At other times, you might want to record important assumptions or document your work. With Microsoft Excel, you can easily attach notes to cells without having to clutter up the worksheet itself. The notes are hidden unless you specifically choose to display them, and they can be printed on a separate page as a handy way of annotating printed worksheets. (You'll learn how to print notes in the next chapter, "Printing Microsoft Excel Documents.")

To attach a note to a cell, follow these steps:

1. Select the cell to which you want to attach the note. For this example, select cell C9 in the *ALSPORTS* worksheet.

2. Choose the Note command from the Formula menu. The following dialog box appears.

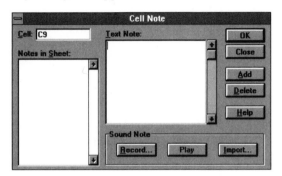

3. Type the following note in the Text Note box. Hold down the Shift key and press Enter to start the second paragraph (beginning *Ask Bob*).

```
We usually see a big increase in August
for this department.
Ask Bob what happened last month.
```

   Notice that you don't need to press Enter to start a new line when your text reaches the right edge of the Note box. Excel automatically moves the text to the next line.

4. Click OK, or press Enter, to attach the note to the cell.

When you return to the worksheet, notice the small square in the top-right corner of cell C9, indicating that this cell has a note attached to it.

To view the note attached to the cell,

1. Double-click cell C9 or choose the Note command again. Excel displays the Cell Note dialog box again.

   Notice that the address of the active cell appears in the Cell box, and the text of the note appears in the Text Note box. The Notes In Sheet box lists the cell reference and part of the note. If more than one note is attached to a worksheet, the Notes In Sheet box lists all their references, and you can choose among them. Whichever note you choose to view will appear in the Text Note box.

2. Click Close or press Esc to close the Cell Note dialog box.

You don't need the note anymore, so delete it. The easiest way to do this is as follows:

1. Select the cell with the attached note—cell C9 in this example.

2. Press the Del key.

3. When the Clear dialog box appears, choose Notes. Click OK or press Enter to delete the note.

If you want, you can also delete a note with the Note command. Highlight the note to delete in the Notes In Sheet box and click the Delete button in the dialog box. Click OK or press Enter when a message appears asking you to confirm the deletion. Click OK or press Enter to complete the command.

ADDING TEXT BOXES

If you want to make your notes and comments immediately noticeable to those who look at your worksheet, you can put your comments in text boxes that appear on the worksheet itself, instead of attaching them to cells as notes. The Text Box tool on the Utility toolbar allows you to create a text box on the worksheet.

To practice creating text boxes, suppose you want to add a few words of congratulations on the *ALSPORTS* worksheet to Harvey Johnson, the manager of the Ski department. Follow these steps:

1. Display the Utility toolbar.

2. Click the Text Box tool shown below. The mouse pointer changes to a cross.

3. Point to the top-left corner of cell F14 and drag the pointer to about the middle of cell H16. A dotted box follows the pointer. When you release the mouse button, a text box appears on the worksheet.

4. Type

```
Good job, Harvey. Kudos to the Ski department!
```

Press Esc or click elsewhere in the worksheet to signal Excel that the box is complete. Your screen now looks like the one in Figure 4-11. (The Format and Utility toolbars have been removed to provide a better look at the overall worksheet.)

5. To keep your screen uncluttered, close the Utility toolbar.

Department	Jul-92	Aug-92	Gain(%)
Skiing	$15,600	$21,270	36.3%
Hunting	27,280	25,900	(5.1%)
Camping	13,750	11,085	(19.4%)
Apparel	15,920	23,540	47.9%
Team Sports	12,500	13,930	11.4%
Golf	10,100	9,705	(3.9%)
	$95,150	$105,430	10.8%

	August	September	Gain(%)
Skiing	21,270	36,560	71.9%
Hunting	25,900	28,710	10.8%
Camping	11,085	7,250	(34.6%)
Apparel	23,540	27,800	18.1%
Team Sports	13,930	22,570	62.0%
Golf	9,705	8,270	(14.8%)
	$105,430	$131,160	24.4%

FIGURE 4-11. *The worksheet with a text box.*

You can apply the full range of Excel formatting options to text boxes. Experiment on your own with fonts, patterns, and colors. To select the box, simply click it. If you want to adjust its size, drag one of the handles that appear when the box is selected. To delete the box, press the Del key while the box is selected.

TIP *The Drawing toolbar contains a varied collection of geometric shapes, curves and lines. With these tools, you can draw lines, curves, boxes, circles and more exotic objects on your worksheets. This book won't go into detail about the drawing tools, but information is readily available through the Help menu or in the Microsoft Excel documentation.*

FAST FORMATTING TECHNIQUES

You now have a good command of Excel's worksheet formatting options. In the remainder of this chapter, you'll see a few useful labor-saving techniques.

AutoFormatting Cells

Excel offers a collection of predesigned formats for tabular data such as the Alan's Sports sales summaries. To see how this works, follow these steps:

1. Select the range A4:D12.

2. Choose the AutoFormat command from the Format menu. This brings up the following dialog box:

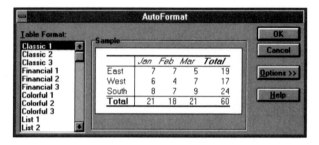

3. Click various options in the Table Format list box. The data in the Sample box illustrates the different formats as you choose them.

4. Double-click the Classic 3 option.

   Your screen should now look like the one in Figure 4-12.

To apply the most recently used AutoFormat to a cell range, select the range and click the AutoFormat tool (shown below) on the Standard or Formatting toolbar.

Return the table to its original format by choosing Undo AutoFormat from the Edit menu.

Copying Cell Formats

When you copy cell contents, Microsoft Excel also copies cell formats. Copying formats along with the cell contents can be very useful if you plan carefully. For example, if you build a worksheet in sections (as you've done

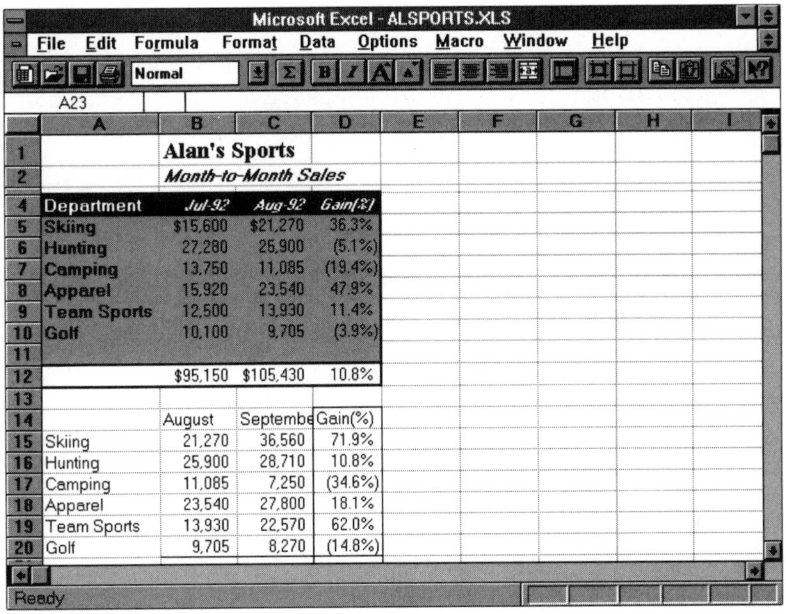

Microsoft Excel - ALSPORTS.XLS									
File	Edit	Formula	Format	Data	Options	Macro	Window	Help	

Normal

A23

	A	B	C	D	E	F	G	H	I
1		**Alan's Sports**							
2		*Month-to-Month Sales*							
4	Department	*Jul-92*	*Aug-92*	*Gain(%)*					
5	Skiing	$15,600	$21,270	36.3%					
6	Hunting	27,280	25,900	(5.1%)					
7	Camping	13,750	11,085	(19.4%)					
8	Apparel	15,920	23,540	47.9%					
9	Team Sports	12,500	13,930	11.4%					
10	Golf	10,100	9,705	(3.9%)					
11									
12		$95,150	$105,430	10.8%					
13									
14		August	September	Gain(%)					
15	Skiing	21,270	36,560	71.9%					
16	Hunting	25,900	28,710	10.8%					
17	Camping	11,085	7,250	(34.6%)					
18	Apparel	23,540	27,800	18.1%					
19	Team Sports	13,930	22,570	62.0%					
20	Golf	9,705	8,270	(14.8%)					

Ready

FIGURE 4-12. *The Classic 3 table format.*

with the Alan's Sports example), you can save time by formatting the first section before copying it to create the next section.

Excel also lets you specify what information you want to copy. To see how, follow these steps:

1. Select cell B1 in the *ALSPORTS* worksheet.

2. Click the Copy tool (shown below) on the Standard toolbar.

3. Select cell B2.

4. Click the Paste Formats tool (shown below) on the Standard toolbar. This tool is a shortcut for the Paste Special command on the Edit menu.

Microsoft Excel copies only the formatting from cell B1, applying it to the subtitle in cell B2 without affecting the data in the destination cell.

Notice that the marquee has remained active. If you wanted, you could repeat the copy by selecting another cell or range of cells and clicking the Paste Formats tool again. To finish this example,

1. Press Esc to turn off the marquee.

2. Return the formatting in cell B2 to its original form by choosing Undo Paste Special from the Edit menu.

If you repeatedly create worksheets with specific formatting, you might want to save one of these worksheets as a template. *See the Microsoft Excel documentation for more information.*

CONCLUSION

This chapter has covered basic formatting techniques for dressing up your data. Now your work will be sharp *and* look sharp. As you've seen, the Formatting toolbar can save you a lot of time, so it's a good idea to display it when you are readying your work for presentation.

In the next chapter, you'll cover the final phase of worksheet production: printing.

Chapter 5

Printing Microsoft Excel Documents

Printing a Microsoft Excel worksheet is simple enough in concept, but when you begin to deal with actual data and reports, you have to make several decisions. For example, how do you want the worksheet to be oriented on the page? What part of the worksheet do you want to print? How many copies do you need? Excel provides many options that make it simple to tailor the printed copy to your needs. This chapter helps you understand these options so that you are able to make decisions quickly when you're ready to print a worksheet.

SETTING UP YOUR PRINTER

The way to learn how to print is to practice with real data, so first,

- Open the *ALSPORTS* worksheet.

To begin looking at your print options,

- Choose the Page Setup command from the File menu. Doing this opens a large dialog box in which you define the overall look of your printed pages.

You'll see more of the Page Setup dialog box later. For now,

- Click the Printer Setup button. This brings up the Printer Setup dialog box.

This dialog box lists the printers you have installed either by specifying them when you first set up Microsoft Windows or, at a later time, by using the Windows Control Panel.

As you can see, the Printer Setup dialog box lists both the printers Windows recognizes and the ports through which they are connected to your computer (LPT1 for the first parallel port, COM1 for the first serial port, and so on). In most cases, you switch from one printer to another simply by selecting the printer you want to use and pressing Enter. If the printer you want is not listed in the dialog box, use the Microsoft Windows Control Panel to install a different printer. For detailed information about how to use the Control Panel, either switch to Program Manager, activate the Main program group, double-click on the Control Panel icon, and use the Help menu, or refer to the Microsoft Windows documentation.

Assuming that your printer or printers are already installed, let's move on to another dialog box:

1. Verify that the printer you want to use is selected in the Printer list box, and then click the Setup button.This brings up the dialog box for the printer you selected a moment ago. (Figure 5-1 shows the dialog box for the Hewlett-Packard LaserJet III.)

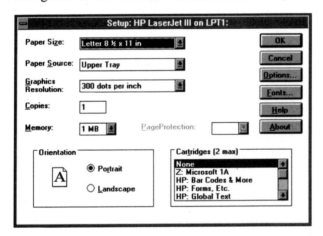

FIGURE 5-1. *The Printer Setup dialog box for the Hewlett-Packard LaserJet III.*

2. Examine the setup options for your printer. When you finish, "back out" of this series of dialog boxes by clicking OK to return to the Printer Setup dialog box. Click OK again to return to the Page Setup dialog box, and click OK once more to end the command and return to the worksheet.

This chapter focuses on printing worksheets, but the principles also apply to printing macro sheets and databases. Printing charts is somewhat different, however; you'll find information in Chapter 7, "Formatting Charts."

PREVIEWING THE PRINTED PAGE

Before printing a worksheet, you will usually want to see how it will look when printed. Previewing is particularly useful when you're printing long or heavily formatted worksheets. Without actually printing a copy, you can see the portion of the worksheet that will be printed and see how the worksheet will be positioned on the printed page(s).

To preview the *ALSPORTS* worksheet,

■ Choose the Print Preview command from the File menu. Your screen now looks like the one in Figure 5-2.

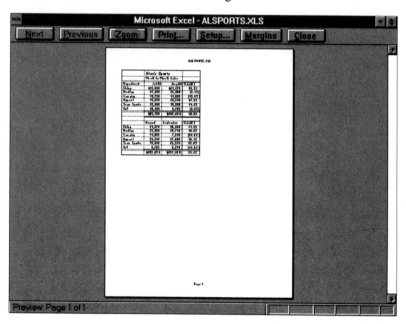

FIGURE 5-2. *Previewing a worksheet before printing.*

As you can see, Print Preview presents a bird's-eye view of the worksheet. Notice that the *ALSPORTS* worksheet will print on a single page, and that the Next and Previous buttons at the top of the Preview window are dimmed. For worksheets longer than one page, click the Next button to display the next page of the worksheet. Click the Previous button to display the previous page.

To examine a particular part of the worksheet in more detail,

1. Point to the worksheet. The pointer changes shape from an arrow to a magnifying glass.

2. Move the magnifying glass over the part of the worksheet that you want to examine, and then click. Microsoft Excel *zooms in* on that area so you can see the area in detail.

3. To return to normal page preview, click any part of the worksheet.

 You can also click the Zoom button to examine the worksheet. Excel zooms in on the top-left corner of the current page. Use the scroll bars to view different areas. Click Zoom again to return to normal page preview.

If you're satisfied with the worksheet at this point, you can click the Print button at the top of the window to print the worksheet. But before you print the *ALSPORTS* worksheet, let's look at the changes you can make from the Preview window.

Suppose you want to adjust the margins. In the Preview window, the margins can be displayed as dotted lines, and the worksheet has margin and column handles that you can move in the same way you move row and column handles in worksheets. To see how this works,

1. Click the Margins button at the top of the window. Your screen now resembles the one in Figure 5-3.

2. Drag the left margin handle (labeled in Figure 5-3) to the right and release the mouse button.

The data shifts to the right. You can also drag a column handle (labeled in Figure 5-3) to change column widths in the Preview window. (You cannot, however, change row heights in the Preview window.)

You can also change printing options from the Preview window by clicking the Setup button. (You'll see these options later in this chapter. For now, simply remember that you can change these options from the Print Preview window.)

If you need to make any other type of revisions to your worksheet (such as deleting unnecessary rows), you can return to the document window by clicking the Close button in the Preview window.

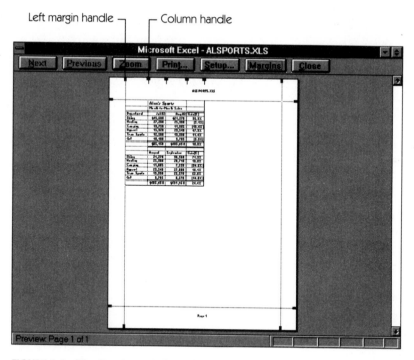

FIGURE 5-3. *The Preview window after you click the Margins button.*

PRINTING THE WORKSHEET

To print your worksheet from the Preview window, simply click the Print button at the top of the window. If you are not previewing the worksheet, choose the Print command from the File menu. Either way, you see a dialog box similar to the one shown in Figure 5-4.

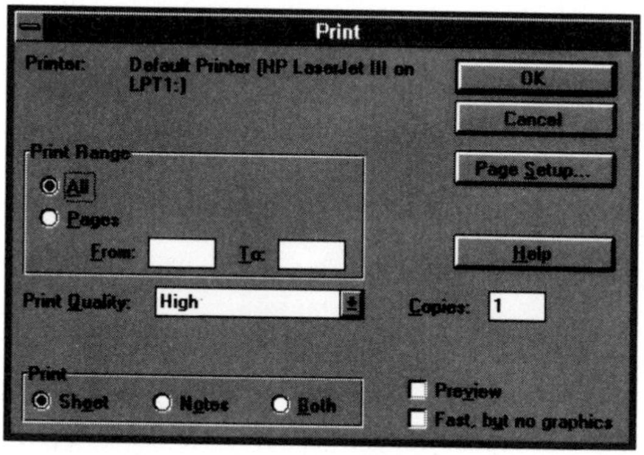

FIGURE 5-4. *The Print dialog box.*

133

After you choose Print from either the Preview window or the document (worksheet) window, follow these general steps to print a worksheet:

1. Turn off the Preview option (in the Print dialog box) if an X in the check box shows that it's turned on.

2. Select the desired options. The following table summarizes the most important ones:

To Specify:	Use: Option	Default	Procedure
Which pages to print	Print Range group	All pages	Type the range of pages to print in the From and To text boxes.
Print resolution	Print Quality list box	Depends on printer	Select the desired resolution from drop-down list.
Number of copies	Copies text box	1	Type the number.
What information to print	Print group	Sheet (worksheet only)	Select Notes to print cell notes only; select Both to print worksheet and notes.

3. Click OK, or press Enter.

Excel then prints the worksheet using the options you specified.

To try printing the *ALSPORTS* worksheet,

1. Click the Print button (if you're in the Preview window) or choose the Print command from the File menu.

2. For this practice, simply accept the defaults in the dialog box. Click OK, or press Enter.

Your printed worksheet should look like the one in Figure 5-5. (If your worksheet doesn't print, see "Resolving Printer Problems" at the end of this chapter.)

If you want to use the default settings to print a worksheet, you can bypass the Print dialog box by clicking the Print tool (pictured below) on the Standard toolbar.

ALSPORTS.XLS

	Alan's Sports		
	Month-to-Month Sales		
Department	Jul-92	Aug-92	Gain(%)
Skiing	$15,600	$21,270	36.3%
Hunting	27,280	25,900	(5.1%)
Camping	13,750	11,085	(19.4%)
Apparel	15,920	23,540	47.9%
Team Sports	12,500	13,930	11.4%
Golf	10,100	9,705	(3.9%)
	$95,150	$105,430	10.8%
	August	September	Gain(%)
Skiing	21,270	36,560	71.9%
Hunting	25,900	28,710	10.8%
Camping	11,085	7,250	(34.6%)
Apparel	23,540	27,800	18.1%
Team Sports	13,930	22,570	62.0%
Golf	9,705	8,270	(14.8%)
	$105,430	$131,160	24.4%

FIGURE 5-5. *The printed* ALSPORTS *worksheet.*

Take a look at the printed *ALSPORTS* worksheet. Excel has printed grid-lines along with the cell entries. It has also printed the filename of the worksheet as a *header* at the top of the page and has included a *footer* showing the page number at the bottom of the page. Later in this chapter, you'll see how to change these options with the Page Setup command.

PRINTING PART OF A WORKSHEET

Unless you specify otherwise, Microsoft Excel prints the entire worksheet. To print certain pages only, remember that you can specify the page range in the Print dialog box.

To specify the *print area* without regard to page count, however, you use the Set Print Area command on the Options menu as follows:

1. First, select the range of cells that you want to print.

2. Next, choose the Set Print Area command from the Options menu. The range you selected is set off by dashed lines.

3. Finally, choose the Print command from the File menu, and follow the steps described earlier for previewing and printing.

If you have the Utility toolbar on the screen, you can set the print area by selecting the cells to print and clicking the Set Print Area tool shown below.

When Excel sets the print area, it assigns the name *Print_Area* to the selected range. When you print the worksheet, Excel prints only the area to which this name is assigned. You can redefine the print area at any time. For example, to reset the print area to encompass two discontinuous (or overlapping) blocks of cells,

1. Select the first block and then hold down the Ctrl key while you select the second block.

2. Choose Set Print Area from the Options menu.

When you choose Print from the File menu, Excel will print each discontinuous block on a separate page.

To reset the print area to the entire worksheet, select the entire cell grid by clicking the rectangle at the top-left corner of the worksheet (at the junction of the row and column headers) and then choose the Remove Print Area command from the Options menu.

If you prefer, you can also reset the print area as follows:

1. Choose the Define Name command from the Formula menu. A dialog box appears, listing all the currently defined names.

2. Select *Print_Area* from the Names In Sheet list box.

3. Click the Delete button. The name disappears from the list, but the dialog box remains on the screen.

4. Click the Close button.

Either way, the next time you choose Print, Excel prints the entire worksheet.

PRINTING LARGE WORKSHEETS

To see how to print worksheets longer than a single page, you need a new example—one with more data than the *ALSPORTS* worksheet contains. To work through the examples in the rest of this chapter, you must create a worksheet like the one shown in Figure 5-6. However, you don't have to painstakingly enter the exact data that appears in the sample worksheet. You simply have to approximate the size of the example, so instead you'll make a few entries and then copy those entries to other cells, as described next.

	B	C	D	E	F	G	H	I	J
1				Sales by Region and Product					
2									
3		Jan-92	Feb-92	Mar-92	Apr-92	May-92	Jun-92	Jul-92	Aug
4	Northeast								
5	Hoisin sauce	$14,583	$15,511	$16,077	$16,028	$16,613	$17,260	$18,131	$18
6	Black beans	9,082	8,923	8,747	9,319	9,598	9,726	9,856	9
7	Sesame oil	13,861	13,621	13,675	13,730	13,493	13,547	13,601	13
8	Bean curd	18,753	18,859	18,547	18,959	18,641	18,692	18,152	18
9	Dried squid	2,673	2,718	2,837	2,805	2,799	2,765	2,795	2
10									
11	Southeast								
12	Hoisin sauce	17,914	17,751	17,940	18,288	18,122	18,474	18,833	19
13	Black beans	9,565	9,876	10,210	10,620	11,119	11,454	11,799	12
14	Sesame oil	16,788	16,842	16,906	16,972	17,038	16,717	16,402	16
15	Bean curd	18,622	18,131	17,653	17,188	16,735	16,296	15,867	15
16	Dried squid	5,248	5,426	5,610	5,802	6,001	6,207	6,421	6
17									
18	North Central								
19	Hoisin sauce	13,574	13,961	14,359	14,768	15,190	15,623	16,069	16
20	Black beans	9,192	9,377	9,564	9,756	9,950	10,150	10,353	10

FIGURE 5-6. *Data to be copied to create the* SALESREG *worksheet.*

To create the sample worksheet,

1. Start by opening a new worksheet and saving it as *SALESREG*.

2. Make the entries shown in cells A4 and B5:B9 of Figure 5-6.

3. Enter *10000* in the range C5:N9. (Do this by selecting the range, typing the number, and then pressing Ctrl-Enter.)

4. Select the range B5:N9. (Include the product names.)

5. Point to any border of the selected range, hold down Ctrl, and use Excel's drag-and-drop feature to copy the range to cell B12. Repeat the operation to copy the range to cells B19, B26, B33, B40, and B47.

6. Press F5, type *A11*, and press Enter to jump to cell A11.

7. Type *Southeast* in cell A11, *North Central* in A18, *Southwest* in A25, *Northwest* in A32, *South Central* in A39, and *Central* in A46.

To enter the dates in row 3, follow these steps:

1. Select cell C3.

2. Type *Jan-92*, and press Enter.

3. Drag the fill handle over the range C3:N3. When you release the mouse button, Excel's AutoFill feature will fill in the dates through Dec-92.

4. To finish up, reduce the width of column A to about 2 characters, widen column B, enter the title *Sales by Region and Product* in cell F1, and then center the title.

You should now have a reasonable facsimile of the worksheet shown in Figure 5-6 for use in the remaining examples in this chapter.

Printing Column and Row Labels

When Microsoft Excel prints a long worksheet, it breaks the worksheet into pages and prints them in a specific sequence. Multiple-page worksheets can be difficult to read. For example, the sample worksheet is two screens (14 columns) wide and several screens (51 rows) long. The worksheet has labels in columns A and B and in rows 1 and 3. Excel prints this worksheet as four separate pages—printing the first set of columns from top to bottom, until all 51 rows have been printed, and then printing the second set of columns from top to bottom. The resulting printout is somewhat difficult to decipher, as Figure 5-7 shows. Pages 1 and 3 have printed column labels, but pages 2 and 4 don't. Pages 1 and 2 have printed row labels, but pages 3 and 4 don't. Without all the descriptive labels, the reader can't be sure what the numbers on pages 2, 3, and 4 represent.

You can make the printout easier to read by using the Set Print Titles command on the Options menu to repeat the labels on all printed pages. Follow these steps:

1. Choose the Set Print Titles command from the Options menu. This brings up the following dialog box:

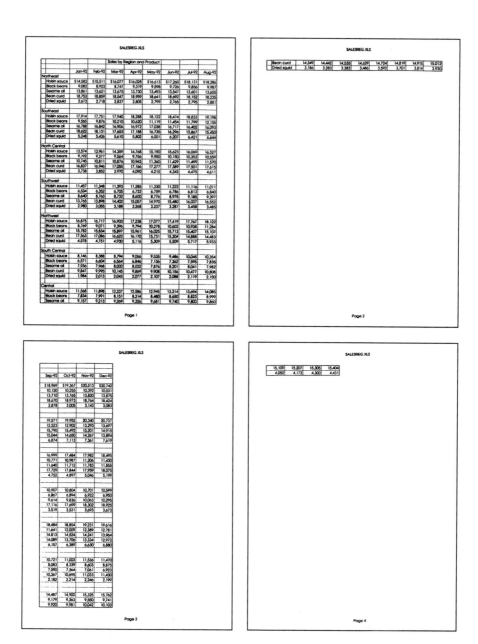

FIGURE 5-7. *A four-page worksheet printed without column and row labels on each page.*

2. Drag through the rows containing the labels you want to print—in this case, rows 1, 2, and 3. (It doesn't matter which column you place the pointer in as you do this.)

3. Select the Titles for Rows box.

4. Drag through the columns you want to print—in this case, columns A and B.

5. Click OK, or press Enter.

6. Switch to Print Preview and click the Next button until page 3 appears. (Page numbers are shown in the status bar at the bottom of the window.) If necessary, zoom in for a clearer view.

As you can see, when you print the worksheet, the top half of page 3 will look like the printout in Figure 5-8.

SALESREG.XLS

	Sep-92	Oct-92	Nov-92	Dec-92
Northeast				
Hoisin sauce	$18,969	$19,367	$20,513	$20,742
Black beans	10,120	10,255	10,392	10,531
Sesame oil	13,710	13,765	13,820	13,875
Bean curd	18,670	18,973	18,764	18,424
Dried squid	2,878	3,005	3,143	3,083
Southeast				
Hoisin sauce	19,571	19,952	20,340	20,737
Black beans	12,523	12,902	13,293	13,697
Sesame oil	15,790	15,492	15,201	14,915
Bean curd	15,044	14,650	14,267	13,894
Dried squid	6,874	7,113	7,361	7,619
North Central				
Hoisin sauce	16,999	17,484	17,982	18,495
Black beans	10,771	10,987	11,206	11,430
Sesame oil	11,640	11,712	11,783	11,855
Bean curd	17,729	17,844	17,959	18,075
Dried squid	4,752	4,897	5,046	5,190

FIGURE 5-8. *The third page of a worksheet with column and row labels.*

Although titles are usually located at the top and far left of a worksheet, they can be placed anywhere in the worksheet. The only restriction is that titles must comprise one or more entire columns or one or more entire rows; the Set Print Titles command does not accept partial rows or columns.

CHANGING THE PAGE SETUP

You've seen how to preview and print, and how to print large documents. Now it's time to see how to use the Page Setup command to control the overall appearance of the pages you print. When you choose Page Setup from the File menu, the dialog box shown in Figure 5-9 appears. (Recall that you can also access this dialog box from the Preview window by clicking the Setup button.) Let's look at some of the Page Setup options.

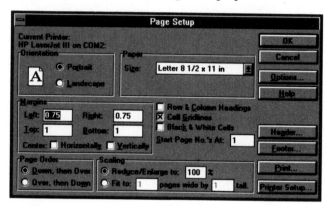

FIGURE 5-9. *The Page Setup dialog box.*

Using Headers and Footers

When you print your worksheets, you may want to add descriptive *headers* and *footers* to the pages. Headers and footers differ from titles. They don't appear in the worksheet on the screen. They are part of the printing information that Excel saves with your worksheet, and they appear only when you print or preview the worksheet. You might want to enter a title or description as a header. Footers are useful for displaying page numbers. However, you can include any information you want in both headers and footers.

When you click the Header button in the Page Setup dialog box, you see the dialog box shown in Figure 5-10 on the following page. You can include header text at the left, center, and right of each page by typing it in the appropriate Left, Center, or Right section box. Excel aligns the text according to the box it's entered in. The Footer dialog box (available through the Footer button in the Page Setup dialog box) works in the same fashion, allowing you to place text at the bottom of each page.

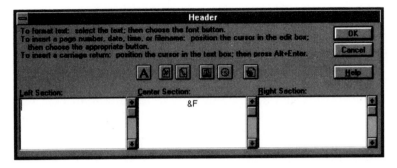

FIGURE 5-10. *The Header dialog box.*

Microsoft Excel provides special codes that specify header and footer content. You can use these codes separately or in combination with each other or with text. Usually, though, you can avoid having to type these codes into the boxes. The Header and Footer dialog boxes provide buttons that enter the most commonly used codes automatically.

To practice using headers, try the following:

1. From the File menu select the Page Setup command to bring up the Page Setup dialog box.

2. Click the Header button.

Select the following options in the Header dialog box:

1. With the insertion point in the Left box, click the Date button shown below.

2. In the Center box, double-click the code *&F* to select it and replace the code by typing *Sales Department Report*.

3. Click in the Right box, type *Page* followed by a space, and then click the Page Number button shown below.

4. Drag to select the text you typed in the Center box, and then click the Font button shown below.

5. In the Font dialog box that appears, format the text as Times New Roman Bold 12-point or as another font of a size and style you like. Click OK.

6. Click OK to close the Header dialog box.

7. To avoid numbering each page at both the top and the bottom, click the Footer button. Select and delete the page-number entry in the Center section of the Footer dialog box.

8. Click OK to close the Footer dialog box, and click OK a second time to close the Page Setup dialog box.

9. Now preview your worksheet.

If you print the worksheet, the header on page 1 will look like the example in Figure 5-11.

7/10/92		Sales Department Report						Page 1

	Jan-92	Feb-92	Mar-92	Apr-92	May-92	Jun-92	Jul-92	Aug-92
Sales by Region and Product								
Northeast								
Hoisin sauce	$14,583	$15,511	$16,077	$16,028	$16,613	$17,260	$18,131	$18,286
Black beans	9,082	8,923	8,747	9,319	9,598	9,726	9,856	9,987
Sesame oil	13,861	13,621	13,675	13,730	13,493	13,547	13,601	13,655
Bean curd	18,753	18,859	18,547	18,959	18,641	18,692	18,152	18,235
Dried squid	2,673	2,718	2,837	2,805	2,799	2,765	2,795	2,881
Southeast								
Hoisin sauce	17,914	17,751	17,940	18,288	18,122	18,474	18,833	19,198
Black beans	9,565	9,876	10,210	10,620	11,119	11,454	11,799	12,155
Sesame oil	16,788	16,842	16,906	16,972	17,038	16,717	16,402	16,093
Bean curd	18,622	18,131	17,653	17,188	16,735	16,296	15,867	15,450
Dried squid	5,248	5,426	5,610	5,802	6,001	6,207	6,421	6,644
North Central								
Hoisin sauce	13,574	13,961	14,359	14,768	15,190	15,623	16,069	16,527
Black beans	9,192	9,377	9,564	9,756	9,950	10,150	10,353	10,559
Sesame oil	10,745	10,811	10,876	10,943	11,360	11,429	11,499	11,570
Bean curd	16,837	16,946	17,055	17,166	17,277	17,389	17,501	17,615
Dried squid	3,738	3,852	3,970	4,090			4,475	4,611

FIGURE 5-11. *Printout of the header defined in the Header dialog box.*

Using Other Page Setup Options

Microsoft Excel specifies the left, right, top, and bottom margins in inches. As you can see in Figure 5-9, Excel accepts decimal fractions. By changing margin specifications in the Page Setup dialog box, you can reposition your worksheet on the printed page (just as you did earlier by dragging the margin handle in the Preview window). If you want, try setting different margins now by using the Page Setup command and then previewing your worksheet.

TIP *If a worksheet won't quite print on one page, you can squeeze it onto a single page by entering a percentage smaller than 100% in the Reduce/Enlarge box—the smaller the percentage, the fewer the pages required to contain the document. Or you can use the Fit To option to specify the width and length of the printed document in pages; Excel will shrink the printed document accordingly.*

Unless you change the default settings, Excel prints gridlines when it prints your worksheet. Printing gridlines can slow down printing and can make the worksheet harder to read. You can eliminate the gridlines from the final printout by turning off the Cell Gridlines option in the Page Setup dialog box.

Similarly, you can print your worksheet with or without the row and column headers (A, B, 1, 2, and so on). Simply click the Row & Column Headings check box to turn this option on and off. (It is turned off by default.)

If you want to start numbering the pages of your worksheet with a number other than 1, you can enter the starting number in the Start Page No.'s At box.

Orienting Worksheets on the Printed Page

Many printers supported by Microsoft Excel allow you to choose the way your worksheet is oriented on the page. Standard orientation, called *portrait mode*, is vertical; that is, the page is taller than it is wide. This book is printed in portrait mode. Sometimes printing your worksheet horizontally makes information more readable. This orientation is called *landscape mode*.

Many of the printers supported by Excel allow you to select either portrait or landscape mode on a worksheet-by-worksheet basis. The Portrait and Landscape buttons are available in the Page Setup dialog box, as shown in Figure 5-9.

CONTROLLING PRINTING

Now that you've mastered the basics of printing your Microsoft Excel worksheets, let's look at some of the additional options Excel offers for controlling the appearance of your printed pages.

The following examples use the Epson 24-pin and the Hewlett-Packard LaserJet families of printers. If you are using a different printer, your dialog boxes may look slightly different, but you will still be able to understand the examples.

Using Soft Fonts

As discussed in Chapter 4, "Formatting Worksheets," the Microsoft Windows 3.1 program includes several TrueType fonts. These fonts are designed to faithfully reproduce Microsoft Excel screen fonts on printed documents. However, you might have added some Windows-compatible soft (printer) fonts that you purchased from another supplier. If so, you must ensure that these fonts are properly installed; otherwise the fonts in your printed documents will not look right.

The Font dialog box tells you which fonts are TrueType and which are soft fonts by displaying little icons next to the font names. Given the variety of fonts and printers available, you will almost certainly have to experiment to get the most out of Excel's print formatting capability.

Changing Page Breaks

As explained earlier, Microsoft Excel breaks worksheets into printed pages in a specific way, taking into account the page dimensions and margins you specify. With long worksheets, you might want to override Excel's automatic page breaks and establish your own. You can insert your own page breaks in order to print less of the worksheet on a page than Excel's page breaks allow, but you cannot use page breaks to increase the size of the print area.

You can set vertical page breaks, horizontal page breaks, or both. To set new page breaks, follow these steps:

1. Select the header of the row or column at which you want the page to break. Excel will break the page *above* the selected row or to the *left* of the selected column. (In this example, select the header for column M.)

2. Choose the Set Page Break command from the Options menu.

Excel displays a dashed line in the worksheet to mark the break. Both manual and automatic page breaks are indicated by dashed lines. Manual breaks are distinguished from automatic breaks by larger dashes, as shown between columns L and M in Figure 5-12 on the next page.

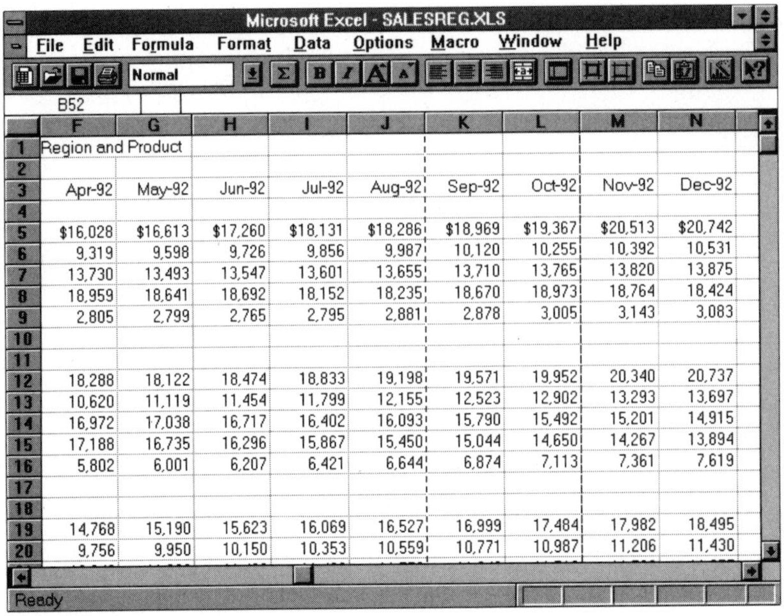

	F	G	H	I	J	K	L	M	N
1	Region and Product								
2									
3	Apr-92	May-92	Jun-92	Jul-92	Aug-92	Sep-92	Oct-92	Nov-92	Dec-92
4									
5	$16,028	$16,613	$17,260	$18,131	$18,286	$18,969	$19,367	$20,513	$20,742
6	9,319	9,598	9,726	9,856	9,987	10,120	10,255	10,392	10,531
7	13,730	13,493	13,547	13,601	13,655	13,710	13,765	13,820	13,875
8	18,959	18,641	18,692	18,152	18,235	18,670	18,973	18,764	18,424
9	2,805	2,799	2,765	2,795	2,881	2,878	3,005	3,143	3,083
10									
11									
12	18,288	18,122	18,474	18,833	19,198	19,571	19,952	20,340	20,737
13	10,620	11,119	11,454	11,799	12,155	12,523	12,902	13,293	13,697
14	16,972	17,038	16,717	16,402	16,093	15,790	15,492	15,201	14,915
15	17,188	16,735	16,296	15,867	15,450	15,044	14,650	14,267	13,894
16	5,802	6,001	6,207	6,421	6,644	6,874	7,113	7,361	7,619
17									
18									
19	14,768	15,190	15,623	16,069	16,527	16,999	17,484	17,982	18,495
20	9,756	9,950	10,150	10,353	10,559	10,771	10,987	11,206	11,430

FIGURE 5-12. *An automatic page break (small vertical dashes between columns J and K) and a page break set with the Set Page Break command (large vertical dashes between columns L and M).*

To set both vertical and horizontal breaks at one time, follow these steps:

1. Select the cell immediately below and to the right of the position where you want the horizontal and vertical breaks to cross. (In this example, select cell G24.)
2. Choose the Set Page Break command from the Options menu.

Your worksheet now looks similar to the one in Figure 5-13.

If your worksheet contains more than one page following a manual page break, Excel resumes its normal automatic page-breaking routine for the remaining pages (unless it encounters another manual page break).

To remove a manual page break, follow these steps:

1. Select any cell directly below a horizontal manual page break or directly to the right of a vertical manual page break. (In this example, select a cell in column M.)
2. Choose Remove Page Break from the Options menu.

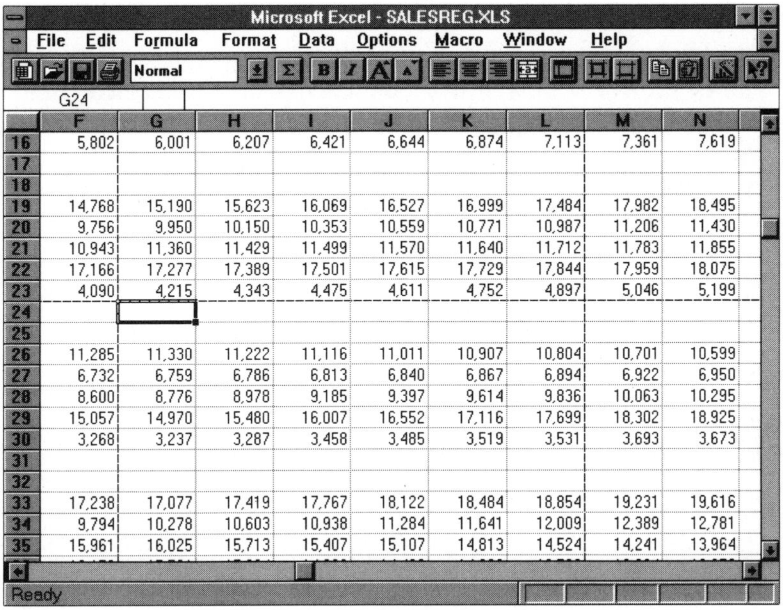

FIGURE 5-13. *A worksheet in which vertical and horizontal manual page breaks were set with a single command.*

You can remove intersecting horizontal and vertical breaks with one command. Follow these steps:

1. Select the cell below and to the right of the intersection of the horizontal and vertical page breaks. (In this example, select cell G24.)

2. Choose Remove Page Break from the Options menu.

RESOLVING PRINTER PROBLEMS

Even experienced Microsoft Excel users can occasionally run into printing difficulties. Sooner or later, you'll choose the Print command and get either odd-looking output or nothing at all. The problem is usually simple and easily corrected. To identify the problem, check the following:

■ Be sure the printer is turned on and properly connected to your computer. A good test is to try printing something else with another program. If that doesn't work properly, run the self-test routine for your printer, or consult your printer manual for guidance.

- If the printer itself is working correctly, check to see whether you configured your printer properly when setting up Microsoft Windows. (To check the settings, double-click the Printers icon in the Windows Control Panel.)

- If you still haven't found the problem, you might be using the wrong printer driver. Your version of Microsoft Excel or Microsoft Windows might not supply drivers for some of the latest-model printers. If you suspect that this is the problem, contact the technical support group at Microsoft or the printer manufacturer for assistance.

CONCLUSION

You've learned how to preview documents before printing them, how to print documents, how to format your printouts with headers and footers, how to control page breaks, and how to print reports. These are the basics of working with Microsoft Excel worksheets. In the next chapter, you'll move on to charting, another important Excel feature.

Section II

Charts and Databases

This section covers the remaining two parts of the Microsoft Excel triad. You'll learn to present data in graphic form to add pep to your presentations. Then you'll learn to perform inquiries on worksheet data you have stored in database form.

Chapter 6

Creating Charts Quickly

The goal of a worksheet is to provide information that fosters better decisions. Accordingly, you will often need to do more than simply lay out words and numbers: You'll want to breathe some life into your worksheet data with charts and graphs. Creating charts in Microsoft Excel has always been convenient; with version 4 the process has become even easier.

USING THE CHARTWIZARD

Microsoft Excel provides you with 14 different chart *types*, including 6 that create three-dimensional charts. You can also combine different types in a single chart. Moreover, Excel offers a wide range of variations within each type and gives you complete control over dozens of chart elements, such as fonts, colors, borders, and patterns.

Creating a Chart

Excel charts can be created in either of two forms. The first form is a document type separate from, but invisibly linked to, the worksheet containing the charted data. Chart documents can be saved under their own filenames. Excel assigns them the extension .XLC. The second chart form is an *embedded* chart, which is part of a worksheet. When you want to print a report that includes both the chart and the worksheet data on the same page, use an embedded chart. To print the chart only, create it as a separate document.

Both chart documents and embedded charts depend on worksheets to supply their data. Charts are linked to worksheet data through cell references that enable Excel to automatically update the information in the chart.

To see how charts work, let's create some sample data for a company called Waterbug Pool Services, Inc.

When creating this sample worksheet, you might want to use the fill handle for the month names in B4:G4, as you did when you entered a series of dates in the example in Chapter 5, "Printing Microsoft Excel Documents."

1. Open a new worksheet and enter the following data:

Cell	Entry
D1	Waterbug Pool Services, Inc.
D2	Sales Analysis—First Half, 1992
B4	Jan
C4	Feb
D4	Mar
E4	Apr
F4	May
G4	Jun
A5	Sales
B5	25916
C5	28374
D5	31416
E5	31568
F5	37782
G5	42930

2. To align the month names over the numbers, select cells B4:G4 and click the Right Align tool on the Standard toolbar.

3. To sharpen your formatting skills, and to make your worksheet match those shown in this chapter, you might also want to apply bold formatting to the titles and headings, as well as center the headings in cells D1 and D2.

4. When you have finished, choose the Save As command from the File menu and give the new worksheet the name *WATERBUG*.

Now create a chart depicting the sales figures from the *WATERBUG* work-sheet. Follow these steps:

1. Select the range A4:G5.

2. Click the ChartWizard tool (shown below) on the Standard toolbar.

   A marquee surrounds the selected range. When you move the mouse pointer back to the worksheet, the pointer changes to a cross.

3. Define the chart area by dragging the mouse from about the middle of cell A6 to the middle of cell H19. When you release the mouse, the Excel ChartWizard appears in a small window titled ChartWizard - Step 1 of 5.

4. Confirm your choice of the range A4:G5 (displayed in the Range box as *=$A$4:$G$5*) by clicking the Next button or by pressing Enter. This brings up the second ChartWizard window.

5. Here, the ChartWizard offers a selection of chart types to choose from. Click the Next button or press Enter to accept the proposed chart type, a column chart. Click Next or press Enter to accept the default responses in Steps 3 and 4 as well.

   Take a moment to look at the options available as you go through the ChartWizard steps. You can return to any previous step by clicking the Back button.

6. In ChartWizard Step 5 (shown below), choose No to answer the Add A Legend? question.

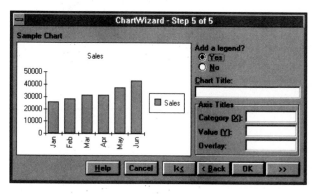

7. Type *Waterbug Pool Services, Inc.* in the Chart Title box. Notice that the Sample Chart box reflects the changes you made.

8. Choose OK, or press Enter.

Your worksheet now contains a chart, as shown in Figure 6-1.

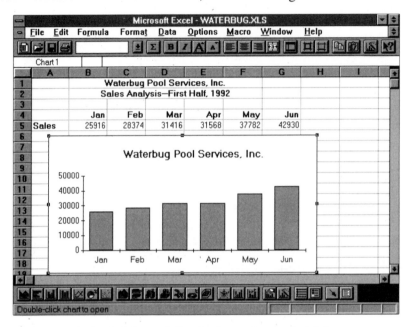

FIGURE 6-1. *A simple Microsoft Excel column chart embedded in a worksheet.*

 If your chart looks different from the one in Figure 6-1, the default "preferred" chart type has been changed. To change the chart to the Column type, refer to the section entitled "Using the Chart Toolbar," later in this chapter.

Creating a Chart with the F11 Key

You've just learned the fastest way to create an *embedded* Excel chart. To create a chart in its own *document window*, follow these steps:

1. Select the range A4:G5.

2. Press F11. (If your keyboard has only 10 function keys, press Alt-F1.)

This creates a new chart document called *Chart1*, as shown in Figure 6-2. Leave this chart open on your screen for the next few minutes.

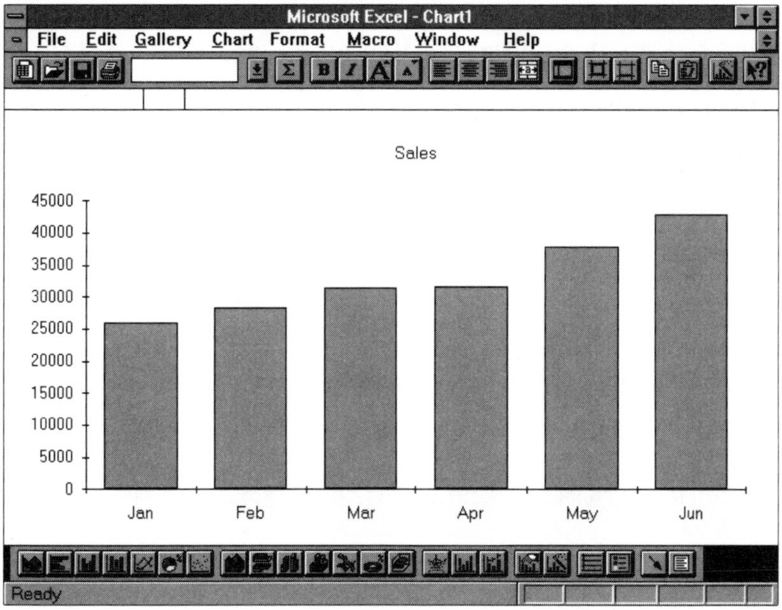

```
                    Microsoft Excel - Chart1
  File  Edit  Gallery  Chart  Format  Macro  Window  Help
```

Sales

FIGURE 6-2. *A chart in its own document window.*

You can also create a chart document by choosing New from the File menu and choosing Chart in the dialog box that appears.

CHART MECHANICS

Behind the scenes, Microsoft Excel determines how to present certain chart elements. For example, Excel sizes the *data-series markers* (the columns in your sample chart) so that they are proportional to the values in the worksheet cells you selected. In the example, Excel also used the dates in row 4 of the worksheet as labels along the X axis. Excel's assumptions about the relationship between worksheets and charts are usually on target, but sometimes you must change these assumptions. You'll learn how to do this in Chapter 7, "Formatting Charts."

How Embedded Charts Work

Embedded charts are graphic objects that Excel treats as whole elements within a worksheet. Though you can't do much with charts using the worksheet menus, you can use the Chart toolbar to work with embedded charts. Unless you close or hide it, the Chart toolbar appears on the screen whenever either a chart window or an embedded chart worksheet is selected. You'll learn how to use this toolbar in a little while.

When you save a worksheet containing an embedded chart, Excel saves the chart with the worksheet. You cannot directly save an embedded chart as a separate document, but you can open an embedded chart and work with it in a chart window at any time simply by double-clicking the chart. Once the embedded chart is displayed in its own window, you can then use the Save As command on the File menu to save the chart as a separate document. Conversely, if you create a chart as a separate document, Excel lets you copy the chart from its own window (with the Copy command or the Copy tool) and paste it into a worksheet as an embedded chart.

How Chart Windows Work

Like the embedded chart, the chart you created with the F11 key is *dynamically linked* to the *WATERBUG.XLS* worksheet data. If you make a change to the contents of a worksheet cell whose value is plotted in the chart, the chart immediately reflects the change.

Microsoft Excel names the first chart document you create in a session Chart1, the second Chart2, and so on. Chart windows always contain the entire chart, so scroll bars are unnecessary. When you shrink or expand the window, Excel shrinks or expands the chart proportionally. You can maximize or minimize chart windows as desired.

Using the Chart Menus

When a chart window is active, as it should be now, Excel displays a chart menu bar that differs from the worksheet menu bar. Most of the commands on the File menu work as they do in a worksheet, but the other menus are quite different. For example, the row-oriented and column-oriented commands on the worksheet Edit menu (Delete, Insert, Fill Right, and Fill Down) are meaningless in a chart window, so they are omitted. The Chart and Gallery menus are unique to the chart menu bar.

- Take a few moments to open and view the chart menus.

You'll learn about the chart menu commands in the next chapter, "Formatting Charts."

 Use the Window menu or press Ctrl-F6 to switch from one window to another.

Saving, and Retrieving Charts

You can save chart documents in the same way you save a worksheet, except that Excel attaches the extension .XLC (rather than .XLS) to the name. To save your chart document:

1. Choose Save As from the File menu.

2. Save Chart1 with the name *WATERBUG*.

Charts are linked to a supporting worksheet and take their values from it, even if the worksheet is closed. When you open an existing chart, it appears with the values it had when you last saved it. But because you might have revised the supporting worksheet in the meantime, Excel displays the message shown in Figure 6-3, asking whether you want to update the references to the supporting worksheet.

FIGURE 6-3. *The Microsoft Excel "update references" message.*

To see how updating works, follow these steps:

1. Close the *WATERBUG* chart by choosing Close from the File menu.

2. In the plotted range of the worksheet, change the value in cell G5 from 42930 to 12930.

3. Close the *WATERBUG* worksheet by choosing the Close command from the File menu.

4. Click Yes when Excel asks if you want to save your changes.

5. Open the File menu and click *WATERBUG.XLC* in the bottom section of the menu.

6. When the message box appears, click the Yes button, or press Enter, to update the chart.

Microsoft Excel updates the chart to reflect the new value in the worksheet: It reduces the height of the rightmost column.

Before continuing,

■ Open *WATERBUG.XLS* and restore the value in cell G5 to 42930.

USING THE CHART TOOLBAR

Most of the tools on the Chart toolbar represent various chart types. To choose a different chart type for the active chart, you click the appropriate tool. The next several pages will cover various chart types that are available through Chart tools. The tools are labeled in the following illustration.

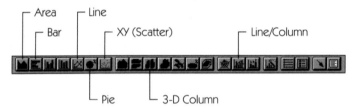

If the Chart toolbar is not on the screen, either the embedded chart is not selected or the Toolbar was closed in a previous Excel session. To display the toolbar, do one of the following:

■ Click on the chart to select it.

■ If the Toolbar does not appear, point to the Standard toolbar, click the right mouse button, and choose Chart from the shortcut menu Excel displays. Click on the embedded chart to select it.

Using Bar Charts

A bar chart is simply a column chart turned on its side. Column charts are useful for illustrating results over time, but bar charts are better suited for making comparisons among items.

■ Click the Bar Chart tool to choose the bar chart format. Your chart will now resemble the one in Figure 6-4.

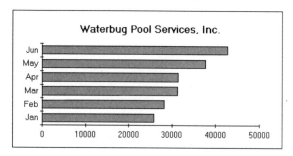

FIGURE 6-4. *A bar chart of the* WATERBUG *data.*

Using Line Charts

A line chart plots the points in a series and connects them with lines. Line charts draw attention to rates of change over time.

■ Click the Line Chart tool to choose the line chart format. The result looks like the chart in Figure 6-5.

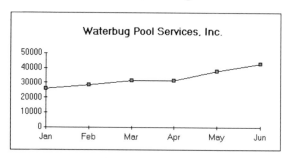

FIGURE 6-5. *A line chart of the* WATERBUG *data.*

Using Area Charts

An area chart connects the values in the data series with lines and fills in the areas below the lines with patterns or color. You might think of an area chart as a colorful line chart. When you're charting a large number of data points, area charts are preferable to column charts because 15 or more data points make the columns too narrow. Area charts also show the contrast in relative trends of data series very well.

■ Click the Area Chart tool to choose the area chart format. The result appears in Figure 6-6.

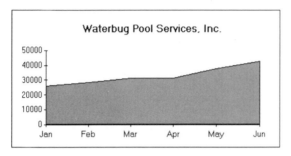

FIGURE 6-6. *An area chart of the* WATERBUG *data.*

Using Pie Charts

A pie chart is a good choice for those times when you want to show relative portions of a 100 percent total. Each slice of the pie represents a single value, and Microsoft Excel sizes the slice in proportion to its share of the total.

■ Click the Pie Chart tool to choose the pie chart format. The result is shown in Figure 6-7.

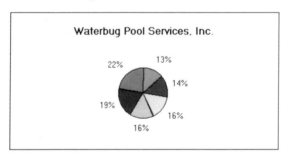

FIGURE 6-7. *A pie chart of the* WATERBUG *data.*

Each slice is displayed in a different color or, if you have a monochrome display, a different pattern. In a chart window you can *explode* a pie slice by dragging it out from the center with the mouse.

The nature of pie charts restricts them to one data series. If several series are selected when the chart is created, Excel uses only the first series to create the pie chart. If you change the chart type to something other than a pie chart, however, the additional data series reappear in the new chart.

You don't need this chart for the rest of the examples, so delete it.

■ Verify that the chart is selected, and then press the Del key.

Using XY (Scatter) Charts

XY charts, or scatter diagrams, appear to be little more than line charts without the lines, but they are really quite different. XY charts don't represent results over time, and they don't use the labels from a worksheet as categories. Instead, they use values on both the X and Y axes to plot the data points on an XY grid, illustrating the correlation between two variables. Your *WATERBUG* data aren't suitable for an XY chart, but you can easily create such a chart by following these steps:

1. Open a new worksheet and enter the data shown in the following illustration.

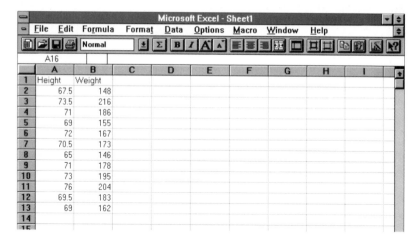

2. In the worksheet, select the pairs of values to be reflected in the chart—in this case, the range A1:B13.

3. Click the ChartWizard tool.

4. Drag the mouse from about cell C2 through cell H13 to define the chart boundaries. Click Next.

5. Click the XY (Scatter) option (shown on the next page) in Step 2.

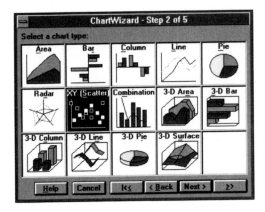

6. Click the ≫ button to accept the remaining defaults and display the chart.

Your chart now looks like the one in Figure 6-8. From this scatter diagram, you can visually judge whether a correlation exists. In this case it looks like there is a relationship between a person's height and weight.

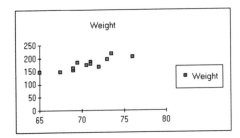

FIGURE 6-8. *An XY chart based on height and weight data.*

You don't need this worksheet and chart anymore. To eliminate them,

1. Choose the Close command from the File menu.

2. Click No when Excel asks if you want to save the worksheet.

Using Combination Charts

If you have more than one series of data, you can mix chart formats in a single chart by creating a combination chart. To try this, create a more interesting chart by adding more data to the *WATERBUG* worksheet.

1. Make the following changes:

Cell	Entry
A6	Cost of sales
A8	Gross profit
B6	12426
B8	=B5–B6
C6	14321
D6	16649
E6	18487
F6	21067
G6	25580

2. Copy the formula in cell B8 to the range C8:G8 by dragging the fill handle to the right, from B8 through G8.

Now follow these steps to create the new chart:

1. Select the range A4:G6. (Row 6 will add the second data series to the chart.)

2. Click the ChartWizard tool and drag over cells B10:G20 to define the chart area. (Drag "below" the visible worksheet area, if necessary, to scroll down a few rows farther.)

3. In Steps 1 through 4, click Next or press Enter to accept the default settings.

4. In Step 5, click No in response to the Add A Legend? question. Type *Waterbug Pool Services, Inc.* in the Chart Title box. Click OK or press Enter when you're finished. The resulting chart looks like the one in Figure 6-9.

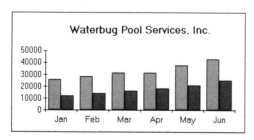

FIGURE 6-9. *A column chart with two data series.*

Now you're ready to turn your two-column chart into a combination line and column chart.

1. Verify that the chart is selected.

2. Click the Line/Column Chart tool.

The result looks like the chart in Figure 6-10. Excel used columns for the first data series and a line for the second series.

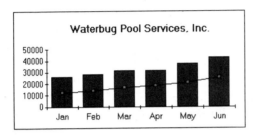

FIGURE 6-10. *A combination line/column chart.*

When you create a combination chart, Microsoft Excel divides the data series evenly between the *main chart* and the *overlay chart*. If the number of data series is uneven, Excel assigns the odd series to the main chart. The first set of data series is plotted on the main chart, and the second set is plotted on the overlay chart.

You can change the type of the main chart by activating the chart window and choosing the Main Chart command from the Format menu. You can change the type of the overlay chart by choosing the Overlay command, also from the Format menu. (These commands are covered in Chapter 7, "Formatting Charts.")

Creating 3-D Charts

Microsoft Excel offers six 3-D (three-dimensional) chart types—area, bar, column, line, pie, and surface.

■ With the *WATERBUG* combination chart selected, click the 3-D Column Chart tool to change to a 3-D chart like the one shown in Figure 6-11.

Choose some of the other 3-D buttons on the toolbar to see what the other chart types look like.

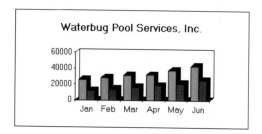

FIGURE 6-11. *A 3-D column chart.*

You'll be using this chart again in Chapter 7, so be sure to save *WATER-BUG.XLS* before quitting Excel. You won't need the *WATERBUG.XLC* chart document again, so you can click either Yes or No if Excel asks you whether you want to save changes to it when you quit.

CONCLUSION

In this chapter, you've learned to create some snappy looking charts with Microsoft Excel. But you have only scratched the surface. In the next chapter, you'll explore Excel's extensive chart-formatting capabilities.

Chapter 7

Formatting Charts

As you have seen, Microsoft Excel does a lot of formatting for you when you use the ChartWizard. Usually, Excel's default assumptions will satisfy your requirements. But for those times when you need something out of the ordinary, this chapter shows you how to create your own unique chart formats.

The first section shows you how to format each of the important parts of a chart. In the latter part of the chapter, you'll learn to blend these pieces of charting knowledge into charting wisdom.

 Whether you've embedded a chart in a worksheet or saved it as a separate document, you format a chart in a chart window. To open the window, remember that you double-click on an embedded chart but that you open the document file if the chart is saved as a separate document.

WORKING WITH CHART ITEMS

To give you the most charting flexibility, Microsoft Excel lets you select individual elements—items—within a chart and change their appearance by using formatting commands.

Types of Chart Items

Figure 7-1 identifies the various kinds of items in Microsoft Excel charts. Not all of these items are present in all types of charts. Pie charts, for instance, have no axes. When you work with chart objects, the menus in the chart window reflect the commands available for use. For example, the Axes command on the Chart menu is not available when the active window contains a pie chart. Other commands on the Chart and Format menus become available only when you select certain chart items. Table 7-1 describes the various types of chart items.

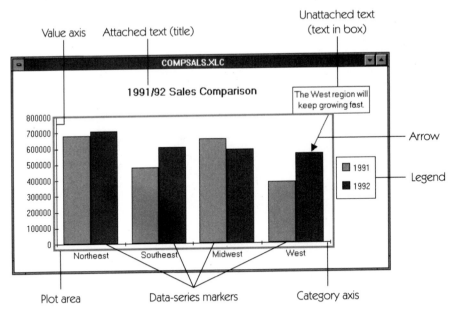

FIGURE 7-1. *The Microsoft Excel chart items.*

Selecting Chart Items

As you do with cells and ranges in worksheets, you must select the chart item you want to format before you choose the formatting command.

To select a chart item,

■ Point to the item and click.

Microsoft Excel marks the currently selected item with white or black *selection squares*. (Black selection squares indicate that the item can be moved.) As you can see in Figure 7-2, sometimes the selection squares surround the item. At other times, such as when you select the data-series markers, the squares appear in the midst of the selected items. If you select an axis, the squares appear at the ends of the axis.

The name of the currently selected item always appears at the left end of the formula bar. The content of the item, which can be text (such as a title) or a SERIES function that defines a data series, always appears in the main section of the formula bar.

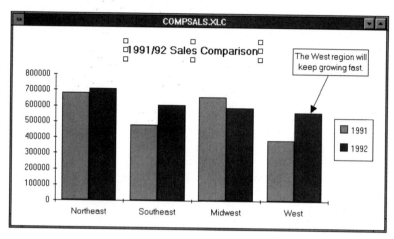

FIGURE 7-2. *A chart with the title selected.*

Chart Item	Description
Chart	The chart as a whole.
Plot area	The rectangular area containing the plotted data, all axes, and data-series markers. The plot area is surrounded by a heavy line in Figure 7-1.
Axes	The lines that provide a frame of reference for plotted data. On a two-dimensional chart, the vertical (value) axis usually indicates amounts and the horizontal (category) axis indicates either points in time or categories.
Attached text	Axis titles, category names, data marker labels, or the chart title.
Unattached text	Freely movable text (usually a subtitle or comments) that you add to the chart.
Data markers	The pictorial representations of values on the chart. Two-dimensional forms include bars, lines, dots, and pie sections, depending on the chart type.
Legend	A cross-reference between data-series names and the patterns or colors representing them in the chart.
Arrow	An arrow symbol you can place on a chart to emphasize a particular item.

TABLE 7-1. *Types of chart items.*

PREPARING *WATERBUG* FOR THE EXAMPLES

The following practice session is based on the chart you embedded in your *WATERBUG* worksheet in Chapter 6. To prepare for the examples,

1. Open the *WATERBUG* worksheet if necessary.

2. Double-click on the embedded chart to move to the chart window.

3. Click the Column Chart tool on the Chart toolbar to change to a simple column chart.

4. Maximize the chart window if it is not already maximized.

5. Hide the Standard toolbar to increase your work area.

Any changes you make now to the version of the chart displayed in the chart window will be reflected in the embedded form in your worksheet.

FORMATTING CHART ITEMS

With charts, the term *formatting* covers a lot of ground. For example, you can format chart text in much the same way you format worksheet text. In addition, however, you can also emphasize any chart item by adding borders, colors, and patterns. Let's start by creating a new chart item.

Adding Axis Titles

Your chart looks good now, but you can make it even easier to interpret. Follow these steps to add descriptive labels to the category (horizontal) axis.

1. Move the mouse pointer over the category axis and click the right mouse button. Doing this brings up a shortcut menu of commands related to formatting axes.

2. Click the Attach Text command. Excel displays the Attach Text dialog box shown below.

3. The Category (X) Axis button is already selected. This is what you want, so click OK, or press Enter. A placeholder *X* label surrounded by white selection squares appears below the category axis.

4. Type *Period* and press Enter. The text is now attached to the Category axis.

5. Click in a blank part of the chart or select a different chart item to remove the selection squares so that you can see the axis title more clearly.

Changing Pattern and Color

The Patterns command on the Format menu provides an outlet for your artistic impulses. You can use any 2 colors from a basic palette of 16 colors. You can also apply color to any one of 18 patterns, many of which visually blend 2 colors, such as red and blue, to create a third (purple). This blending comes about because patterns are made up of combinations of foreground and background colors. For example, a pattern consisting of an equal number of black foreground dots and white background dots can produce an even gray color. If you change the foreground and background colors to red and blue, the visual result is solid purple.

 On a black-and-white monitor, colors are represented in shades of gray, but you can still use the color controls. To see color names, open the Color list in the Patterns dialog box.

To add a pattern to the title of your chart, follow these steps:

1. Select the title.

2. Choose the Patterns command from the Format menu. The following dialog box appears:

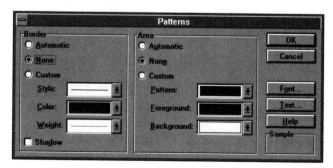

3. Experiment with various color combinations by making selections from the Foreground and Background list boxes and then clicking on different patterns in the Pattern list box. (Try to use an open pattern and combinations of light colors so that the title remains readable.) The Sample box in the bottom-right corner of the Patterns dialog box shows you how the currently selected combination of colors and pattern will appear on the chart.

4. When you have made the selections you want, click OK or press Enter and click on an open area of the chart to view the result.

Your chart title now looks something like the one in Figure 7-3. You can follow the same basic procedure to add patterns to the legend, labels, and unattached text in a chart.

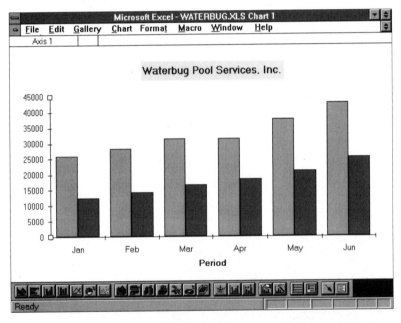

FIGURE 7-3. *The* WATERBUG *chart with a patterned title.*

Formatting Axes

You can display axes in many different ways by adjusting the line style and thickness, as well as the scaling and tick marks.

To format the axes on your chart, follow these steps:

1. Point to the horizontal Category axis and click the right mouse button.

2. Choose the Patterns command from the shortcut menu. A somewhat different Patterns dialog box appears.

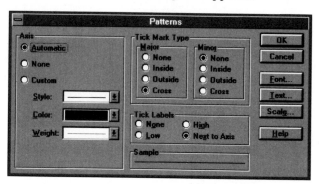

3. In the Weight list box, select the heaviest weight for the axis (the last one in the list), and then click OK or press Enter. The horizontal axis and its tick marks now appear as thick lines.

4. Click the vertical axis with the right mouse button and choose the Scale command. The Axis Scale dialog box appears.

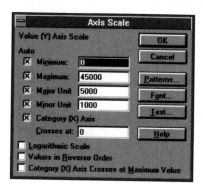

5. Change the Major Unit amount from 5000 to 10000, and then click OK or press Enter.

If you did not maximize your chart window, Excel might already be using 10000 as the major unit. This difference in default settings happens because Excel adjusts the scale to match the size of the chart. If you see 10000 in the Major Unit box, simply click OK.

Your chart now looks like the one in Figure 7-4. Notice that every unit of 10000, instead of every unit of 5000, now has a tick mark.

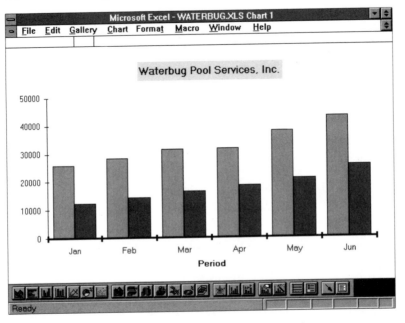

FIGURE 7-4. *The WATERBUG chart after the axes have been formatted.*

FORMATTING CHART TEXT

Microsoft Excel gives you full control over chart text. You can align and orient chart text in a variety of ways, and you can use fonts and colors to emphasize and enhance the words.

Adding Unattached Text to a Chart

Sometimes you'll want to add notes or comments to a chart. The process is simple, although you must remember that you can add text to an embedded chart only when you are working in a chart window, as you are now with the *WATERBUG* chart.

To add unattached text to a chart, you can use the Text Box tool on the Chart toolbar, or you can simply type when nothing else in a chart is selected.

First, use the Text Box tool to add a comment. Follow these steps:

1. In the chart window, click the Text Box tool shown below.

   The word *Text*, surrounded by black selection squares indicating a movable object, appears in the middle of your chart.

2. Replace the word *Text* with your own comment. Type the following, breaking to a new line by holding down Ctrl and pressing Enter where you see <Ctrl-Enter>:

```
June figures are<Ctrl-Enter>
preliminary.
```

   Press Enter to indicate that your comment is complete.

The comment does little good parked in the middle of the chart. To move it,

1. Place the mouse pointer inside the area marked by the selection squares. Hold down the left mouse button, and a rectangular box appears.

2. Drag the box to the upper-right corner of the chart. Click in a blank area of the chart to see the result.

Your chart should now look like the one in Figure 7-5.

 You can use arrows to draw attention to particular parts of a chart. Click the Arrow tool to the left of the Text Box tool or choose the Add Arrow command from the Chart menu, and Excel will display a large arrow with a selection square at each end. Move the arrow by dragging it. Change its size or orientation by dragging either of the selection squares.

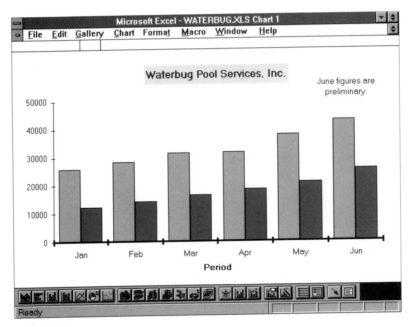

FIGURE 7-5. *The chart with unattached (movable) text added.*

Although the Text Box tool is easy to use, adding unattached text simply by typing is even easier. To try it,

1. Select the comment you just added and press Del to delete it.

2. Type

```
June figures<Ctrl-Enter>
are preliminary.
```

Press Enter. Your new comment, surrounded by black selection squares, appears in the middle of the chart.

3. Drag the comment to the upper-right corner of the chart as you did before and deselect the comment by clicking in a blank area of the chart.

You achieve the same result but take a slightly different route to get there.

 Use the same technique of pointing and dragging to move any graphic object in an Excel document—a chart item, an embedded chart, or a graphic object you have imported from another program. Remember, though, that in a chart you can move only those items surrounded by black selection squares.

176

Formatting Unattached Text

Notice that Excel used its default font and font size for your comment and automatically centered the lines within an area it defined as belonging to the comment. You can use the Standard and Formatting toolbars to change font, size, and alignment, as well as add character formatting such as bold or italic.

You can also resize and reshape the ''box'' surrounding an item by selecting the item and dragging any of the black selection squares. You'll find this feature useful if you decide to enclose unattached text in a box, as described in the next section.

To practice some formatting alternatives without changing what you've done so far,

1. Switch to the worksheet window by opening the Window menu and choosing *WATERBUG.XLS* from the list at the bottom. Now, use the Save command on the File menu. (Saving in this way saves your changes in the embedded chart; using Save from the chart window would save the chart as a separate document.)

2. After the save, double-click on the embedded chart to return to the chart window.

3. Experiment with fonts, font sizes, alignment, and character styles as much as you want.

4. When you're finished, return to the worksheet window, choose Close from the File menu, and click No when Excel asks if you want to save your changes.

5. Reopen the *WATERBUG* worksheet, double-click on the embedded chart, and you're ready to continue with the remainder of this chapter.

Putting Boxes Around Text

Chart titles and unattached text look more impressive when they're boxed. To put a shadowed box around the chart title, follow these steps:

1. Double-click the title. This brings up the Patterns dialog box. (You can display the Patterns dialog box for an item at any time; double-clicking selects the item and chooses the Patterns command.)

2. The Border options control the appearance of the box frame. From the Color drop-down list, select the dark blue color. (If you have a monochrome monitor, select one of the dark gray shades.) Excel changes the sample lines in the Style and Weight groups to the color you select.

3. Open the Weight list box, and select the heaviest line.

4. Turn on the Shadow option by clicking its check box.

5. Click OK, or press Enter.

With the title nicely boxed, your *June figures...* comment now looks a little plain. To add a box around the comment as well,

1. Double-click the comment to select it and open the Patterns dialog box.

2. Double-click Automatic in the Border options. Click elsewhere on the screen to deselect the text box.

Your chart now looks like the one in Figure 7-6.

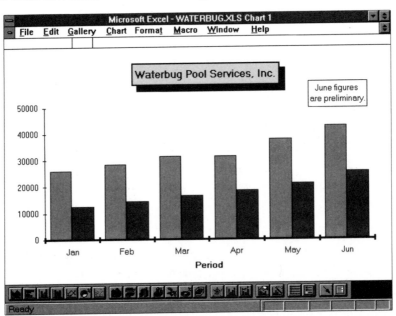

FIGURE 7-6. *The* WATERBUG *chart with a shadowed box around the title.*

Positioning Text

Let's look at some ways you can position various types of text in your charts. Notice that not all of the positioning commands work with all text items.

To position the title text,

1. Select the title box, click the right mouse button for a shortcut menu, and then choose the Text command. The dialog box shown in Figure 7-7 appears.

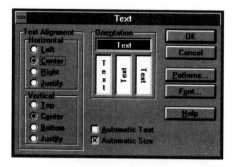

FIGURE 7-7. *The Text dialog box.*

The options in the Horizontal and Vertical Alignment groups are intuitive. Horizontal aligns text to the left, center, or right within the item boundaries. Vertical aligns text toward the top, center, or bottom of the item area.

2. Experiment by changing the Alignment settings for the title. Return the title to its centered position when you are done.

If all you want to do is format text horizontally, remember you can simply click on one of the alignment tools when the Standard toolbar is displayed.

The Orientation option group in the Text dialog box (Figure 7-7) offers four possible text alignments. Each option button shows the effect clicking the button has on the chart. Obviously, horizontal text is most appropriate for title boxes. But vertical text can be useful for labels along the value (vertical) axis. To see how vertical text looks, follow these steps:

1. If necessary, click Cancel, or press Esc, to remove the Text dialog box from the screen.

2. Click the vertical axis with the right mouse button.

179

3. Choose the Attach Text command from the shortcut menu. Click OK, or press Enter, to confirm the default selection, Value (Y) Axis.

4. Type the word *Dollars* and press Enter. The *Dollars* label is oriented sideways, bottom-to-top—the default orientation.

5. Use the Text command to orient *Dollars* in other ways. Return to the default orientation when you're done.

Changing the Font

The shadowed box adds interest to the title, but the title text itself still looks like all the other text in the chart, so add more emphasis by changing the text font to Roman 18-point bold. Follow these steps:

1. Select the title again, click the right mouse button, and choose the Font command. The following dialog box appears:

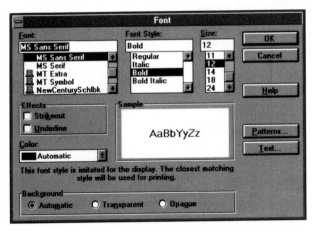

The fonts available depend on your version of Windows and on the printer you have installed, but Roman should be available in all cases.

2. Select Roman in the Font list box.

3. Select 18 in the Size list box.

4. If the Bold option is not selected in the Font Style box, click it.

180

5. If you have a color monitor, select Dark Red from the Color drop-down list. Click OK, or press Enter.

FORMATTING THE CHART ITSELF

The quickest way to format a chart as a whole is to click one of the chart type tools on the Chart toolbar or to select one of the chart type options on the Gallery menu. Microsoft Excel then creates the type of chart you requested.

Suppose, however, you don't want a different chart type, but you do want something other than Excel's predefined formats. You can make changes to the entire chart just as you have done with individual chart items.

Selecting the Entire Chart

To format an entire chart, you must first select the chart, which itself is an object. Follow these steps:

1. Move the mouse pointer outside the plot area, to a blank space either above the top or below the bottom of the value (Y) axis.

2. Click.

Selection squares encompass the whole chart, meaning that the chart itself is selected.

Now that you know where to click to select the chart, try a faster way.

■ Move the pointer outside the plot area and double-click.

This one action selects the chart and brings up the Patterns dialog box. Now, formatting the chart is a breeze.

Adding Borders and Patterns to the Chart

With the chart selected, follow these steps:

1. Create a border around the chart by using the options in the Border group of the Patterns dialog box. Select the solid line style, the blue color (if you have a color monitor), and a medium line weight. Turn on the Shadow option by clicking its check box.

2. Create a background pattern for the whole chart by using the options in the Area group. Select a pattern and new foreground and background colors. Click OK, or press Enter.

Your chart now looks something like the one in Figure 7-8.

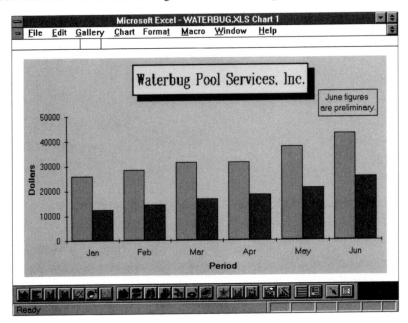

FIGURE 7-8. *The chart after a background pattern is added.*

You'll probably spend quite a bit of time experimenting with formatting patterns. If you come up with a pattern you particularly like, you can save the formatting as a reusable chart template. *For information on templates, see your Excel documentation.*

DESIGNING A CHART TO HIGHLIGHT IMPORTANT INFORMATION

You have seen a number of ways to format charts, but there's more to creating interesting charts than fancy formatting. The most important goal is to present data accurately and in an easy-to-understand form. The key is choosing the right chart type for the data.

In this section, you'll add more data to the Waterbug Pool Services worksheet in order to explore some of the decisions you must make when creating a chart for presentation.

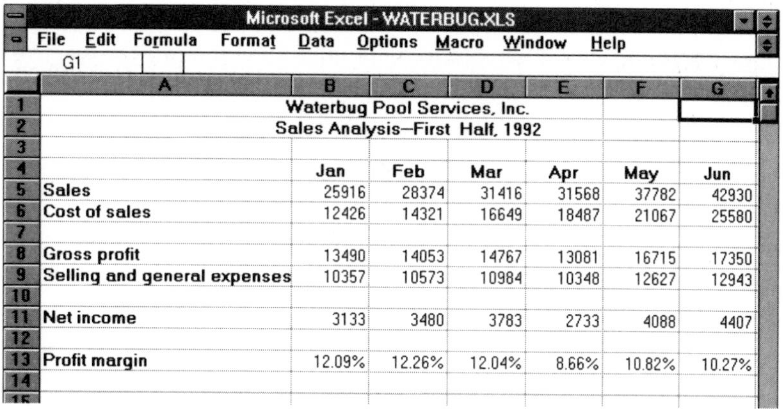

Microsoft Excel - WATERBUG.XLS

File Edit Formula Format Data Options Macro Window Help

G1

	A	B	C	D	E	F	G
1		Waterbug Pool Services, Inc.					
2		Sales Analysis—First Half, 1992					
3							
4		Jan	Feb	Mar	Apr	May	Jun
5	Sales	25916	28374	31416	31568	37782	42930
6	Cost of sales	12426	14321	16649	18487	21067	25580
7							
8	Gross profit	13490	14053	14767	13081	16715	17350
9	Selling and general expenses	10357	10573	10984	10348	12627	12943
10							
11	Net income	3133	3480	3783	2733	4088	4407
12							
13	Profit margin	12.09%	12.26%	12.04%	8.66%	10.82%	10.27%
14							

FIGURE 7-9. *Sales, expense, and profit data for Waterbug Pool Services.*

The finished worksheet is shown in Figure 7-9, above. Follow these steps to make the changes:

1. Double-click the document control menu or choose Close from the file menu to close the chart window.
2. If necessary, make room for the new data in the *WATERBUG* worksheet by dragging your embedded chart to a location below row 13.
3. Enter the new labels in cells A9, A11, and A13.
4. Format the labels as bold. Widen column A by dragging the header boundary.
5. Enter the amounts in cells B9 through G9.
6. Enter the following formula in cell B11:

   `=B8–B9`

7. Enter the following formula in cell B13:

   `=B11/B5`

8. Use the fill handle to copy the formulas in B11:B13 into columns C through G.
9. Apply the 0.00% format to row 13.

Now suppose you've been asked to make a presentation at a management meeting, highlighting significant aspects of the company's performance in the first half of 1992. You see immediately that the worksheet contains too much information to present in one chart. You must determine what information is most important for your presentation.

The *WATERBUG* chart you produced earlier shows that business seems to be going well. Sales are increasing briskly, and the cost of sales appears to be appropriate. Row 11 in the worksheet indicates that net income shows a general upward trend. But something in the worksheet strikes a sour note. Notice that net income as a *percentage* of total sales (profit margin) has declined over the six-month period. You're aware of the reasons behind the severe drop in April, but you still think the overall downward trend should be discussed at the meeting. How can you show the significance of this trend in a chart?

The answer is a combination chart. To contrast the good news (steady sales growth) with the bad news (lagging profit margins), you can create a chart with the sales data series plotted on a main chart and the profit margin data series plotted on an overlay chart. Combining two different chart types will highlight the divergent trends in the two data series. For this example, you'll use a column chart for sales and a line chart for profit margin. Follow these steps:

1. Select the range A4:G5, and then hold down the Ctrl key and select A13:G13.

2. Press F11 (Alt-F1 if you don't have an F11 key).

Your chart looks like the one in Figure 7-10. Only the sales figures appear in this chart. Because the value axis is scaled in increments of 5000, the percentage values are too small to show up.

To show the percentage values,

1. Choose the Combination command from the Gallery menu.

2. Select option 2 (which shows a second value axis on the right) and click OK.

Excel redraws the chart so you can see the contrast between the sales trends on the main (column) chart and the profit-margin trends on the overlay (line) chart, as shown in Figure 7-11.

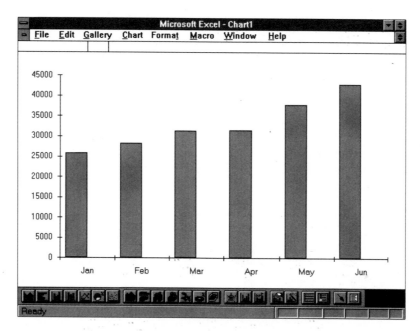

FIGURE 7-10. *A column chart of the* WATERBUG *sales data.*

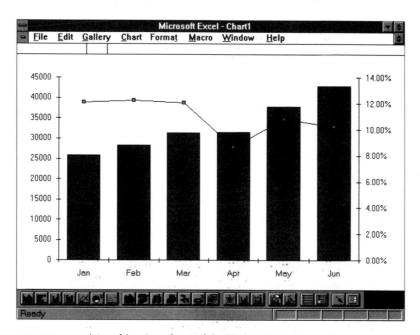

FIGURE 7-11. *A combination chart of the* WATERBUG *sales data versus profit-margin data with two value axes.*

Notice that the scale of the axis on the right causes Excel to plot the profit-margin data toward the top of the chart. You can dramatize the profit-margin trend by overriding the automatic scaling of the percentage axis.

To change the scaling, follow these steps:

1. Point to the value axis on the right side of the chart.

2. Click the right mouse button. This brings up the shortcut menu for formatting axes.

3. Click Scale. Doing this brings up the Axis Scale dialog box shown below.

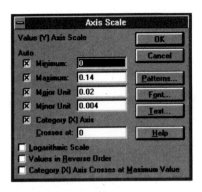

4. Change the value for the Minimum option to *0.07* to make 7 percent the lowest value on the scale. Click OK, or press Enter.

Because the vertical range of the overlay chart is now from 7.00% to 13.00%, Excel redraws the overlay chart in a way that accentuates the downward trend of net income as a percentage of sales, as shown in Figure 7-12.

CAUTION *The previous example demonstrates how you can bring some creativity to bear on business data. Microsoft Excel can point out troublesome trends before they become big problems. On the other hand, you can easily go overboard if you're not careful. For example, it's possible to make an insignificant trend look overly important by severely narrowing the range of an axis.*

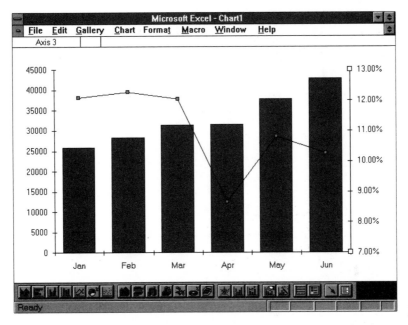

FIGURE 7-12. *The combination chart from Figure 7-11 after the scale of the percentage-value axis has been adjusted.*

Changing the Type of a Formatted Chart

Once you have added formatting to such items as series markers and axes, you should generally avoid using the Chart toolbar or the Gallery menu commands to change the chart type. Such changes can wipe out some of your formatting. Instead,

■ Choose the Main Chart command from the Format menu.

Excel displays the dialog box shown in Figure 7-13.

To change the chart type, you select the desired type from the drop-down list in the Main Chart Type box. Each time you select a different chart type, the examples in the Data View group change to show charts of the type you've selected.

 The other options in the Format Chart dialog box provide global options relating to data-series markers. For more information on these options, press F1 or click the Help button in the dialog box, or see the Excel documentation.

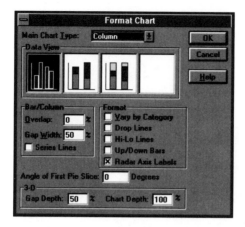

FIGURE 7-13. *The Format Chart dialog box.*

Choosing the Overlay command from the Format menu brings up a similar dialog box that allows you to format the overlay part of a combination chart.

Choosing a Preferred Chart Type

Whenever you begin a session with Excel, the program uses a simple column chart as its default, or preferred, chart type. This is the type of chart you created early in Chapter 6, and it is the one you see highlighted in the dialog box that appears whenever you choose Column from the Gallery menu.

During a given session, however, you might be concentrating on producing a different kind of chart, such as a set of pie charts or bar charts. Instead of creating each chart in the default column format and then changing to the type you want, you can tell Excel to temporarily change the preferred chart type. To do this, you use the Set Preferred command, as follows:

1. Create a chart of the type you want.

2. From the chart window, choose the Set Preferred command from the Gallery menu.

During the remainder of your current session, Excel will use the same chart type as its default.

If you change a chart to a different type and want to return it to the previously defined preferred format,

1. Select the chart, if it is embedded, or display the chart in a chart window.

188

2. Click the Preferred Chart tool (shown below) on the Chart toolbar, or choose Preferred from the Gallery menu.

If you have more than one chart window open, the Preferred command affects only the active chart.

PRINTING CHARTS

You've seen that you can create charts either as embedded objects within a worksheet or as separate documents in their own right. When it comes to printing, you have the same two choices. If you have an embedded chart and want to print it as part of the worksheet that contains it, all you do is use the commands and options described in Chapter 5, ''Printing Microsoft Excel Documents.''

If you want to print a chart as a separate document, you begin by displaying the chart in a chart window. (You can use this approach to print an embedded chart as well as one you've saved as a separate document.) Once you have displayed the chart, you follow the same general procedures you use for printing worksheets. You do, however, have a few different sizing options. These options (shown below) are located in the Chart Size box at the bottom of the Page Setup dialog box you see when you choose the command from the File menu in the chart window. Table 7-2 explains the options.

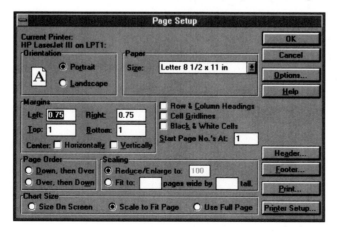

Option	Dimensions of Printed Chart
Size On Screen	Identical to size on screen.
Scale To Fit Page	Expanded as large as possible while retaining the height-to-width proportions shown on the screen. This is the default option.
Use Full Page	Expanded to fill the entire page, regardless of the effect on the chart's proportions.

TABLE 7-2. *Page-setup options and their effects on printed charts.*

The Row & Column Headings and Cell Gridlines options have no meaning for charts, so they are not available in the Page Setup dialog box when you're printing a chart from a chart window. The Scaling options, which would be incompatible with the Chart Size options, are also unavailable when you print a chart as a separate document.

Having made your selections in the Page Setup dialog box, choose the Print command to print your chart. The Print dialog box for charts is identical to the one for worksheets, except that options not applicable to charts are dimmed.

CONCLUSION

You've still seen only part of what Microsoft Excel can do in formatting charts, but you are now well equipped to experiment on your own. Try changing the colors or patterns of other items, such as data-series markers, legends, unattached text, or the chart axes. Try the Arrow tool to point to important items on a chart. Three-dimensional charts offer a whole host of formatting options. Excel's charting features are so extensive most users will never need a dedicated charting program.

Chapter 8

Managing Databases

Now that you've learned how to create and use Microsoft Excel worksheets and charts, it's time to move on to the third major Excel component: databases. A database is a set of related data items. The set is stored in a worksheet and is structured so that individual items can be located and summarized efficiently. You are already familiar with many databases that exist outside of computers—for example, the telephone book and other printed listings.

The first part of this chapter covers such basics as creating databases, adding and deleting records, and sorting data. In the latter part of the chapter you'll learn to use *selection criteria* to manipulate data.

UNDERSTANDING DATABASES

Consider a typical address file made up of cards like the one pictured in Figure 8-1. Each card shows a name, company, address, and telephone number. The fact that each card contains the same types of information makes the address file a database.

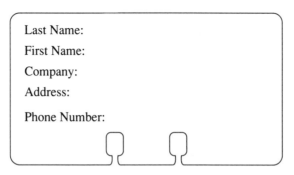

FIGURE 8-1. *A Rolodex card—one record in a database.*

Figure 8-2 shows how the address database might look in a Microsoft Excel worksheet. The column headings, called *field names,* serve the same purpose as the printed categories on each card. Each row, called a *record,* is equivalent to one card. For example, the information in row 2 of the database is equivalent to the information you might record on the card for Harrison Small. Each column, called a *field,* is equivalent to one of the categories that appear on all the cards.

Storing this type of data electronically provides capabilities that you don't have with telephone books and address files. Using commands on the Data menu, you can have Excel find all the records that meet specific conditions. This approach is much quicker than flipping through your Rolodex cards. You can also tell Excel to sort the records, rearranging the database records in whatever order you specify.

	Last Name	First Name	Company	Address	City, State	Phone No.
1	Last Name	First Name	Company	Address	City, State	Phone No.
2	Small	Harrison	Flite Manufacturing	10500 Barnes Highway	Denver, CO	(303) 332-5786
3	Smathers	William	Walker Bearings	1098 10th Street	Springfield, MO	(417) 442-1585
4	Smedley	Charles	Smedley & Smedley	One Flagship Avenue	Tampa, FL	(813) 442-8731
5	Smith	Lawrence	King Sprockets	650 "E" Street	Lompoc, CA	(805) 221-1789
6	Smith	Nick	Burns Chemical	5600 Telegraph Road	Detroit, MI	(313) 696-2461
7	Smith	Stephen	Zippo Office Supply	2500 Center Street	Chicago IL	(312) 332-4000
8	Smithers	Lester	Ames Janitorial	2960 Industrial Ave.	St. Louis, MO	(314) 442-1264
9	Smoot	Alvin	HTZ Corporation	3400 Tobacco Road	Knoxville, TN	(615) 343-8921
10	Smothers	Jordan	New Age Widgets	2000 Parkway Drive	New York, NY	(212) 331-6845
11	Snidely	Jonathan	Snidely Insurance	15695 Everett Road	Boston, MA	(617) 332-6347

FIGURE 8-2. *An address database in a Microsoft Excel worksheet.*

CREATING A DATABASE

For the examples in this chapter, suppose you are a stockbroker and you want to use Excel to maintain information on each of your clients. To start off, you must create a database containing the following client information:

- Last name

- First name

- Account balance

- Commissions generated in 1991

- Commissions generated to date in 1992

- Total commissions generated in 1991 and 1992

- Date you last met with the client

These items will be the fields in your database. For reasons explained later in the chapter, it's best to leave some blank rows at the top of the worksheet. Accordingly, you will enter the field names in row 6 of your worksheet.

To create the sample database, follow these steps:

1. Open a new, blank worksheet.

2. Type the following field names in the specified cells. Note that field names must be text entries; numeric entries and formulas are not allowed.

Cell	Field Name	Cell	Field Name
A6	Last Name	E6	1992 Commissions
B6	First Name	F6	Total Commissions
C6	Account Balance	G6	Last Meeting
D6	1991 Commissions		

3. Click the row 6 header to select the entire row, and then choose the Alignment command from the Format menu.

4. Select the Center and Wrap Text options in the Alignment dialog box, and then click OK or press Enter.

5. Click the Bold button on the toolbar.

6. Widen the columns and reduce the row height, so that the field names wrap neatly in two lines of text.

7. Enter the first record in row 7, using the following data:

Cell	Entry	Cell	Entry
A7	Walton	E7	159
B7	Wilbur	F7	=D7+E7
C7	43870	G7	1/11/92
D7	916		

8. Choose the Save As command from the File menu, and name the worksheet *CLIENTS*.

9. Take a minute now to format the cells of your database. For example, assign fields that contain numbers the #,##0 format.

Notice that, although field names must be text entries, the data itself can contain formulas. Fields that contain formulas are called *computed fields*. In Figure 8-3, the formula bar shows the computed field in F7. (The worksheet in the illustration has been scrolled so that the five blank rows at the top are no longer visible.) The formula =D7+E7 adds the values in the 1991 Commissions and 1992 Commissions fields (D7 and E7) and returns the sum in cell F7.

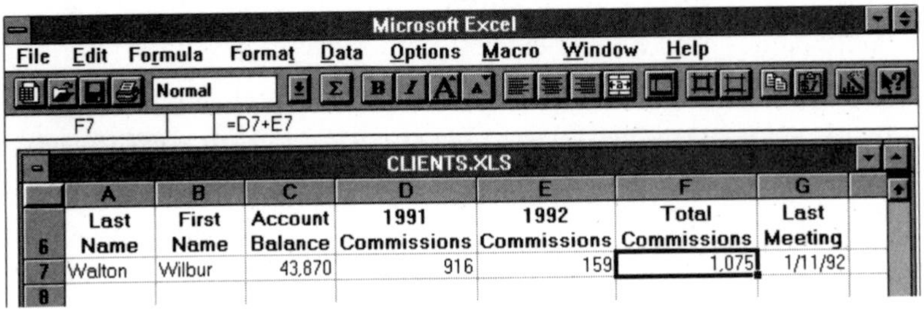

FIGURE 8-3. *The first record in the* CLIENTS *database, with the formula bar showing the computed field in cell F7.*

Setting the Database

To carry out most of the commands on the Data menu, Microsoft Excel needs to know which part of the worksheet contains the active database. Although you can have several databases on a worksheet, only one of them can be active at a time. Designating the active database is called *setting the database*.

To set the database you just created, follow these steps:

1. Select the range A6:G8.

2. Choose the Set Database command from the Data menu.

Although nothing appears to happen, behind the scenes Excel assigns the name *Database* to the selected range. From now on, Excel will recognize only the range A6:G8 as a database, unless you do one of the following:

- Select a new range and choose Set Database again.

- Choose the Define Name command from the Formula menu and delete the name *Database*.

■ Choose the Define Name command from the Formula menu and assign *Database* to a different range.

The range you defined contains three rows: the field names in row 6, the record in row 7, and the blank row 8. Including at least one blank row at the end of the database makes it easier to add new records to a database that you expect will grow. For example, you could add a second record to the example database simply by selecting the blank row 8, choosing the Insert command from the Edit menu, and entering the information for the new record in the new row 8 that Excel inserted above the selected blank row.

When you insert rows, Excel extends the range defined with the name *Database* so that it continues to include the last (blank) row. Excel does not count blank rows at the end of the database in determining the total number of records in the database.

Inserting rows is not the only way to add records to a database, however. A better way is to use a special *data form,* as described next.

USING THE DATA FORM

To help you create and edit your databases, Microsoft Excel provides a type of dialog box called the data form. You can use the data form to add entries to your database, change entries, and view specific entries. Choose the Form command from the Data menu to see the default data form, which is shown in Figure 8-4 on the following page.

When you choose the Form command from the Data menu, Excel displays the record located in the first row of the database. The title bar at the top of the data form displays the name of the worksheet that contains the active database. The *record indicator* at the top right shows the sequence number of the displayed record (*New Record* if you display a blank record).

The scroll bar in the data form is similar to the vertical worksheet scroll bar. You can move among the records in the database by clicking the scroll-bar arrows or by dragging the scroll box. You can move through the database 10 records at a time by clicking above or below the scroll box.

You'll find out about the *command buttons* in a moment, after you enter some more data.

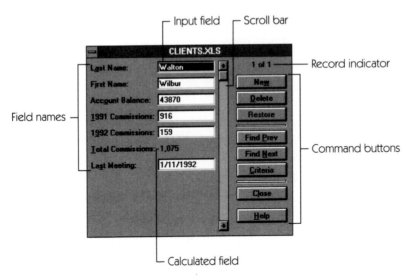

FIGURE 8-4. *The Microsoft Excel default data form.*

Using Input Fields

The data form displays the field names in text boxes called *input fields*. To enter or revise a record, you simply select an input field and type or edit the information for that field, using ordinary mouse or keyboard methods. (You cannot edit the Total Commissions field, however, because that entry is the result of a calculation.)

In the next set of steps, you'll enter a new record with the following data:

Field Name	Entry
Last Name	Miller
First Name	Herman
Account Balance	6960
1991 Commissions	459
1992 Commissions	55
Last Meeting	3/30/92

Follow these steps to create this record:

1. Click the New command button at the top right of the data form. The data form's input fields are now blank, and the record indicator displays *New Record*.

196

2. Type the last name in the Last Name text box.

3. Press the Tab key to move to the next field (First Name), and type the first name.

4. Type the rest of the data, pressing the Tab key to move through the remaining input fields.

5. Press Enter when you're ready to add the record to the database.

Excel uses the information you enter in the 1991 Commissions and 1992 Commissions fields to calculate the value for the Total Commissions field.

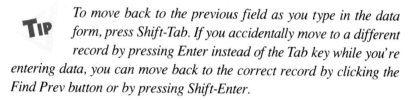

To move back to the previous field as you type in the data form, press Shift-Tab. If you accidentally move to a different record by pressing Enter instead of the Tab key while you're entering data, you can move back to the correct record by clicking the Find Prev button or by pressing Shift-Enter.

Now use the data form to enter the following data for the remaining 13 records in the sample database:

Last Name	First Name	Account Balance	1991 Commissions	1992 Commissions	Last Meeting
Williams	Oliver	10940	137	73	8/12/91
Hendricks	Margaret	48750	1014	387	10/1/91
Smith	Jeffrey	62550	1718	299	8/7/91
Johnson	Johnny	57248	1101	296	5/9/92
Baker	Abel	55080	1386	379	7/15/92
Devine	Dennis	112300	2712	553	6/13/92
Spencer	David	8145	121	0	10/13/91
Terry	Florence	74640	1236	294	2/20/92
Green	Scott	36460	867	224	3/27/92
Merrill	L.Y.	54153	770	346	12/8/91
Smith	Harvey	12690	190	122	5/5/92
Wilson	Harry	29240	439	249	5/10/92
Nevin	John	90890	868	391	6/28/92

When you've finished adding records,

1. Click Close to close the data form.

2. Save the worksheet again.

Using the data form to add a new record automatically extends the database range to include the new record, provided that blank rows are available in the worksheet immediately below the existing database range. Excel extends the range whether or not you include a blank row in the selected range when you set the database.

Form the habit of using the data form to add new records. Doing so means that you'll never have to worry about an incorrect data range.

Performing Operations Within the Data Form

The command buttons mentioned earlier enable you to do much more with the data form than enter data. Table 8-1 describes the effects of these buttons.

Command Button	Effect
New	Creates blank fields for a new record and inserts the record after the last record (row) in the database.
Delete	Removes the currently displayed record from the database.
Restore	Undoes all current edits to the displayed record.
Find Prev	Searches up from the current record in the database and displays the first previous record that meets criteria defined in the data form with the Criteria button. If no criteria are defined, Find Prev displays the immediately preceding record in the database.
Find Next	Searches down from the current record in the database and displays the next record that meets criteria defined in the data form with the Criteria command. If no criteria are defined, Find Next displays the next record in the database.
Criteria	Lets you define the criteria to be used in searching for specific records.
Close	Closes the data form, saving any unsaved changes to the current record, and also reactivates the worksheet proper.
Help	Displays the Help window for the Data Form command.

TABLE 8-1. *The effects of the data-form command buttons.*

You've already learned how to use the data form to add new records. Now you'll see some other useful operations.

Finding records

Some databases, such as address files, are relatively static—you'll rarely need to update records. Other databases are more dynamic and change frequently, sometimes even daily. For example, suppose today is October 1, 1992, and you've just had lunch with Scott Green, one of your clients. You need to update your database to reflect this meeting. To find Green's record, follow these steps:

1. Choose the Form command from the Data menu.

2. Click the Criteria button. The input fields go blank, and the data form itself undergoes some subtle changes, as shown in the following illustration:

Notice that the word *Criteria* appears where the record indicator is normally displayed. The command buttons differ somewhat, and—importantly—notice that you can now make an entry in the Total Commissions field to search for matching records based on the results of this computed field.

3. To specify the record you want, type *green* in the Last Name input field. (Capitalization doesn't matter.)

4. Press Enter, or click the Find Next button.

The Scott Green record is now displayed in the form.

By filling in more input fields, you can be even more specific about the record you want to locate. For example, to locate the record for Harvey Smith, not Jeffrey Smith, you would type *Smith* in the Last Name input field and *Harvey* in the First Name input field.

Editing records

Using the data form, you can easily revise the data in your database. In the record for Scott Green, the Last Meeting input field currently contains the date 3/27/1992. To edit this entry, follow these steps:

1. Point to the Last Meeting field and double-click to select the entry.

2. Type *10/1/92* in the text box.

3. Press Enter.

Microsoft Excel makes the change in the database, and the data form displays the next record.

To make one of a series of editing changes permanent, press Enter. In contrast, to make your final editing change permanent and remove the data form from the screen at the same time, click the Close button.

Deleting records

You can use the data form to quickly delete entire records. For example, to delete the currently displayed record without returning to the database in the worksheet, follow these steps:

1. Click the Delete button. Excel displays the following message telling you the deletion will be permanent:

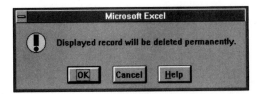

2. Click OK, or press Enter to confirm the deletion.

The record vanishes, and the next record in the database appears in its place. On the worksheet, Excel clears the database cells that contained the record you deleted and then moves subsequent records up to fill the gap. The database range also moves up one row.

Closing the Data Form

When you finish working with the data form, you remove it from the screen by clicking the Close button or by pressing Esc. Excel returns you to the place in the worksheet where you were working when you chose the Form command from the Data menu.

Before continuing,

1. Close the data form if you have not already done so.

2. Use the Open File tool or the Open command on the File menu to reopen the *CLIENTS* worksheet. Click OK or press Enter when Excel asks whether to revert to the version you saved earlier.

All subsequent examples in this chapter use this earlier version of the worksheet, which contains the 15 records you originally entered.

FILLING A RANGE WITH A SERIES

Later in the chapter you will learn about sorting records in a database. Immediately after you sort a database, you can restore the records to their original sequence by choosing the Undo Sort command from the Edit menu. But what if you don't realize until later that you need to put the database records back in their original sequence?

Excel can help you restore the original sequence only if you have planned ahead. You can protect yourself against erroneous sorts by using the Series command on the Data menu. You can number the records in a database so that you can, if necessary, restore the database to its original order after you have sorted it.

As an example, let's number the records in the *CLIENTS* database. Follow these steps:

1. Click the column A header, and choose Insert from the Edit menu to insert a new, blank column in front of the Last Name column.

2. Select cell A6, and enter the pound sign (#) as a new field name.

3. Enter *1* in cell A7.

4. Select the range A7:A21.

5. Choose the Series command from the Data menu. The dialog box shown on the next page appears.

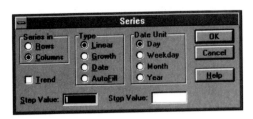

6. Be sure Columns in the Series In box and Linear in the Type box are selected.

7. Click OK, or press Enter.

Excel enters a set of sequential numbers from 1 through 15 in the selected range. As you will see later in this chapter, you can sort the database any way you want and return it to its original arrangement simply by sorting in ascending numeric order based on the # (Number) field.

Note that Excel did not automatically expand the *Database* range name to include the new column you added at the edge of the database. If you want column A to be included in the *Database* range name, you will have to reset the database. Also note that if you add new records to the database, they are not automatically assigned a sequential number in column A. You must either type in the number or expand the series by selecting a new range that includes the cells in column A adjacent to the new records and using the Series command again.

SORTING RECORDS

Depending on the kind of information you store in your databases, you might want to arrange a given database in numeric, chronological, or alphabetic order. *Sorting,* or arranging your data in particular ways, is an important database feature.

Simple Sorting

For a simple numeric or alphabetic sort that arranges records in ascending (A to Z, 0 to 9) or descending (Z to A, 9 to 0) order, you can use the Sort Ascending and Sort Descending tools on the Utility toolbar. (The tools are illustrated and labeled on the next page.)

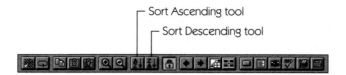

Sort Ascending tool
Sort Descending tool

To try these tools,

1. Display the Utility toolbar. If necessary, drag it out of the way.

2. To make all fields in the database visible, narrow column A until it is two or three characters wide.

3. Select cells A7:H16, which contain the complete sets of data for the first 10 records in your database. Selecting whole records is important. If you select partial records, Excel will sort only those fields, and the result will be scrambled—and unreliable—data.

The records are already sorted in ascending numeric order, thanks to the sequential numbers you entered in column A, so start with a descending sort.

1. Click the Sort Descending tool. Excel immediately rearranges the selected records, listing them in descending numeric order, from 10 down through 1.

2. Return your database to its original order by clicking the Sort Ascending tool. Once again, Excel arranges the records, this time reversing the sort to list the records in order from 1 through 10.

3. Close the Utility toolbar.

Sorting with Keys

In addition to simple sorts, Microsoft Excel gives you the ability to sort records according to values in particular fields, using up to three *keys* with the Sort command on the Data menu. A key is simply a cell address that indicates which field you want Excel to use as a basis for sorting the records.

You can sort the entire database, or you can sort only a specific range of records. In either case, the Sort command requires that you first select the range of cells to be sorted. (Most of the other commands on the Data menu use the defined database as the object of the command, regardless of which cells are currently selected in the worksheet.)

Figure 8-5 shows how your clients rank, from highest to lowest, in 1991 commissions. To get these results, you must sort the database by commissions generated. Follow these steps:

1. Select the range A7:H21 in the *CLIENTS* worksheet.

Don't include field names in any range you select for sorting. If you do, Excel will sort the names along with the data.

2. Choose the Sort command from the Data menu. The following dialog box appears.

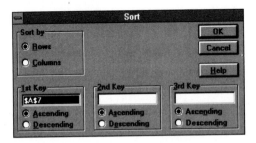

3. Be sure the Rows option in the Sort By group is selected.

4. The 1st Key text box should be selected. Replace the proposed $A$7 by typing *E7*. This cell reference will tell Excel to sort on the basis of the values in the 1991 Commissions field. (You can use the address of any cell in column E.) Ignore the 2nd Key and 3rd Key options.

5. Click the Descending option to sort the database from highest 1991 commission to lowest.

6. Click OK, or press Enter.

To sort your client database alphabetically, using last names as the first key and first names as the second key, specify both fields. Simply enter B7 as the 1st Key and C7 as the 2nd Key, and the database will be sorted by last name and then by first name within last name.

	#	Last Name	First Name	Account Balance	1991 Commissions	1992 Commissions	Total Commissions	Last Meeting
7	8	Devine	Dennis	112,300	2,712	553	3,265	6/13/92
8	5	Smith	Jeffrey	62,550	1,718	299	2,017	8/7/91
9	7	Baker	Abel	55,080	1,386	379	1,765	7/15/92
10	10	Terry	Florence	74,640	1,236	294	1,530	2/20/92
11	6	Johnson	Johnny	57,248	1,101	296	1,397	5/9/92
12	4	Hendricks	Margaret	48,750	1,014	387	1,401	10/1/91
13	1	Walton	Wilbur	43,870	916	159	1,075	1/11/92
14	15	Nevin	John	90,890	868	391	1,259	6/28/92
15	11	Green	Scott	36,460	867	224	1,091	3/27/92
16	12	Merrill	L.Y.	54,153	770	346	1,116	12/8/91
17	2	Miller	Herman	6,960	459	55	514	3/30/92
18	14	Wilson	Harry	29,240	439	249	688	5/10/92
19	13	Smith	Harvey	12,690	190	122	312	5/5/92
20	3	Williams	Oliver	10,940	137	73	210	8/12/91
21	9	Spencer	David	8,145	121	0	121	10/13/91

FIGURE 8-5. *The* CLIENTS *database sorted from highest to lowest based on the 1991 Commissions field.*

Excel can also perform sorts based on fields that contain text, because every character that you can enter in a cell has a specific ranking. In an ascending sort, special characters such as @, #, and & are sorted first. Next come numeric characters that you have entered as text. (Numeric characters entered as numbers are sorted before any text or special characters.) Next come alphabetic characters. Because Excel ignores capitalization when sorting, *A* has the same ranking as *a*. Highest are the logical values FALSE and TRUE and Excel error values. Excel always puts blank cells at the bottom of the sorted range, whether you are sorting in ascending or descending order.

Before you move on, restore the records to the order in which they were entered. Use either of the following methods:

■ Choose Undo Sort from the Edit menu.

■ Sort the database on column *A* (the field with the # sign).

The records will be restored to the order in which you entered them.

To clean up for the next examples,

■ Delete your sequentially numbered column A by clicking on the column header and choosing Delete from the Edit menu.

USING CRITERIA TO SELECT RECORDS

You've learned the basics of using the Microsoft Excel database-management tools, including the Criteria button in the data form. Now it's time to learn more about how criteria can help you create and extract useful subsets of database records. First, you establish *selection criteria* to tell Excel which records you are interested in. Excel then uses these criteria to determine which records are affected when you choose the Find, Extract, or Delete command from the Data menu.

Entering Criteria

The best way to understand selection criteria is to actually walk through an example. Along the way, you'll learn the underlying concepts so that you can apply the same procedures to your own work.

Using as an example the *CLIENTS* database you created earlier, suppose you want Microsoft Excel to list all clients with the last name *Smith*. You need to tell Excel to look for records that match the criterion *Last Name equals Smith*. You start by creating a *criteria range* in a blank area of your worksheet. The criteria range must be at least two rows deep, and the top row must contain the names of all the database fields you intend to use in selecting records.

You don't have to include every database field name in the top row of the criteria range. Doing so, however, allows you to add other criteria later without having to add field names. Copying all the database field names also ensures that the database names and the names in the criteria range are exactly the same. For clarity and consistency, all the examples in this chapter include all the database field names in the criteria range.

The first step in creating the criteria range, then, is to copy the field names into the area you plan to use as the criteria range.

1. Select cells A6:G6.

2. Copy the database field names into row 1, which will be the top row of the criteria range.

3. Adjust the row height so that you can see the complete field names.

Now you see why you started the database in row 6. Leaving some blank rows at the top of the worksheet for a criteria range makes revising criteria more convenient, because you can easily jump to the top-left corner of the worksheet.

Next you need to specify the actual selection criteria. For this example, you'll enter only one, the last name of the person whose record you want to work with.

1. Select cell A2 and type *smith*, the criterion you want in the Last Name field.

2. Press Enter.

Your criteria range now looks like the one in Figure 8-6.

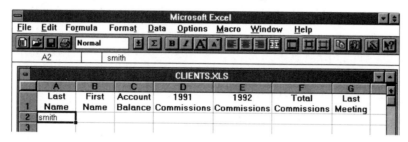

FIGURE 8-6. *The criterion* smith *entered in the Last Name field of the criteria range.*

Setting the Criteria Range

You can enter several different criteria ranges containing different sets of criteria on a single worksheet, but only one criteria range at a time can be active. Just as Microsoft Excel needs to know which is the active database, it needs to know which is the active criteria range. Designating the active criteria range is called *setting the criteria range*.

To set the criteria range for the *CLIENTS* worksheet, follow these steps:

1. Select the range A1:G2.

2. Choose the Set Criteria command from the Data menu.

Although you see no change in the worksheet, Excel has now assigned the name *Criteria* to the range you selected and will recognize only the range A1:G2 as a criteria range unless you do one of the following:

■ Select a new range and choose the Set Criteria command again.

■ Choose the Define Name command from the Formula menu and delete the name *Criteria*.

■ Choose Define Name and assign *Criteria* to a different range.

As mentioned, the criteria range must be a single rectangular range. The range you defined for this example contains only the minimum two rows required. You kept the range small because including blank rows in a criteria range causes Excel to select all records in the database, and such a broad selection defeats the purpose of defining criteria. If you later need to add a new criteria row, you can reset the criteria range to include that row. (You'll see how to use more than one criterion later in this chapter.)

Extracting Records

Now that you have specified a criterion, you're well on the way to seeing what it can do. The process of producing a list of all records that meet a criterion or a set of criteria is called *extracting*. To extract records that match criteria, you use the Extract command on the Data menu. When you choose this command, Microsoft Excel checks the criteria range and identifies all matching records. It then copies those records to an area of the worksheet called the *extract range*, the place you designate for receiving the matching records.

Defining the extract range

The first step in designating the extract range is to copy the field names to an empty area of the worksheet. Once again, you don't have to include every field name. For example, if you aren't interested in displaying the first names in the selected records, you can omit the First Name field from the extract range. As with the criteria range, however, for clarity and consistency the examples here include all the database field names in the extract range.

To define an extract range on your *CLIENTS* worksheet,

1. Copy the field names in row 1 of the worksheet to row 25.

2. Adjust the row height so that you can see the field names.

3. If necessary, select the range A25:G25 again.

4. Choose the Set Extract command from the Data menu.

Extracting the data

Now that you've defined the criteria range and the extract range, you can choose the Extract command from the Data menu to tell Microsoft Excel to extract all matching records. To extract the records for *Smith* in the *CLIENTS* database, follow these steps:

1. Choose the Extract command from the Data menu. The following dialog box appears:

2. Turn on the Unique Records Only option. Excel includes this option because you can sometimes erroneously enter records into the database twice. Selecting Unique Records Only eliminates duplicates from the extract range. Turning the option on is a good habit to form—unless, of course, you want to search a database for duplicate records.

3. Click OK, or press Enter.

Your worksheet looks like the one in Figure 8-7. Excel copied the records of both Jeffrey Smith and Harvey Smith, in the order in which they appear in the database, into the rows below the field names in the extract range.

	A	B	C	D	E	F	G
	Last Name	First Name	Account Balance	1991 Commissions	1992 Commissions	Total Commissions	Last Meeting
25							
26	Smith	Jeffrey	62,550	1,718	299	2,017	8/7/91
27	Smith	Harvey	12,690	190	122	312	5/5/92
28							

FIGURE 8-7. *The records extracted using the criterion* smith.
(Worksheet is scrolled to display the filename and column labels.)

When you choose the Extract command, Excel displays the message shown in Figure 8-8 if the top row of your extract range contains either blank cells or any entries other than field names. If this message appears, click OK or press Enter to close the message box. Then use the Define Name command on the Formula menu to verify that the Database and Criteria names refer to the correct cells, define a valid extract range, and choose the Extract command again.

FIGURE 8-8. *The message telling you an extract range is invalid.*

When the extract range is in a single row (like A25:G25 in the preceding example), Excel displays all matching records in the rows directly below this range. In the process, Excel deletes any preexisting entries in the columns below the defined extract range. In this example, if there were preexisting data in the rows below row 25, the data in columns A through G would be deleted. To avoid this problem, be sure the extract area does not have any rows of data below it.

Alternatively, you can select a limited extract range that contains only a certain number of rows. For example, suppose you selected the range A25:G35 and then chose Set Extract to define those cells as the extract range. You could then use the Extract command knowing that, no matter how many records matched your selection criteria, Excel would fill no more than the 10 rows you specified as the extract range. If the Extract command produced more records than Excel could copy into the extract range, Excel would display a message saying that the extract range was full. You could then either move or expand the extract range and repeat the extraction.

If you want to preserve a group of extracted records intact, copy them to another part of the worksheet. Otherwise, the next time you use the Extract command, Excel will overwrite the previously extracted records.

Using Criteria to Best Advantage

You can search text and numeric fields in ingenious ways, and you can mix and match criteria to produce useful subsets of the overall database. Let's look now at some of the fine points of defining criteria.

Searching for text

In preceding examples, you knew exactly how to spell the last names of the clients you were searching for, but you won't always be so fortunate. Suppose you have several hundred clients and you want to contact one of them about a special opportunity. The trouble is, you can't remember the client's name—it's something like Wilson or Wellman. How can you find the client's record?

With Microsoft Excel, the solution is simple. Excel can extract records using your best guess about selection criteria. Follow these steps to extract the records of all clients whose last names begin with the letter *W:*

1. First, delete *smith* and any other entries you've typed in cells A2:G2 of your criteria range.

2. Now, enter *w* in cell A2.

3. Choose the Extract command from the Data menu.

4. When the Extract dialog box appears, click OK, or press Enter.

The extract range now includes the records of the three clients whose last names begin with *W*, as shown in Figure 8-9.

Last Name	First Name	Account Balance	1991 Commissions	1992 Commissions	Total Commissions	Last Meeting
Walton	Wilbur	43,870	916	159	1,075	1/11/92
Williams	Oliver	10,940	137	73	210	8/12/91
Wilson	Harry	29,240	439	249	688	5/10/92

FIGURE 8-9. *The records of all clients whose last names begin with* W.

You can further refine the selection by using *wildcard characters* in the criteria you specify. An asterisk (*) substitutes for any number of characters in whatever position it occupies in the criterion. For example, if you entered *w*n* instead of *w* as your criterion, Excel would extract only names beginning with *W* and ending with *n*, such as Walton and Wilson. If records with last names of Winn and Williamson were included in the database, Excel would also extract those records.

For even greater precision, you can use a question mark (?), which substitutes for a single character in a criterion. For example, the criterion *w????n* limits the extraction to records with six-letter names beginning with *W* and ending with *n*, such as Walton and Wilson.

Using comparison criteria

You'll often need to find records with values that fall within a certain range in a given field. To limit the extraction in this way, you can enter a criterion that consists of a numeric value preceded by a comparison operator—for example, = (equal to), < (less than), or > (greater than).

Suppose you want a list of all clients whose account balances exceed $40,000. To extract this list, follow these steps:

1. Delete the entry in cell A2.

2. Enter *>40000* in cell C2. The criteria range should now look like the following screen.

	A	B	C	D	E	F	G
	Last Name	First Name	Account Balance	1991 Commissions	1992 Commissions	Total Commissions	Last Meeting
1							
2			>40000				

CLIENTS.XLS

3. Choose the Extract command from the Data menu. When the Extract dialog box appears, click OK, or press Enter.

Your extract range now looks like the one in Figure 8-10.

	A	B	C.	D	E	F	G
25	Last Name	First Name	Account Balance	1991 Commissions	1992 Commissions	Total Commissions	Last Meeting
26	Walton	Wilbur	43,870	916	159	1,075	1/11/92
27	Hendricks	Margaret	48,750	1,014	387	1,401	10/1/91
28	Smith	Jeffrey	62,550	1,718	299	2,017	8/7/91
29	Johnson	Johnny	57,248	1,101	296	1,397	5/9/92
30	Baker	Abel	55,080	1,386	379	1,765	7/15/92
31	Devine	Dennis	112,300	2,712	553	3,265	6/13/92
32	Terry	Florence	74,640	1,236	294	1,530	2/20/92
33	Merrill	L.Y.	54,153	770	346	1,116	12/8/91
34	Nevin	John	90,890	868	391	1,259	6/28/92

CLIENTS.XLS

FIGURE 8-10. *The records of all clients who have account balances greater than $40,000.*

To produce a list of clients who have account balances *greater than or equal to* $40,000, you can use the >= operator. Excel also accepts the <= (less than or equal to) operator and the <> (not equal to) operator.

Combining criteria

Suppose that, despite your best efforts to keep in close touch with your most important clients, you have a feeling you haven't met with a few of them in quite a while. You decide to create a list of all clients about whom *both* of the following statements are true:

■ The client's account balance exceeds $50,000.

■ You haven't met with the client since February 1992.

Such criteria are called *AND criteria,* because both the first *and* the second criterion must be matched for a record to be selected. Microsoft Excel requires you to enter both these criteria *in the same row* in the criteria range.

To extract the records that meet both criteria, follow these steps:

1. Enter *>50000* in cell C2.

2. Enter *<3/1/92* in cell G2 (meaning *before March 1, 1992*).

3. Choose the Extract command from the Data menu. When the Extract dialog box appears, click OK, or press Enter.

Your extract range looks like the one in Figure 8-11. Now all you have to do is pick up the telephone and set up meetings with these neglected clients.

	A	B	C	D	E	F	G	
	Last Name	First Name	Account Balance	1991 Commissions	1992 Commissions	Total Commissions	Last Meeting	
25								
26	Smith	Jeffrey	62,550	1,718	299	2,017	8/7/91	
27	Terry	Florence	74,640	1,236	294	1,530	2/20/92	
28	Merrill	L.Y.	54,153	770	346	1,116	12/8/91	

FIGURE 8-11. *Important clients you need to meet with soon.*

You can also define two AND criteria for the same field. For example, to extract the records of clients with account balances between $50,000 and $60,000, follow these steps:

1. Copy the field name *Account Balance* to cell H1.

2. Select the new criteria range (cells A1:H2).

3. Choose the Set Criteria command from the Data menu to redefine the criteria range.

4. Delete the criterion in cell G2.

5. Enter *<60000* in cell H2.

6. Choose the Extract command from the Data menu. When the Extract dialog box appears, click OK, or press Enter.

As you can see in Figure 8-12, three clients have account balances between $50,000 and $60,000.

	A	B	C	D	E	F	G	
	Last Name	First Name	Account Balance	1991 Commissions	1992 Commissions	Total Commissions	Last Meeting	
25								
26	Johnson	Johnny	57,248	1,101	296	1,397	5/9/92	
27	Baker	Abel	55,080	1,386	379	1,765	7/15/92	
28	Merrill	L.Y.	54,153	770	346	1,116	12/8/91	

FIGURE 8-12. *The records of all clients that meet two AND criteria in the same field.*

Before you continue with this chapter,

■ Delete the entries in cells H1 and H2.

Using alternative criteria

Sometimes you'll want to select records that meet either, not both, of two criteria. Such criteria are called *OR criteria*. They must be entered *in separate
rows* in the criteria range.

For the example shown in Figure 8-10, you extracted records of clients
with account balances exceeding $40,000. Suppose you've decided to send a
mailing to clients who have balances of more than $60,000 as well as to clients
whose accounts generated more than $1,000 in commissions in 1991, regard-
less of their current balances.

To extract the records that meet either (or both) of these criteria, follow
these steps:

1. Select the range A1:G3.

2. Choose the Set Criteria command from the Data menu to redefine
   the criteria range.

3. Enter the criterion *>60000* in cell C2.

4. Enter the criterion *>1000* in cell D3. Your criteria range now looks
   like the one in the following illustration.

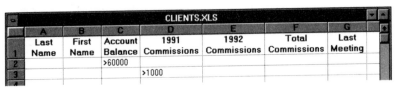

5. Choose the Extract command from the Data menu. When the Extract dialog box appears, click OK, or press Enter.

Figure 8-13 shows the results of this extraction. Because rows 2 and 3 contain
OR criteria, the extract range includes three clients (Margaret Hendricks,
Johnny Johnson, and Abel Baker) who have account balances of less than
$60,000 but 1991 commissions of more than $1,000 and one client (John
Nevin) who has an account balance of more than $60,000 but 1991 commis-
sions of less than $1,000. In addition, the range includes three clients (Jeffrey
Smith, Dennis Devine, and Florence Terry) who have both account balances
of more than $60,000 *and* 1991 commissions of more than $1,000.

	CLIENTS.XLS						
	A	B	C	D	E	F	G
25	Last Name	First Name	Account Balance	1991 Commissions	1992 Commissions	Total Commissions	Last Meeting
26	Hendricks	Margaret	48,750	1,014	387	1,401	10/1/91
27	Smith	Jeffrey	62,550	1,718	299	2,017	8/7/91
28	Johnson	Johnny	57,248	1,101	296	1,397	5/9/92
29	Baker	Abel	55,080	1,386	379	1,765	7/15/92
30	Devine	Dennis	112,300	2,712	553	3,265	6/13/92
31	Terry	Florence	74,640	1,236	294	1,530	2/20/92
32	Nevin	John	90,890	868	391	1,259	6/28/92

FIGURE 8-13. *The records of all clients whose accounts generated more than $1,000 in commissions in 1991, who have account balances greater than $60,000, or who match both criteria.*

You can combine AND and OR criteria. In the sample criteria range shown below, row 2 contains AND criteria and rows 2 and 3 constitute an OR criterion. These criteria instruct Excel to find records with account balances between $60,000 *AND* $70,000 *OR* those with total commissions greater than or equal to $600:

	CLIENTS.XLS							
	A	B	C	D	E	F	G	H
1	Last Name	First Name	Account Balance	1991 Commissions	1992 Commissions	Total Commissions	Last Meeting	Account Balance
2			>60000					<70000
3						>=600		

CAUTION *If you define a criteria range of more than two rows and later want to perform another search with only one row of criteria, you must redefine the criteria range to two rows (the field-name row and the criteria row). Do this even if you delete all the entries in the second criteria row. Remember, a blank row in a criteria range causes Microsoft Excel to select all records in the database.*

FINDING RECORDS QUICKLY

The Extract command on the Data menu helps you create subsets of your database. Sometimes, though, you may simply want a "quick read" of the records that meet specific criteria. That's where using the Find command on the Data menu is handy. The Find command allows you to look at matching records one at a time, without having to copy them to another part of your worksheet.

To see how the Extract and Find commands differ, follow these steps:

1. Keeping the criteria you used in the preceding example, choose the Find command from the Data menu. Excel highlights the record of Margaret Hendricks, the first client in the database who meets the current criteria. The status bar message *Use arrow keys to view records* indicates that the program is in Find mode. Your screen now looks like the one in the following illustration.

	Last Name	First Name	Account Balance	1991 Commissions	1992 Commissions	Total Commissions	Last Meeting
7	Walton	Wilbur	43,870	916	159	1,075	1/11/92
8	Miller	Herman	6,960	459	55	514	3/30/92
9	Williams	Oliver	10,940	137	73	210	8/12/91
10	Hendricks	Margaret	48,750	1,014	387	1,401	10/1/91
11	Smith	Jeffrey	62,550	1,718	299	2,017	8/7/91
12	Johnson	Johnny	57,248	1,101	296	1,397	5/9/92
13	Baker	Abel	55,080	1,386	379	1,765	7/15/92
14	Devine	Dennis	112,300	2,712	553	3,265	6/13/92
15	Spencer	David	8,145	121	0	121	10/13/91
16	Terry	Florence	74,640	1,236	294	1,530	2/20/92
17	Green	Scott	36,460	867	224	1,091	3/27/92
18	Merrill	L.Y.	54,153	770	346	1,116	12/8/91
19	Smith	Harvey	12,690	190	122	312	5/5/92
20	Wilson	Harry	29,240	439	249	688	5/10/92
21	Nevin	John	90,890	868	391	1,259	6/28/92

CLIENTS.XLS

2. Click the up and down arrows in the vertical scroll bar (or press the Up and Down direction keys) repeatedly to move among the matching records. Excel skips over nonmatching records.

3. When you have finished, press Esc or choose the Exit Find command from the Data menu to turn off Find mode.

If you want to print a list of matching records, choose the Extract command from the Data menu, select the extract range, and use the Set Print Area command on the Options menu.

Using Criteria in the Data Form

Early in this chapter, you used the Criteria button in the data form to find the record for a particular person. You can also search quickly through your database by setting comparison criteria within the data form. To use the data-form method, follow these steps:

1. Choose the Form command from the Data menu.

2. Click the Criteria button to turn on Criteria mode and display the criteria form.

3. Type *>60000* in the Account Balance field.

4. Type *>1000* in the 1991 Commissions field. Your criteria form now looks like the following:

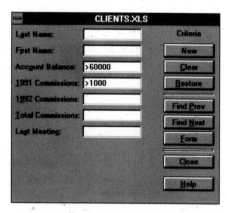

5. Click the Find Next button. The data form now displays the first matching record.

6. Click the Find Next button to move forward through the database from one matching record to the next; Click the Find Prev button to move backward.

7. Click the Close button, or press Esc, to return to the worksheet.

If you change your mind about the criteria you want to use and the criteria form is still on your screen, you can click the Clear button to remove all the criteria from the form. To return to the data form without carrying out the search, click the Form button.

CAUTION *If you've moved partway through your database with previous searches and haven't closed the data form before you set new criteria, Microsoft Excel begins searching the database for matching records from the most recent position in the data form. Therefore, you shouldn't assume that the first matching record displayed is the first matching record in the database.*

The data-form criteria are completely independent of those in the criteria range of the worksheet. After you remove the data form, all Find and Extract operations revert to using the worksheet criteria range.

You can use wildcards in criteria in a data form. However, because the data form contains only one input field for each field name, you can't specify OR criteria, nor can you specify two criteria for a single field as you did when you extracted the records shown in the example in Figure 8-12.

DELETING MULTIPLE RECORDS

On occasion, you'll probably want to delete old or unneeded records from your database. You can use criteria to find the records and then use the Delete command from the Data menu to remove from the database all records matching the criteria you specify in the criteria range.

When you choose the Delete command, Microsoft Excel displays the warning message shown in Figure 8-14. Always take this warning seriously, because using the Delete command can be risky. In particular, remember that including a blank row in the criteria range means that *all* records in the database are matching records and will therefore be destroyed if you click OK or press Enter to tell Excel to go ahead with the Delete command.

FIGURE 8-14. *Excel's deletion warning message.*

To avoid losing data, be sure to double-check the criteria range before you choose Delete. To quickly determine which range is currently assigned the name *Criteria*, follow these steps:

1. Choose Goto from the Formula menu (or press F5).

2. Double-click Criteria in the Goto list box.

Excel highlights the criteria range. When you're certain nothing in the criteria range will cause Excel to destroy important records, choose the Delete command from the Data menu. After deleting the matching records, Excel reduces the range defined with the name *Database* accordingly.

As an added precaution, you might want to use the Extract command to extract the records that match your criteria. You can then review the records before choosing Delete. If the extract range contains records you don't want to delete, modify the criteria and repeat the extract process until you are sure the Delete command won't destroy records you want to retain.

ADVANCED DATABASE TOOLS

Microsoft Excel offers powerful statistical functions that help you analyze data. For example, you can compute totals, averages, and variances, either for matching records or for the entire database. You can also create a table that displays results based on the use of different values for a specified argument in a formula. Use the Search command on the Help menu to find the topic *database functions*, or consult the Microsoft Excel documentation to learn more about either of these topics.

CONCLUSION

Having finished this chapter, you've completed your basic training in Microsoft Excel worksheets, charts, and databases. You're ready to round out your skills. The next section of the book covers some more complex aspects of Excel: linked worksheets, customization, analysis tools, and macros.

Section III

Worksheet Analysis and Management

You're now ready to move beyond the basics. The chapters in this section tell you how to deal with situations that require worksheet linking and analysis techniques. You'll also be introduced to the basics of recording and replaying macros—sets of often-used Excel commands.

Chapter 9

Working with Multiple Worksheets

You can open several Microsoft Excel worksheets at one time, displaying each worksheet in a separate window. You can also link worksheets so that one worksheet can feed the results of its computations into another. In this chapter, you will first learn how to link worksheets and then you'll learn about two Excel features, group editing and workbooks, that help you work more efficiently with sets of worksheets.

MOVING DATA BETWEEN WORKSHEETS

Before you can link worksheets, you must know how to copy data from one worksheet to another. Copying data saves time when you need to create a worksheet that is similar in structure to a worksheet you created earlier, and copying also reduces the chance of error. Copying also is your means of creating a common bond between worksheets that you want to link.

To experiment with copying data,

1. Open a blank worksheet, and enter the sales data shown in Figure 9-1 (on the next page) for Balloon World, Inc. Enter the titles in cells B1 and B2.

2. Center and boldface the titles to match the illustration.

3. Save the worksheet with the name *NORTH*.

To copy the Balloon World, Inc. data from the first worksheet, follow these steps:

1. Select the range A1:B7. Click the Copy tool or press Ctrl-C (the shortcut for the Copy command).

```
 ━                         Microsoft Excel                    ▼ ▲
  File  Edit  Formula  Format  Data  Options  Macro  Window  Help
 ┌──┬──┬──┬──┐ ┌──────┐ ┌───────────────────────────────────────┐
 │  │  │  │  │ │Normal│ ±  Σ  D  I  A  ⋯
 └──┴──┴──┴──┘ └──────┘
        A11
 ──────────────────────────────────────────────────────────────
 ━                          NORTH.XLS                        ▼ ▲
        A       B      C     D     E     F     G     H     I
  1        Balloon World, Inc.
  2        Sales Summary─
  3
  4   Blue      180
  5   Red       200
  6   Yellow    100
  7   Green     120
  8
```

FIGURE 9-1. *The Balloon World, Inc. data.*

2. Open a new worksheet. It will have the name *Sheet2* in its title bar, and cell A1, the top-left corner of the destination range, will be selected.

3. Notice the message in the status bar: *Select destination and press ENTER or choose PASTE.* The destination is selected, so simply press Enter.

A copy of the *NORTH* data immediately appears in Sheet2. As you see, copying data from one worksheet to another can be very straightforward.

 In this example the worksheet you copied to was clearly visible. When you work with your own data, if the document you want to display is obscured by other documents, open the Window menu, which lists all the open documents in the menu. Then select the document you want to move to. You can also press Ctrl-F6 to cycle through the open documents.

LINKING WORKSHEETS

In a minute, you'll copy the worksheet again, thereby creating three worksheets you'll use to summarize sales for three Balloon World, Inc. regions: North, Central, and South. From these three *source documents*, or supporting worksheets, you'll create a fourth worksheet, called a *dependent worksheet*, that consolidates sales from the three regions into company totals. The links you create will allow Microsoft Excel to update the information in the dependent worksheet if the information in any of the source worksheets changes.

Why Use Linked Worksheets?

Rapid updating of separate worksheets is obviously a great benefit, but using linked worksheets can make your work simpler, faster, and more accurate in other ways too. Here are some of the benefits of using linked worksheets:

- Easier summarizing of data. When you need to summarize information from several locations or departments, maintaining the consolidated totals in a separate worksheet can be helpful.

- Easier reporting. Often, breaking a large worksheet into separate worksheets is the most convenient way to generate a variety of reports from a large mass of data. When you want a particular report, simply print the appropriate worksheet. (Incidentally, you can also design different reports in a single worksheet. You'll learn to do this in Chapter 10, "Rearranging Microsoft Excel.")

- Less clutter on the screen. Instead of scrolling through a massive worksheet looking for the information you need, you can view only the data that interests you by opening the worksheet in which that data is stored.

- Conservation of computer memory. You do not need to open the source worksheets in order to work with a dependent worksheet. Breaking up a large worksheet into small worksheets allows you to work easily with the information when you might otherwise encounter memory limitations.

Summarizing Data from Multiple Worksheets

Now we'll explore the concept of linked worksheets by working through an example. Before you continue, follow these steps to create the regional and consolidated worksheets:

1. Save the Sheet2 worksheet with the name *SOUTH*.

2. Click on a visible portion of the *NORTH* worksheet, or choose the worksheet from the list at the bottom of the Window menu.

3. Copy cells A1:B7 in the *NORTH* worksheet.

4. Open two new worksheets.

5. Use the Paste command or press Ctrl-V to copy the range A1:B7 to one of the two new worksheets.

6. Switch to the second new worksheet. Cell A1 should be selected. Press Enter to copy the cells a second time.

7. Save one new worksheet with the name *CENTRAL* and the other with the name *TOTALS*.

You now have four worksheets, three that will show regional sales data and one that will contain total sales for the company.

You used this exercise to practice copying between work-sheets, but there's an even quicker way to create dependent worksheets. You can use the Save As command on the File menu three times to save one worksheet with three different names. Then you can open the newly created worksheets by clicking their names at the bottom of the File menu.

Arranging windows on the screen

The four open worksheets are somewhat awkward to work with as they appear on the screen right now. To remedy this,

1. Choose the Arrange command from the Window menu. This brings up the following dialog box:

2. Click OK to select the default option, Tiled, which divides the screen as evenly as possible among the open documents, without overlapping them.

Your screen now looks something like the one shown in Figure 9-2. (Your worksheets might appear in different positions.)

Creating linking formulas

Now that you have created the necessary worksheets, you can summarize the regional sales information in the *TOTALS* worksheet. You summarize the data by creating a *linking formula*. Follow these steps:

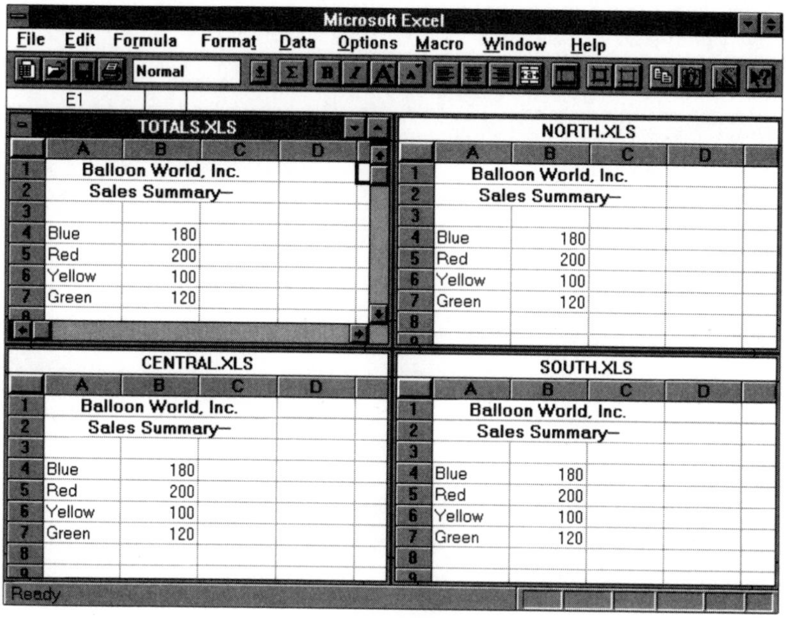

FIGURE 9-2. *The Balloon World, Inc. worksheets after you choose the Arrange command.*

1. Click on the *TOTALS* worksheet if it is not the active worksheet.

2. Select cell B4, and type =.

3. Select cell B4 in the *NORTH* worksheet (in the same manner as in steps 1 and 2 above), and type +.

4. Select cell B4 in the *SOUTH* worksheet, and type +.

5. Select cell B4 in the *CENTRAL* worksheet, and press Enter.

Your worksheet now looks like the one in Figure 9-3 on the next page. Notice the linking formula in the formula bar.

The linking formula contains *external cell references* that link the *TOTALS* worksheet (the dependent worksheet) to the three source worksheets. An external cell reference consists of two components: the name of the source worksheet followed by an exclamation point (!) and a reference to a cell or range within that worksheet.

You could have entered this formula by typing it in the formula bar, but when the source worksheet is open, it's usually easier to simply click the cell that you want to reference. When you create an external cell reference by

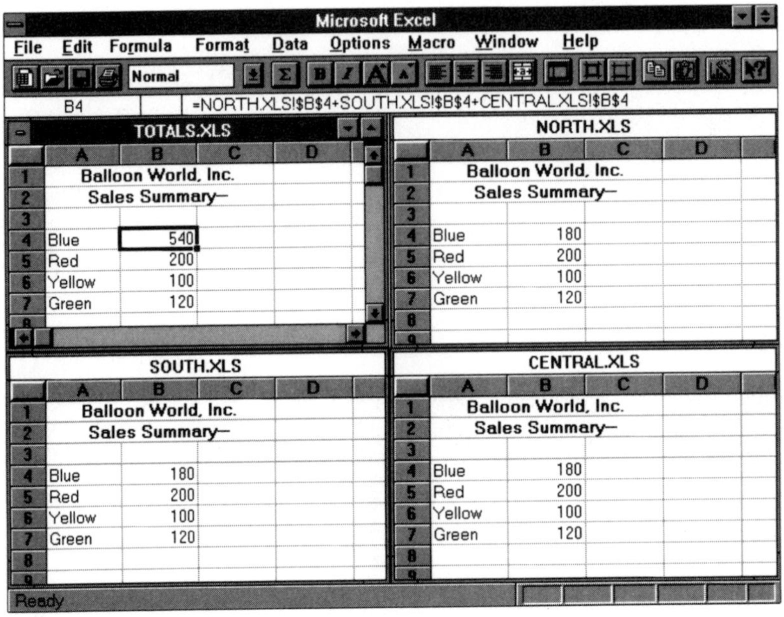

FIGURE 9-3. *The* TOTALS *worksheet with a linking formula in the formula bar.*

clicking a cell in a source worksheet, Microsoft Excel uses the cell's fixed address in the formula. (Recall that a fixed address always refers to a specific cell, whereas a relative address refers to a cell that is a certain number of columns and rows from the cell containing the reference.)

If you anticipate copying a formula containing an external cell reference to other parts of your worksheet, you can also use relative addressing. To see how this works, follow these steps:

1. With cell B4 in the *TOTALS* worksheet selected, drag the mouse pointer over the entire entry in the formula bar.

2. Press F4 three times to change the cell references from fixed to relative. Press Enter.

3. Drag the fill handle down to cell B7 to copy the formula in B4.

The *TOTALS* worksheet now displays the overall company sales totals.

Updating the Dependent Worksheet

When you open a worksheet containing one or more linking formulas, Microsoft Excel checks to see if the source worksheets are open. If they are, Excel simply updates the dependent worksheet with the current values from the source worksheets. Otherwise, Excel displays the message shown in Figure 9-4. To tell Excel to read all source worksheets and supply the current values for all external cell references, click Yes, or press Enter, when you see the message. To retain the values the cells had when you last saved the dependent worksheet, click No.

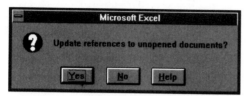

FIGURE 9-4. *The message displayed when a dependent worksheet's supporting worksheets are not open.*

At this point, the Balloon World, Inc. worksheets are not complete. First, to properly identify the regions, you must revise the text entries in cell B2 of each worksheet.

1. Widen column A in each worksheet to 12 characters so that the revised titles will fit nicely on screen.

2. Add the text in the second column of the following table to the end of the existing entries in the worksheet indicated in the first column:

Worksheet	Text to Add to Cell B2
TOTALS	Company Totals
NORTH	North Region
SOUTH	South Region
CENTRAL	Central Region

Later in this chapter, you'll learn how to edit worksheets as a group.

Saving Linked Worksheets

You save linked worksheets the same way you save any other file, by clicking the Save File tool on the Standard toolbar or by choosing Save or Save As from the File menu. However, you should make a point of saving the source worksheets before saving the dependent worksheet. Here's why:

- If you save a source worksheet under a new name while the dependent worksheet is open, Microsoft Excel updates the name of the source worksheet in the external cell reference in the linking formulas, and all is well for the future.

- If you save and close the dependent worksheet and then save a source worksheet under a new name, Excel cannot update the external cell reference. The next time you open the dependent worksheet, Excel won't be able to update the information because it won't "know" the new name of the source worksheet.

To put this policy to work now,

1. Save the source worksheets (*NORTH*, *SOUTH*, and *CENTRAL*).

2. Now save the dependent *TOTALS* worksheet.

It's best to save linked worksheets in the same directory. Otherwise, you must use the Save As command on the File menu to save all source worksheets to ensure that external references in the dependent worksheet are saved correctly. For more information, refer to the topic linking *in Excel's online help, or see your Excel documentation.*

Opening Linked Worksheets

Later in this chapter, you'll see a technique for opening a group of linked worksheets with one command. For now, however, suppose you have opened only the dependent worksheet and then find that you need to revise one or more of the source worksheets. Instead of opening the source worksheets one by one, you can use the Links command on the File menu.

To see how this works, follow these steps:

1. Close all open worksheets. Click OK or press Enter if Excel asks whether you want to save changes to the *TOTALS* worksheet.

2. Now open the *TOTALS.XLS* worksheet. Click OK or press Enter in response to the dialog box that appears.

3. Choose the Links command from the File menu. The following dialog box appears:

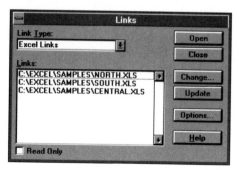

4. Be sure *Excel Links* is shown in the Link Type drop-down list box.

5. Select *NORTH.XLS*, *SOUTH.XLS*, and *CENTRAL.XLS* by holding down the Ctrl key and clicking their filenames.

6. Click the Open button.

7. Use the Arrange command on the Window menu, if necessary, to arrange the document windows on screen. Your screen once again looks something like the following:

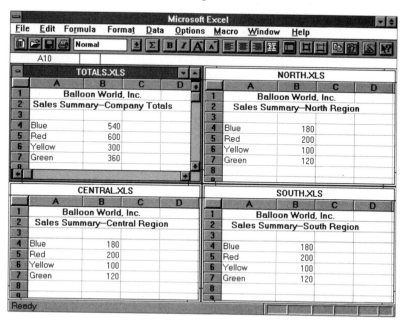

EDITING WORKSHEETS AS A GROUP

If you have a collection of related worksheets, you can save time and enhance accuracy by editing them as a *group*. A group is a temporary association of worksheets collected for editing purposes. When you work with a group, only one worksheet is active, but any changes you make to that worksheet also appear in the same location in every other worksheet in the group. Group editing is therefore a "one change fits all" approach that saves time and increases accuracy.

You define a group by selecting the worksheets you want to include. Once defined, the grouping remains in effect until you change the active worksheet by switching to a different document. You can include any open document except a chart in a group-editing session, including documents you "bind" permanently into a *workbook*, as described later in this chapter.

Starting a Group-Editing Session

To edit the Balloon World, Inc. worksheets as a group, follow these steps:

1. Choose Group Edit from the Options menu. This brings up the following dialog box:

2. All the open files are automatically selected. To edit them as a group, click OK or press Enter.

Your screen now looks like the one in Figure 9-5. Notice that *[Group]* appears in each title bar.

Editing a Group

You can now save time and labor by editing the active worksheet and having your changes carried through to all the other worksheets in the group. To see how this works, follow these steps:

1. Scroll down and enter the following formula in cell B9 of the active worksheet:

   =SUM(B4:B7)

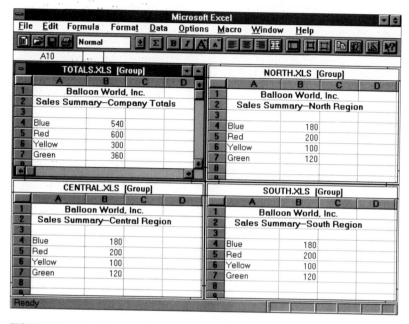

FIGURE 9-5. *The Balloon World, Inc. worksheets after you carry out the Group Edit command.*

2. After creating the formula, hold down Ctrl and click cell B7.

3. Click the Bottom Border tool on the Standard toolbar or, if you prefer, choose the Border command from the Format menu, select the Bottom option, and click OK. Either way, an underline appears in cells B7 and B9.

The active worksheet now looks like the one in Figure 9-6 on the next page. Because you created a group, all the changes—cell entries as well as formatting—have affected every worksheet in the group.

Ending a Group-Editing Session

To end group editing, you activate any worksheet other than the one that was active when you created the group. To ungroup the Balloon World, Inc. worksheets,

■ Point to any inactive worksheet and click to activate it.

Notice that, as soon as you change the active worksheet, the word *Group* no longer appears in any of the title bars.

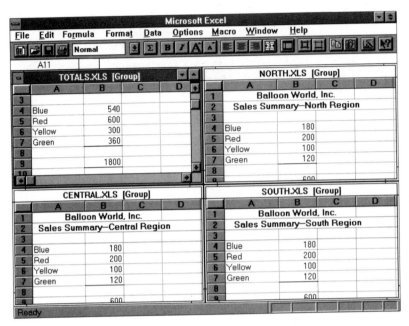

FIGURE 9-6. *The Balloon World, Inc. worksheets after you enter a formula and format cells B7 and B9 in the active worksheet.*

If you want, scroll down in each worksheet to see that Excel applied your formula and formatting to each member of the group. Scroll back to the top of each document when you finish.

Arranging a Group on the Screen

If you have a number of open worksheets, some of which are grouped, the ungrouped documents can get in your way at times. To eliminate the clutter on your screen, you can use the Arrange command on the Window menu to display grouped documents only. Follow these steps:

1. Choose the Group Edit command from the Options menu.

2. Select *NORTH* and *CENTRAL* (using the Ctrl-click method), and then click OK or press Enter.

3. Choose the Arrange command from the Window menu.

4. In the Arrange Windows dialog box, turn on the Documents Of Active Group check box, and then click OK or press Enter.

Microsoft Excel splits the screen vertically between the two worksheets in the group, as shown in Figure 9-7.

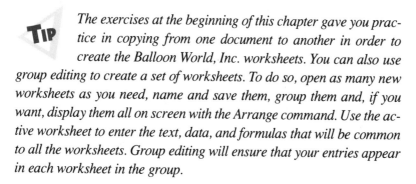

FIGURE 9-7. *The results of the Arrange command when only the documents in the active group are included.*

Before going on,

1. Ungroup the documents by clicking in the window of the inactive document.

2. Close the *CENTRAL.XLS* window. Click Yes or press Enter if Excel asks whether you want to save changes.

> **TIP** *The exercises at the beginning of this chapter gave you practice in copying from one document to another in order to create the Balloon World, Inc. worksheets. You can also use group editing to create a set of worksheets. To do so, open as many new worksheets as you need, name and save them, group them and, if you want, display them all on screen with the Arrange command. Use the active worksheet to enter the text, data, and formulas that will be common to all the worksheets. Group editing will ensure that your entries appear in each worksheet in the group.*

USING WORKBOOKS

When you have created a group of linked worksheets, opening the worksheets one by one can be tedious. To save time, Microsoft Excel allows you to include a set of related files in a *workbook* so that you can manage them as if they were parts of a single unit.

Creating a Workbook

Unlike a group, which is a temporary association of worksheets, a workbook is a file-management tool. A worksheet in a workbook can be either *bound* or *unbound*. A bound worksheet becomes part of the workbook file and can exist in only one workbook. An unbound worksheet remains an independent file; it can be part of several workbooks and can also be worked on without opening a workbook. When you create a workbook, the worksheets are bound in the workbook by default. Follow the steps below to bind your Balloon World, Inc. worksheets in a workbook.

1. From the File menu, choose the New command. The following dialog box appears:

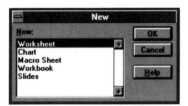

2. Select Workbook.

3. Click OK or press Enter.

Excel displays a blank Workbook Contents window with the title *Book1*.

Adding Documents to a Workbook

Now you'll add the Balloon World worksheets to the workbook. Follow the steps below:

1. Click the Add button at the lower-left corner of the Workbook Contents window. Doing this brings up a dialog box titled Add To Workbook, which lists the names of all the open files.

2. Hold down the Ctrl key and click on the filenames to select all three files (*NORTH.XLS*, *SOUTH.XLS*, and *TOTALS.XLS*) shown in the list box.

3. Click OK or press Enter to both add the worksheets and close the dialog box.

Your Workbook Contents window should now look like the following:

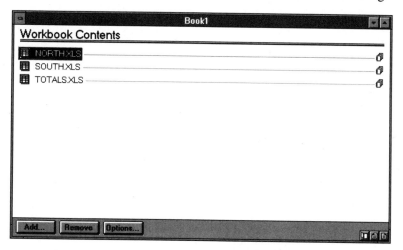

When you add a document to a workbook, a copy *of the worksheet file is placed in the workbook and the original worksheet is closed. As long as a document is bound in the workbook, changes made to the worksheet are made to this copy and are not passed to the original file.*

To add a document that is not currently open to the workbook, follow these steps:

1. Click the Add button in the Workbook Contents window. The Add To Workbook dialog box appears again.

2. Click the Open button in the dialog box. Microsoft Excel displays another dialog box containing a list of all documents in the current directory. (If the file you wanted was in a different location, you could, at this point, use the File Name and Directories boxes as you normally would to find a file.)

3. Double-click *CENTRAL.XLS*. Excel adds the *CENTRAL* worksheet to the workbook. Click OK or press Enter to close the dialog box.

To add a brand-new document to a workbook, follow these steps:

1. Click the Add button in the Workbook Contents window.

2. In the Add To Workbook dialog box, click the New button. The New dialog box appears.

3. Click Worksheet if it is not already highlighted.

4. Click OK or press Enter to close the New dialog box. Excel adds a blank, new worksheet to the workbook.

5. Click OK or press Enter to close the Add To Workbook dialog box.

To change the name of a new worksheet, select it and click the Options button in the Workbook Contents window. Enter a name in the Document Options dialog box, and click OK or press Enter. A worksheet bound in a Workbook can have a name up to 31 characters long.

Managing Worksheets in the Workbook Window

Having created a workbook, you need to know how to use it effectively.

Paging through sheets in a workbook

When your workbook contains only a few documents, as yours currently does, the fastest way to move from viewing one document window to viewing another is to use the paging buttons at the bottom right of the Workbook Contents window and the document window of each sheet in the workbook:

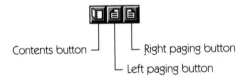

Contents button ⌐ ⌐ Right paging button
⌐ Left paging button

Clicking the Right paging button lets you view and work on the next document in the sequence shown in the Workbook Contents window. Clicking the Left paging button moves you to the previous document.

If your workbook has many documents and you want to move from one document to another, it's usually best to click the Contents button to display the Workbook Contents window. From there, you can simply click the name of the document you want to view.

If you want to reorganize the sheets in a workbook, you can change the sequence of documents in the Workbook Contents window by dragging document icons up or down.

To start a group-editing session, point to any of the paging buttons and click the right mouse button. Choose Group Edit from the shortcut menu that appears.

"Unbinding" worksheets in a workbook

When you add a document to a workbook, it is "bound" into the workbook and can be used only within that workbook. To use the document in other workbooks or without opening a workbook, you must first unbind it. To unbind a document, click the icon to the right of the document name in the Workbook Contents window, as shown below.

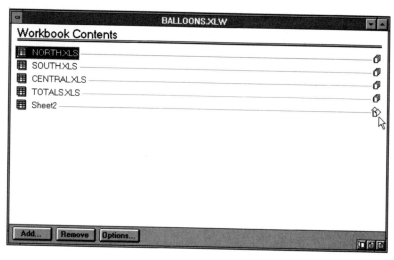

Once a workbook file is unbound, you can save it as a separate file. To incorporate any changes made to the copy of a document you added to a workbook, modified, and then unbound, save the document using the original filename. To save the changes in the workbook copy without overwriting the original file, save the file under a different name. If the document name was changed in the workbook to include more than eight letters, you must save the file with a new name that contains eight or fewer characters.

Removing a worksheet from a workbook

To remove a document from a workbook, simply drag the document out of the Workbook Contents window and release the mouse button. Try it now.

■ Drag the new, blank worksheet from the workbook.

The worksheet no longer appears in the Workbook Contents window. If you open the Window menu, you will see that the worksheet is still open but is not part of the workbook. If you wanted to remove several documents, you would follow the steps below.

1. Open the Workbook Contents window.

2. Hold down Ctrl while clicking the names of the documents you want to remove.

3. Click the Remove button.

The document or documents become unbound and remain open. They can be saved as separate files, added to other workbooks, or discarded.

Saving Workbooks

Now it's time to save your sample workbook. Follow the steps below:

1. Activate the Workbook Contents window and ascertain that all four Balloon World, Inc. worksheets are still included in the workbook.

2. Choose the Save Workbook command from the File menu. If you are saving a workbook for the first time, this command brings up the Save As dialog box.

3. Type *balloons*, and then click OK or press Enter.

Excel saves the workbook file on your disk as *BALLOONS.XLW*. Now you can open the workbook and all associated documents whenever you want by opening *BALLOONS.XLW*.

Opening Microsoft Excel Version 3.0 Workspace Documents

If you're using version 4.0 of Excel and you open a workspace file that was created with an earlier version of the program, Excel converts the file to a workbook. You can then save the documents in the workbook. (You cannot, however, save them as a workspace.)

MOVING DATA BETWEEN MICROSOFT EXCEL AND OTHER PROGRAMS

As you become more proficient with Microsoft Excel, you'll probably start to see ways that you could use the information in your Excel files in documents you create with other programs. Or you might want to import information into Excel from documents created with other programs. You might, for example, want to transfer a table of Excel data into a report you are writing with your word processor, or you might want to include in an Excel worksheet data obtained from a colleague who uses a different spreadsheet program.

Microsoft Excel provides three methods of sharing your information with other programs:

- You can save Excel files in formats that can be directly imported into other programs. To do this, use the Save As command on the File menu and select the appropriate format from the Save File As Type drop-down list box. (These formats were discussed briefly at the end of Chapter 1, "Getting Acquainted.") Conversely, many other programs allow you to save files in formats that can be imported into Excel.

- If you want to move data to or from a program that runs under Microsoft Windows, you can copy the data to the Clipboard from within one program, and then activate the second program and paste the data from the Clipboard.

- If you want to exchange data with a program that supports Object Linking and Embedding (OLE) or Dynamic Data Exchange (DDE), you can create links between documents so that if the data in the source document changes, the data in the dependent document is updated accordingly.

For more information, see your Excel documentation.

CONCLUSION

Worksheet linking offers a number of advantages if used wisely. As you have seen, you can break down large worksheets into smaller, more manageable elements. You've also seen how, by using workbooks and group editing, you can work more efficiently with sets of worksheets. In the next chapter, you'll learn to handle large Excel projects and use screen space efficiently.

Chapter 10

Rearranging Microsoft Excel

Microsoft Excel is highly malleable. To maximize your productivity, you can customize the screen display to make Excel work the way you want it to. Even better, you can customize Excel itself so that it manages and presents your data in ways that let you do more with the information. Features such as views and scenarios help you analyze your worksheet data better. Get ready to use some of Excel's most powerful features.

CUSTOMIZING THE MICROSOFT EXCEL SCREEN

Excel's many onscreen tools streamline your work, but there might be times when you want to maximize screen space available for data. Or maybe you just want a change of scenery. If this is the case, there's no reason to feel shy about doing the screen your way.

Changing the Worksheet Display Options

For practice in this chapter, you'll use the *SALESREG* worksheet you created in Chapter 5, so begin by doing the following:

1. Open the *SALESREG* worksheet.

2. Maximize the document window.

3. Now choose the Display command from the Options menu. This brings up the Display Options dialog box shown on the next page.

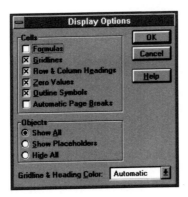

The items in the Display Options dialog box control what you see on screen in the active Excel document. By default, the Gridlines and the Row & Column Headings options are turned on. To see how the screen changes when you turn them off, follow these steps:

1. Click Gridlines.

2. Click Row & Column Headings.

3. Click OK or press Enter.

This removes the gridlines and the row and column headings from the *SALESREG* worksheet. Notice, however, that a selected cell or range is still surrounded by a rectangular outline. If you set display options, remember, too, that the settings affect only the active worksheet.

Changing the Workspace

In the Workspace Options dialog box you can change numerous other, global, settings. Follow these steps:

1. Choose the Workspace command from the Options menu. This brings up the dialog box at the top of the next page.

    The six options in the Display group change the appearance of the screen. The other options change the way Microsoft Excel operates. You'll change one option of each type.

2. Scroll Bars should be turned on. Click to turn this option off.

3. Move Selection After Enter should be off. Click to turn it on.

4. Click OK, or press Enter.

244

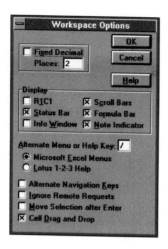

Your screen now looks like the one in Figure 10-1. The scroll bars are gone, as you can see. What you can't see is the change you made to the way Excel moves the cursor. Press Enter repeatedly. Each time you do so, Excel selects the cell immediately below the previous active cell. This feature is useful when you have to enter long columns of figures.

Microsoft Excel - SALESREG.XLS								
File Edit Formula Format Data Options Macro Window Help								

C5 | 14583

Sales by Region and Product

	Jan-92	Feb-92	Mar-92	Apr-92	May-92	Jun-92	Jul-92	Aug-92
Northeast								
Hoisin sauce	$14,583	$15,511	$16,077	$16,028	$16,613	$17,260	$18,131	$18,286
Black beans	9,082	8,923	8,747	9,319	9,598	9,726	9,856	9,987
Sesame oil	13,861	13,621	13,675	13,730	13,493	13,547	13,601	13,655
Bean curd	18,753	18,859	18,547	18,959	18,641	18,692	18,152	18,235
Dried squid	2,673	2,718	2,837	2,805	2,799	2,765	2,795	2,881

FIGURE 10-1. *Part of the screen after gridlines, row and column headings, and scroll bars are removed.*

Another useful data-entry feature is the Fixed Decimal option, which allows you to enter data in "adding machine" mode. Follow these steps:

1. Choose the Workspace command from the Options menu again.

2. Click Fixed Decimal to turn it on.

3. Click OK or press Enter. Notice that *FIX* appears as a reminder at the right side of the status bar.

4. Use the PgDn key to select a cell in a blank area of the worksheet.

5. Enter a series of whole numbers.

As you can see, Excel automatically interpreted the entries as decimal values and inserted a decimal point for you.

All the changes you made in the preceding examples will remain in place until you change them again. Most of the screen features you removed are quite useful, however, so restore them before continuing.

1. Bring up the Display Options dialog box and turn on the Gridlines and Row & Column Headings options.

2. Bring up the Workspace Options dialog box. Turn off Fixed Decimal, turn on Scroll Bars, and (if you want) turn off Move Selection After Enter.

Summary of Display and Workspace Options

The following table summarizes the effects of various options in the Display Options and Workspace Options dialog boxes.

Options Dialog Box	Option	Effect When Turned On
Display	Formulas	Displays formulas rather than returned values
Display	Gridlines	Displays gridlines
Display	Row & Column Headings	Displays row and column headings
Display	Zero Values	Displays a zero when a formula returns a zero value
Display	Outline Symbols	Displays special symbols that help you interpret and manipulate subsections of a worksheet built around an outline
Display	Automatic Page Breaks	Displays page breaks set by Excel
Workspace	Fixed Decimal	Inserts decimal point during data entry
Workspace	R1C1	Displays cell addresses in R1C1 notation

(continued)

Options Dialog Box	Option	Effect When Turned On
Workspace	Status Bar	Displays status bar
Workspace	Info Window	Displays a separate window containing information about the selected cell
Workspace	Scroll Bars	Displays scroll bars
Workspace	Formula Bar	Displays the formula bar
Workspace	Note Indicator	Displays a small square in any cell with an attached note

Managing Toolbars

You're not limited to the standard toolbar designs provided with Microsoft Excel. In a moment you'll learn how to rearrange existing toolbars and create new ones. First, though, here's a closer look at displaying toolbars.

Displaying toolbars

You've seen in earlier chapters that you can display an additional toolbar in either of the following two ways:

- By using the Toolbars command on the Options menu, selecting the toolbar you want in the Toolbars dialog box, and clicking the Show button.

- By moving the mouse pointer over any part of an open toolbar, clicking the right mouse button, and choosing a new toolbar from the shortcut menu that appears.

When you use the shortcut menu, Excel displays a check mark next to each open toolbar.

With a system on which you've installed Excel for the first time, the first toolbar you open floats on the screen like the one in Figure 10-2 on the next page. From that point on, however, Excel keeps track of toolbars and their most recent positions on the screen, so as you open and close toolbars, move them around, and start and stop Excel, the toolbar display you see begins to reflect your own use of Excel.

Often, you'll want to use a specialized toolbar, such as the Formatting toolbar, for part of a task, and then you'll want to put the toolbar away to unclutter the screen.

You can hide a toolbar in any of the following ways:

- By opening the toolbar shortcut menu and clicking next to the toolbar name.

- By choosing the Toolbars command from the Options menu, selecting the toolbar from the list, and clicking the Hide button.

- By clicking the Control-menu box in the upper-left corner of a floating toolbar. (Note that this box appears only when the toolbar is floating as in Figure 10-2.)

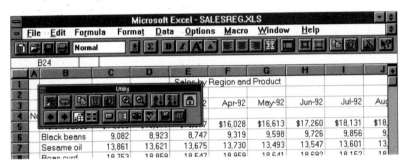

FIGURE 10-2. *The Utility toolbar.*

Reshaping toolbars

You can change the shape of toolbars as needed. To see how this works, do the following:

1. Display the Utility toolbar. If the toolbar is *not* floating (that is, if it is "docked" at the top or side of the screen), drag it onto the worksheet.

2. Move the mouse pointer over the bottom border of the Utility toolbar until the pointer changes to the shape of a double-headed arrow.

3. Press the mouse button and drag the border downward. As you do so, a rectangular shadow border appears.

4. Continue dragging the mouse. The farther you drag, the taller and narrower the rectangle becomes. Release the mouse button when the rectangle won't become any narrower. The tools are arranged vertically in a single column.

Moving toolbars

You learned in an earlier chapter how to drag a floating toolbar up to the toolbar dock under the menu bar. Actually, Excel has four toolbar docks, one at each vertical and horizontal edge. To try one out,

■ Drag the Utility toolbar to the right dock.

The result is shown in Figure 10-3.

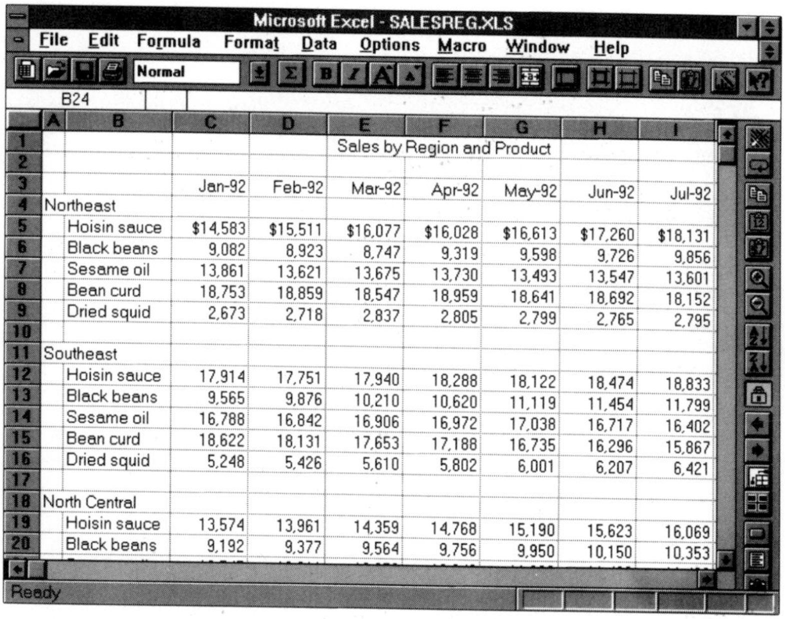

FIGURE 10-3. *The Utility toolbar in the right toolbar dock.*

You can move most toolbars to any of the four toolbar docks. The exceptions are the toolbars that contain list boxes; they cannot be moved to the right or left docks.

You can move a toolbar off a toolbar dock either by dragging it with the mouse or by pointing to a blank area of the toolbar and double-clicking. Conversely, you can double-click on any blank area on a floating toolbar to move it to the last toolbar dock it had previously occupied.

Hide the Utility toolbar now in the following way:

1. Point to a blank area and double-click to move the toolbar into the middle of the worksheet.

2. Click on the Control-menu box, labeled with a hyphen, in the upper-left corner of the toolbar window.

Modifying toolbars

If one of your favorite tools is on the Formatting or the Utility toolbar, you might want to move it to the Standard toolbar so that it's always available. Fortunately, as the next example shows, you can move tools around easily.

Adding tools Follow these steps to add a tool to the Formatting toolbar:

1. Display the Formatting toolbar as a floating toolbar.

2. Point to the toolbar and open the shortcut menu or choose Toolbars from the Option menu.

3. Choose Customize. Doing this brings up the following dialog box:

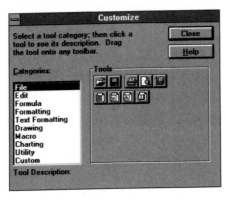

4. Choose Text Formatting from the list.

5. Drag the Text Color tool (shown below) to a blank area on the Formatting toolbar. (Move the Customize dialog box aside if you have to by dragging its title bar.)

6. Click Close or press Enter to close the Customize dialog box.

The Formatting toolbar now looks like the one in Figure 10-4. Leave the customized toolbar on screen for a few minutes.

FIGURE 10-4. *The Formatting toolbar with the Text Color tool added.*

Creating and naming a new toolbar You can also create a toolbar of your own design. In the following example, you'll create a toolbar that contains tools for outlining worksheets. (You'll use this new toolbar later in the chapter when outlining is explained.) Follow these steps:

1. Choose the Toolbars command.

2. When the Toolbars dialog box appears, double-click in the Toolbar Name text box and type *Outlining*.

3. Click the Customize button. When you do, the Customize dialog box opens and a small, blank floating toolbar appears on screen.

4. Click Utility in the Categories list box. The Tools section of the dialog box changes to display the available utility tools.

5. Click on several of the tools. Note that as you do so, a description of the selected tool appears in the lower-left corner of the dialog box.

6. Drag the Promote tool (the one with the left-pointing arrow) out of the Customize dialog box and onto the new toolbar. When you release the mouse button, Excel adds that tool to the toolbar, as pictured below.

7. Drag each of the three remaining outlining tools (shown in Figure 10-5) to the new toolbar, releasing the mouse button when the tool overlaps the right edge of the toolbar, as shown below.

8. Click Close or press Enter when all four tools are on the new toolbar.

When finished, your toolbar should look like the one in Figure 10-5.

FIGURE 10-5. *A custom toolbar containing buttons for worksheet outlining.*

Bring up the toolbar shortcut menu. Outlining is listed along with Excel's built-in toolbars. When you quit Excel, your toolbar configuration, including new toolbars, is saved. When you start Excel again, the toolbars will be just as you left them, and Outlining will be displayed both in the shortcut menu and in the Categories list of the Toolbars dialog box.

If you're not interested in assigning a name to a new toolbar, you can create one even more quickly than you just did. Open the Customize dialog box and click on the category containing the tools you want. To create the toolbar, simply drag a tool out of the Customize dialog box. When you release the mouse button, Excel creates a new toolbar and assigns it a generic name, such as Toolbar 1. *To add other tools, drag them until they overlap part of the new toolbar. When you finish creating the toolbar, close the Customize dialog box.*

Deleting tools and toolbars To remove a tool from a toolbar, do the following:

1. Display the toolbar and choose the Toolbars command or the Customize command. (Either will do the job.)

2. When the Toolbars or Customize dialog box appears, simply drag the unwanted tool off the toolbar.

You can also delete entire toolbars, but only those you have created. You cannot delete toolbars that are built into Excel. To delete a custom toolbar, follow these steps:

1. Choose the Toolbars command.

2. Select the toolbar to delete in the Show Toolbars list box.

3. Click the Delete button. Click OK or press Enter when Excel asks you to confirm the deletion.

4. Click the Close button to close the Toolbars dialog box.

Resetting a toolbar After customizing a built-in toolbar with additional tools, you can restore it to its original "shipped" configuration. Restore your customized Formatting toolbar by following these steps:

1. Choose the Toolbars command.

2. Click Formatting in the Show Toolbars list box if it is not already selected.

3. Click the Reset button in the Toolbars dialog box.

4. Click the Close button to close the dialog box.

You've finished investigating toolbars, so prepare for the next examples in the following way:

1. Close the Formatting toolbar.

2. Close your new Outlining toolbar.

Splitting Document Windows into Panes

When you create a large worksheet you might spend a great deal of time moving from one part of the worksheet to another. You can minimize this travel time by creating *panes*. The *SALESREG* worksheet should be displayed. Follow the steps below to divide the document window into smaller panes:

1. Press Ctrl-Home to move the top-left corner of the worksheet, and then select cell F10.

2. Choose the Split command from the Window menu. Your screen now looks like Figure 10-6.

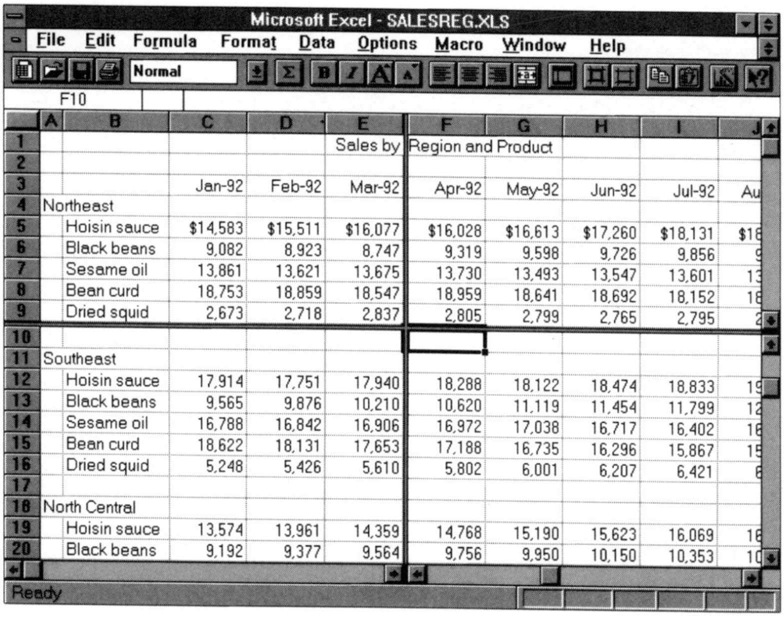

FIGURE 10-6. *The SALESREG worksheet split into panes.*

The panes are "frozen," and you can now scroll each of the quadrants of the *SALESREG* worksheet independently—to a degree, that is. To illustrate scrolling within panes,

1. Click repeatedly to the right of the scroll box in the scroll bar below the bottom-right quadrant to scroll the screen to the right. Notice that the upper-right quadrant scrolls in unison with its lower companion on the right side of the vertical split line.

2. Now click on the vertical scroll bar in the bottom-right quadrant. The bottom-left quadrant scrolls with it.

As you can see, the scroll bars operate on quadrant pairs, rather than on individual quadrants.

You can also split a window with another Split command, this one on the Control menu in the upper-left corner of the document window. When you use the Split command on the Control menu, Excel displays split indicators—gray lines you can drag into position. When the split indicators are where you want the split to occur, click the mouse button or press Enter to lock the split bars into place.

Removing panes

Remove the panes by performing one of the following actions:

- Double-click the intersection of the two split bars, or drag the intersection to the upper-left or upper-right corner of the screen. (To remove a single split bar, double-click or drag it to the edge of the screen.)

- Double-click the *split boxes*, or drag them toward the appropriate borders. Split boxes are small black bars on the scroll bars. They are always located next to a scroll arrow, as pictured below:

Split box

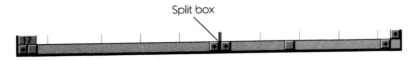

To split a window quickly with the mouse, drag the appropriate split box. Release the mouse button when the split indicator is where you want the split to appear.

254

Freezing titles

One of the better uses for panes is freezing titles in place so that they remain in view as you move around in a worksheet. Follow these steps:

1. Select cell C4.

2. Choose the Freeze Panes command from the Window menu.

Excel splits the window above and to the left of the selected cell, marking the split with dark horizontal and vertical lines. These new panes in your worksheet will serve much the same purpose as print titles for printed documents. No matter where you scroll in the lower-right quadrant, the periods (at the top) and descriptions (to the left) always appear on the screen.

Before moving on, unfreeze the titles and remove the split as follows:

■ Choose Unfreeze Panes from the Window menu.

If you use this feature frequently, you can speed your work with the Freeze Panes tool on the Utility toolbar. Click the tool once to freeze panes, click again to unfreeze them.

Zooming a Worksheet

To get a bird's-eye view of a worksheet, you can "zoom" out by choosing the Zoom command from the Window menu or the Zoom Out tool on the Utility toolbar. To see how this works, do the following:

1. Choose Zoom from the Window menu.

2. In the Zoom dialog box (shown below), select 50% to shrink the *SALESREG* worksheet to 50 percent of its normal size. (If this results in cells filled with # signs, try again with 75%.)

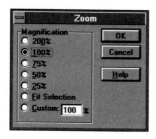

Your screen now looks like the one in Figure 10-7 on the next page.

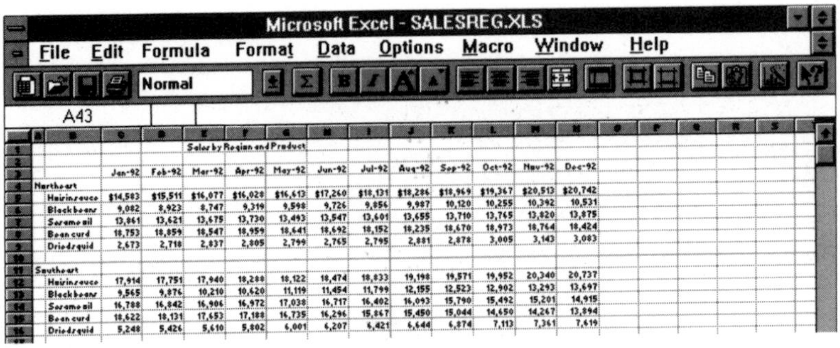

FIGURE 10-7. *The SALESREG worksheet after "zooming" to 50% view.*

To restore the worksheet to normal size,

■ Choose Zoom again and select the 100% option in the dialog box.

USING VIEWS

A worksheet like *SALESREG* can be used in many ways, each requiring a slightly different slant on the information. For these purposes, you can create different *views* into the same Microsoft Excel worksheet. By designing the views to address the diverse uses for the information, you can enhance the value of that information.

The following examples require use of the View command. If the View command does not appear when you bring down the Window menu, run the Excel Setup program to install the View Manager add-in utility. For more details, see Appendix A, "Installing Microsoft Excel."

Creating a Worksheet View

Suppose you'd like to distribute the *SALESREG* worksheet to the regional sales managers, but you want the managers to see only the figures that apply to their individual territories. Follow these steps to create a new view:

1. Use the Zoom command on the Window menu to reduce the *SALESREG* worksheet to 75 percent magnification. (This will make it easier to work with.)

2. Choose the View command from the Window menu. This brings up the Views dialog box.

3. Click the Add button. This brings up the Add View dialog box shown below:

4. Type *Whole Company* in the Name box.

5. Click OK or press Enter.

Excel adds the Whole Company view to the worksheet. The view name will appear in the Views dialog box the next time you choose the View command. Now you'll create a second view. Follow these steps:

1. Select rows 1 and 2 and 10 through 51.

2. Choose the Row Height command from the Format menu and click Hide to hide the selected rows.

3. Choose the View command from the Window menu and click the Add button.

4. When the Add View dialog box appears, type *Northeast* in the Name box and click OK, or press Enter.

5. Choose the View command again. The dialog box should look like the one below:

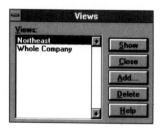

Currently, your worksheet displays only the Northeast region sales figures. To switch to a different view and see the figures for all regions,

■ Double-click the Whole Company view in the list.

As you can see, views can help you zero in on a particular portion of a large worksheet. Because Excel saves views along with the worksheet when you save to a different disk, views are also handy when you want other people to be able to see selected portions of a worksheet. Views do not, however, offer much protection for confidential information.

In the *SALESREG* worksheet, for example, another person could easily choose to unhide the rows in the Northeast view or, for that matter, simply choose the Whole Company view with the View command. One way to address this would be to distribute printed reports instead of the worksheet file itself.

Using Views to Print Reports

If you accept the default settings in the Add View dialog box (as you have), views include the full range of print settings, so you can customize and print a variety of different reports from the same Excel document.

To see how this works, follow these steps:

1. Choose the View command from the Window menu.

2. Choose the Northeast view by double-clicking it or by clicking the Show button.

3. Choose the Page Setup command from the File menu.

4. Click the Cell Gridlines box to turn gridlines off.

5. Click the Header button, delete the text in the Left and Right sections, and edit the Center section as shown in the following dialog box (The displayed header is in bold 12-point type.)

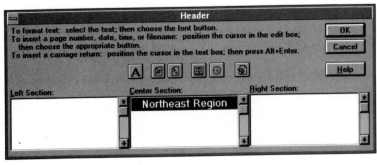

6. Click OK twice: once to close the Header dialog box, and a second time to apply the changes you made to the Northeast view.

7. Now add a view called Report with the Window View command. Preview or print the worksheet. The report will reflect the changes you made in the Page Setup dialog box, and should look like the one in Figure 10-8.

Northeast Region

Northeast	Jan-92	Feb-92	Mar-92	Apr-92	May-92	Jun-92	Jul-92	Aug-92
Hoisin sauce	$14,583	$15,511	$16,077	$16,028	$16,613	$17,260	$18,131	$18,286
Black beans	9,082	8,923	8,747	9,319	9,598	9,726	9,856	9,987
Sesame oil	13,861	13,621	13,675	13,730	13,493	13,547	13,601	13,655
Bean curd	18,753	18,859	18,547	18,959	18,641	18,692	18,152	18,235
Dried squid	2,673	2,718	2,837	2,805	2,799	2,765	2,795	2,881

FIGURE 10-8. *The printed Northeast report.*

8. Change to the Whole Company view and preview or print that worksheet view.

The printed document, unlike the Report view, will have gridlines and a header that includes the date and page number.

You could extend the example by creating and naming a similar view for each of the regions, editing the header and print settings for each. For your Company Totals view, you could revise the header to read *Import Food Distributors*, and leave in the gridlines and a page-number footer for ease of reference. By creating views tailored to specific audiences or purposes, you can do your part in reducing the information glut in your organization.

OUTLINING YOUR WORKSHEETS

By outlining a worksheet, you can better manage data that is combined into several levels of subtotals and totals. Though the concept of outlining a worksheet takes some getting used to, you'll find that it is a powerful tool for summarizing and analyzing data.

Entering the Data

Suppose you work in the marketing department of a company called Junk Food Distributors. Your company sells in three states: Ohio, Michigan, and Illinois. It's your responsibility to summarize monthly sales data by state.

To try outlining, follow the steps below.

1. Open a new worksheet, maximize it, and enter the following text descriptions in the cells indicated.

Cell	Entry
A2	Salted snacks
A3	Candy
A4	Soft drinks
A5	Pastry

2. Use the fill handle to enter *100* (the number of units sold) in each of the cells in the range B2:B5.

3. Use the Autosum button on the toolbar, to enter the formula

    `=SUM(B2:B5)`

    in cell B6.

4. Copy the range A2:B6 to the ranges A8:B12 and A14:B18.

5. Type the names of the regional offices (Ohio, Michigan, and Illinois) in cells A6, A12, and A18, respectively.

6. Enter the text labels for the months January through June in cells B1 through G1.

7. Select cell B20, and enter the formula

    `=SUM(B6,B12,B18)`

8. Use the fill handle to copy the range B2:B20 into columns C through G.

9. Display the outlining toolbar you created earlier in this chapter. If it is floating, move it into the top dock.

You might also want to widen column A and zoom the window to 90 percent so that you can see the data in the worksheet. The contents of your worksheet should look like the screen in Figure 10-9.

	A	B	C	D	E	F	G	H	I	J
1		January	February	March	April	May	June			
2	Salted snacks	100	100	100	100	100	100			
3	Candy	100	100	100	100	100	100			
4	Soft drinks	100	100	100	100	100	100			
5	Pastry	100	100	100	100	100	100			
6	Ohio	400	400	400	400	400	400			
7										
8	Salted snacks	100	100	100	100	100	100			
9	Candy	100	100	100	100	100	100			
10	Soft drinks	100	100	100	100	100	100			
11	Pastry	100	100	100	100	100	100			
12	Michigan	400	400	400	400	400	400			
13										
14	Salted snacks	100	100	100	100	100	100			
15	Candy	100	100	100	100	100	100			
16	Soft drinks	100	100	100	100	100	100			
17	Pastry	100	100	100	100	100	100			
18	Illinois	400	400	400	400	400	400			
19										
20		1200	1200	1200	1200	1200	1200			
21										

FIGURE 10-9. *The worksheet for the outlining example.*

Creating the Outline

Now that you've entered the basic sales data in your worksheet, you're ready to create the outline. Follow these steps:

1. Select the range A1:G20.

2. Choose the Outline command from the Formula menu. The following dialog box appears:

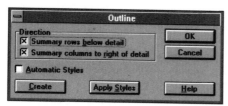

3. Click the Automatic Styles box. This choice ''autoformats'' summary rows in the outline.

4. Click Create.

Your worksheet now looks like the one in Figure 10-10. Notice the outline symbols displayed to the left of the worksheet.

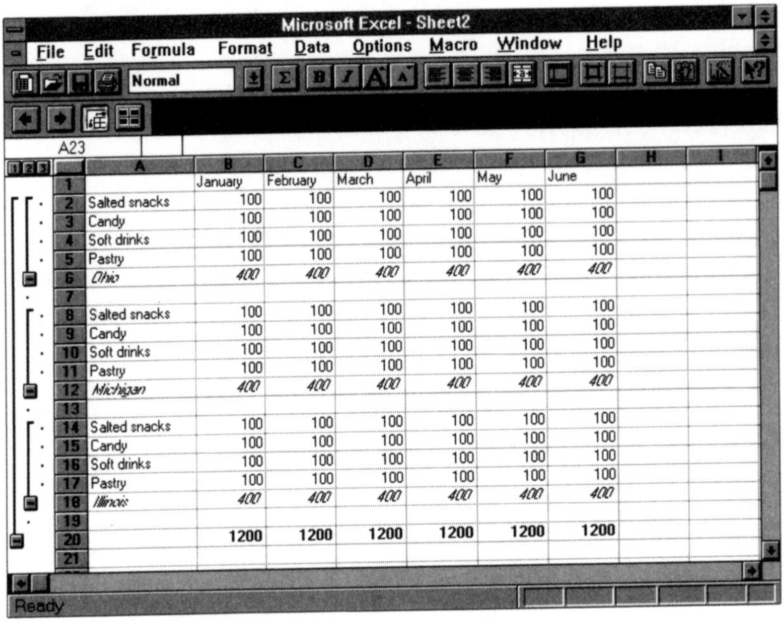

FIGURE 10-10. *The sample worksheet after you create an outline.*

Microsoft Excel has used references in the cells to assign each row to an appropriate level—1, 2, or 3, in the outline. Because row 20 contains references to cells in rows 6, 12, and 18, it is assigned a higher level that encompasses the latter three rows. Hence, row 20 is a level 1 row, while rows 6, 12, and 18 are level 2 rows. The lowest-level rows (level 3) are those that contain numeric constants.

The outline symbols (the small boxes containing minus signs to the left of the worksheet) mark the level 1 and level 2 rows. The lines connected to these boxes indicate visually which rows contain the detail figures included in the total and subtotal amounts.

Working with Outlines

Now it's time to demonstrate how Excel's outlining feature can help you reorganize and summarize data.

Outlining columns

Include quarterly totals in the worksheet by following the steps below.

1. Insert a new column in front of column E.

2. Select the ranges E2:E20 and I2:I20.

3. Double-click the Autosum button.

4. Clear the cells in columns E and I containing zero values.

5. Enter *Quarter1 and Quarter2* in cells E1 and I1, respectively.

6. Choose the Outline command from the Formula menu and click Create. Click OK or press Enter when Excel displays a message asking whether you want to modify the existing outline.

Excel now displays additional outline symbols above the worksheet. These symbols show that Excel is using the quarterly summaries in columns E and I to outline the worksheet horizontally as well as vertically.

Collapsing outline levels

Suppose your manager wants to see a summary of sales by quarter and region, without the product-line detail. You can provide such a report very quickly by collapsing the outline to row level 2 and column level 1.

1. Click the row level 2 button, as shown below:

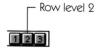

2. Now click the column level 1 button, as shown below:

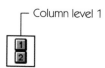

Your worksheet now looks like the one in Figure 10-11 on the next page.

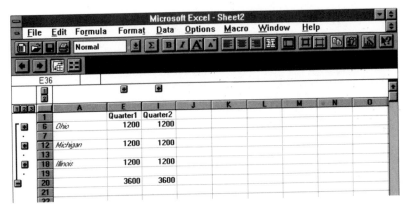

FIGURE 10-11. *The worksheet after the outline has been collapsed to column level 1 and row level 2.*

To expand the outline back to three levels,

■ Click the lowest-level buttons (3 for rows and 2 for columns) in the top-left corner of the document window.

You can collapse part of an outline by clicking one of the minus buttons above or to the left of your outline. For example, if you click the minus button next to one of the level 2 rows, all the level 3 rows bracketed by the line connected to that particular minus button collapse. The minus button also then changes to a plus button. Clicking the plus button expands the outline once again.

Promoting and demoting items in the outline

As you organize your worksheet, you might want to promote or demote rows within the outline hierarchy. To do this in the sample worksheet, you will make use of the Outlining toolbar you created at the beginning of this chapter. To refresh your memory, Figure 10-12 shows and names the four tools on the Outlining toolbar.

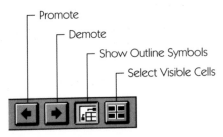

FIGURE 10-12. *The outline tools on your custom toolbar.*

264

To promote row 4, follow these steps:

1. Select any cell in row 4.

2. Click the Promote tool. Doing this brings up the following dialog box:

3. Click OK or press Enter to accept the default response.

The Ohio portion of your worksheet now looks like the one in Figure 10-13. Notice the outline symbols to the left of the worksheet, which indicate that row 4 is now a level 2 row.

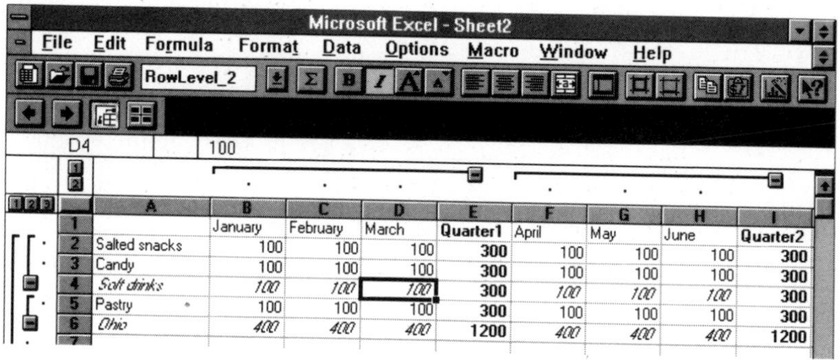

FIGURE 10-13. *The outlined worksheet after row 4 is promoted to level 2.*

To return the Ohio soft-drink sales row to level 3,

- Click the Demote tool, and click OK or press Enter when the Demote dialog box appears.

Using outlining to build large worksheets

Outlining comes in handy when you need to copy ranges that are so large that they extend past the limits of the screen. By creating and collapsing an outline, you can easily copy and move large portions of a worksheet.

To see how copying in outline mode works with your sales figures, follow the steps listed on the next page.

1. Collapse the outline to row level 2.

2. Select the range A1:B20.

3. Copy the selected range to cell B23. (If you use the mouse to drag and drop the range, drag down slowly to avoid overshooting when you reach row 23.)

All the text, data, and formulas in rows 1 through 20, including those which are currently hidden, have been copied into rows 23 through 42.

Collapsing an outline, as you can see, is a handy way of compressing a large range into a relatively small area on the screen. Before you continue, undo the copy.

 To hide the Outline symbols, simply select any cell on the worksheet, and then click the Show Outline Symbols tool. Click the tool a second time to redisplay the outline symbols.

Selecting visible cells

Often you will want to copy the summary figures only. Follow these steps:

1. Be sure the outline symbols are displayed.

2. Select the range A1:E20.

3. Click the column level 1 button above the worksheet.

4. Click the Select Visible Cells tool.

5. Use the Copy command or the Copy tool to copy the selected range to cell A23.

6. Expand the outline to show all levels.

7. Now page down so that you can see rows 23 through 42 in the worksheet.

Because you clicked the Select Visible Cells button before copying the data, Excel copied only the cells visible when the outline was collapsed.

As you have seen, outlining is a useful worksheet organization tool. It can also help in reporting. Suppose, for example, that you work with monthly figures, but your boss wants to look at quarterly figures only. Create an outline, collapse it to the quarterly level, and you can quickly summarize the figures without changing the structure of the worksheet.

To prepare for the next set of examples,

1. Remove the outline symbols.

2. Hide the Outlining toolbar.

3. Save the Junk Food Distributors worksheet, or keep it open on screen. You'll be using the worksheet briefly again later.

USING MULTIPLE SCENARIOS IN YOUR WORKSHEETS

Microsoft Excel version 4 takes the spreadsheet concept beyond its traditional role as a computational engine. In this section, you will see how to create a typical decision-support worksheet, and then infuse it with the ability to analyze alternative scenarios.

The Mortgage Loan Problem

Suppose you are about to apply for a new mortgage loan and want to project your monthly payments under different interest-rate assumptions.

1. Open a new, blank worksheet and enter the following data:

Cell	Entry
A1	Rate
A2	Term
A3	Loan amount
A6	Payment
B3	80000
B6	=−PMT(B1/12,B2*12,B3)

Don't let the error value in cell B6 bother you; you'll make it go away in a moment.

2. Widen column A.

3. Select the range A1:B6.

4. Choose the Create Names command from the Formula menu and click OK or press Enter to accept the defaults in the dialog box.

5. Enter some values for the interest rate and loan term in cells B1 and B2. Type *9.75%* as the rate and *25* as the term.

Cell B6 computes the required monthly payment to pay off a loan, given the loan terms you enter in cells B1:B3.

This modest computation represents what original spreadsheet programs were designed to do: compute results whenever you vary the assumptions by entering new values. You are about to see how Microsoft Excel version 4 handles this type of planning situation.

Creating Scenarios

Version 4 of Microsoft Excel includes a program called the Scenario Manager, which enables you to set up, and save, sets of data that represent differing alternatives you might want to consider in a particular situation. The Scenario Manager (along with the View Manager) is one of a set of add-in programs that you choose to install when you run the Excel Setup program. If you do not see the Scenario Manager command on your Formula menu, you'll have to run Setup again.

Follow the steps below to create four different scenarios.

1. Choose the Scenario Manager command from the Formula menu. Doing this brings up the following dialog box:

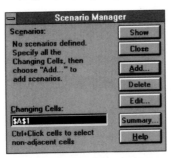

2. Select the range B1:B2 and click the Add button. Now the Add Scenario dialog box appears.

3. In the Name text box, type *8.50% 30 year*.

4. In the Rate box, type *8.5%*.

5. In the Term box, type *30*.

6. Click the Add button. The Add Scenario dialog box reappears.

7. To create the other three scenarios, use the same procedure with the information in the following table.

Name of Scenario	Rate	Term
8.25% 30 year	8.25%	30
8.00% 15 year	8%	15
7.75% 15 year	7.75%	15

When you finish, press Esc or click the Cancel button to remove the Add Scenario dialog box and return to the Scenario Manager dialog box, which lists all the scenarios you added.

Using Scenarios

Now that you've defined the scenarios, you can switch from one to another any time you want with the help of the Scenario Manager dialog box. To use the scenarios, follow these steps:

1. Double-click 8.00% 15 year. The required monthly payment, shown in cell B6, changes to $764.52.

2. Now double-click 8.50% 30 year. The required monthly payment changes to $615.13.

Editing a Scenario

If you create a scenario and then decide your assumptions aren't quite right, you can delete, edit, or edit and rename the scenario.

To delete a scenario, you would do the following:

1. Choose the Scenario Manager command.

2. Select the scenario in the Scenario Manager dialog box.

3. Click the Delete button, and then click the Close button to close the Scenario Manager dialog box.

To change the input values for a scenario, you would do the following:

1. Select the scenario in the Scenario Manager dialog box.

2. Click the Edit button.

3. In the Edit Scenario dialog box that appears, you can edit the input values to change the assumptions, edit the name to change the scenario name, or edit both the input values and the name, effectively creating a new scenario.

4. Click OK to close the Edit Scenario dialog box.

Creating a Summary Report

One of the advantages of creating scenarios is in being able to compare the results of your assumptions. To view the four scenario results side by side, follow these steps:

1. If the Scenario Manager dialog box is not already on the screen, choose the Scenario Manager command from the Formula menu.

2. Click the Summary button. Doing this brings up the following dialog box:

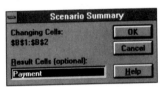

The highlight is in the Result Cells box.

3. Select cell B6, the cell that displays the result calculated for each set of input values if it is not already selected.

4. Click OK or press Enter.

In a few moments, the Scenario Manager builds a summary report that includes your four scenarios. The result on your screen looks like the report in Figure 10-14. Notice that the Scenario Manager has supplied the names of the changing cells and the result cells as labels. If you had not created names for those cells, the cell addresses would be displayed instead.

A summary report is displayed in a new worksheet window and is separate from the worksheet you use for building the scenarios. As a result, you can print, save, or print and save a summary report with the usual Print and Save As commands on the File menu.

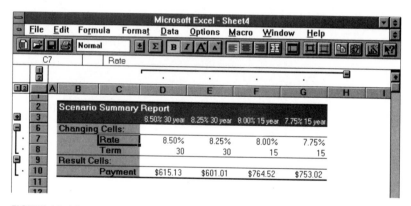

FIGURE 10-14. *A summary report created by the Scenario Manager.*

In a moment, you're going to create an even better report, so discard this summary report.

■ Choose the Close command from the File menu and click No when Excel asks if you want to save the changes.

 You can specify multiple result cells in the Scenario Summary dialog box by separating the cell references with commas. To enter multiple nonadjacent cell references in either this dialog box or the Changing Cells box in the Scenario Manager dialog box, use commas or hold down Ctrl as you click on the appropriate cells.

Changing the "Changing Cells" for a Scenario

Your mortgage payment model is not as useful as it could be. In its present form, it doesn't really represent the true trade-off involved in choosing between a 15-year and 30-year mortgage. The benefit of a 15-year mortgage is that you can obtain a lower interest rate; the drawback, of course, is that your monthly payments will be higher.

Assume that, in your area, a typical 15-year mortgage loan carries an interest rate that is one-half percent lower than that of an equivalent 30-year mortgage. The question you are trying to answer is whether the benefit of the shorter-term loan is worth the discomfort of higher payments over the next 15 years. You want to incorporate that trade-off into your scenarios.

To do this you will have to design the worksheet differently.

1. Open a new worksheet and enter the following formulas:

Cell	Entry	Cell	Entry
A1	Rate differential for 15-year loan	B1	.5%
A2	Rate for 30-year loan	B2	8.5%
A3	Loan amount	B3	80000
A6	Payment on 30-year loan	B6	=−PMT(B2/12,360,B3)
A7	Payment on 15-year loan	B7	=−PMT((B2-B1)/12,180,B3)

2. Widen column A. Select the range A1:B7 and create names for the amounts in column B as you did before.

3. Create three scenarios with B2 as the changing cell. Use 8%, 8.25%, and 8.5% as input values.

When you are finished, your Scenario Manager dialog box should look like the one in Figure 10-15.

FIGURE 10-15. *The Scenario Manager dialog box after new scenarios are created.*

4. Click Summary and select the range B6:B7 as the result cells.

5. Click OK, and the Scenario Manager creates the summary report shown in Figure 10-16.

Now you have a schedule that, within the specified range of interest rates, tells you the required payments for both the 15-year and the 30-year options.

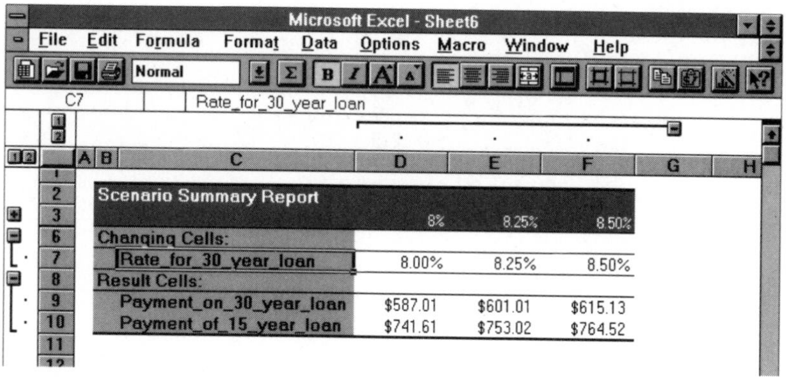

FIGURE 10-16. *The revised scenario summary report.*

Using Models

The Scenario Manager transforms the humble worksheet into something more proactive: a dynamic *model* that resembles a moving picture rather than a snapshot.

This chapter has only scratched the surface of the concept of spreadsheet modeling. By incorporating other advanced Excel features, such as data tables, the Goal Seek command on the Formula menu, the Solver and the What If add-in macro, you can mold Excel to your decision-making process, rather than try to define your business problems in terms of a rigid row-and-column structure.

USING THE CROSSTAB REPORTWIZARD

Excel's Crosstab add-in macro sifts through databases in a flash to create useful summary reports. Suppose you're doing some demographic research using a large database of households and you'd like to see how many families of four or more live in each ZIP code area. If your data is in Excel or in one of the file formats Excel can read, you need only define the database and run the Crosstab ReportWizard to get your totals.

Look again at the Junk Food Distributors example you were working with earlier. In that example, you received sales data that was already summarized by month, product line, and region. Obviously, though, someone had to do some work to group all the individual sales transactions into those categories. In the next example, you'll learn how to create such a summary from a database of sales transactions.

Creating a Crosstabbed Sales Report

To enter the example data, follow these steps:

1. Open a new worksheet and enter the data shown in Figure 10-17.
2. Select the range A1:C16.
3. Choose the Set Database command from the Data menu.

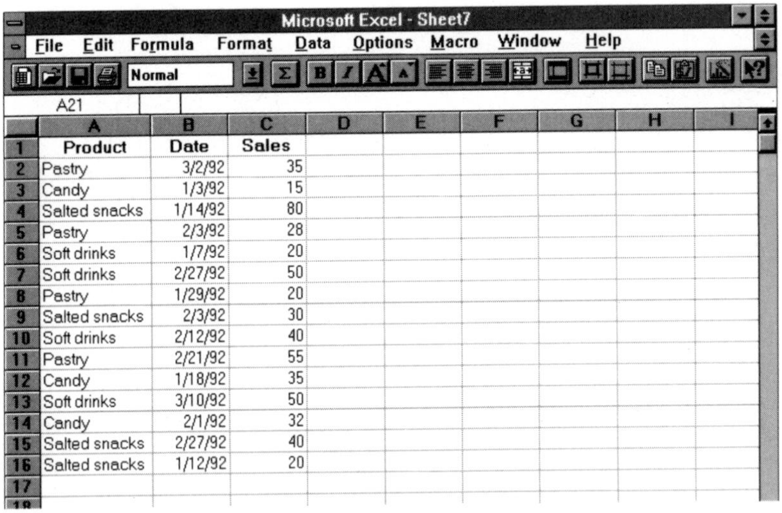

	A	B	C
1	Product	Date	Sales
2	Pastry	3/2/92	35
3	Candy	1/3/92	15
4	Salted snacks	1/14/92	80
5	Pastry	2/3/92	28
6	Soft drinks	1/7/92	20
7	Soft drinks	2/27/92	50
8	Pastry	1/29/92	20
9	Salted snacks	2/3/92	30
10	Soft drinks	2/12/92	40
11	Pastry	2/21/92	55
12	Candy	1/18/92	35
13	Soft drinks	3/10/92	50
14	Candy	2/1/92	32
15	Salted snacks	2/27/92	40
16	Salted snacks	1/12/92	20

FIGURE 10-17. *Data for the Junk Food Distributors sales report.*

Each row of the worksheet now contains the following information:

- The type of product that was sold
- The date the goods were sold
- The amount of the sale

All of the listed transactions occurred in the first three months of the year. Your goal is to summarize this information in the format used in the worksheet you created earlier: a table of sales amounts, with a row for each product line, and a column for each month in the first quarter. To do this, follow the steps on the next page.

1. Select Crosstab from the Data menu. Doing this brings up the large dialog box shown in Figure 10-18. The dialog box explains what you are about to do.

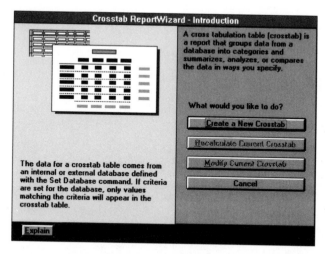

FIGURE 10-18. *The Introduction dialog box of the Crosstab ReportWizard.*

2. Each screen in the Crosstab ReportWizard contains an Explain button, which displays more information. Click the Explain button now. When you finish reading, click the Explain button again to return to the Crosstab ReportWizard.

3. Click Create A New Crosstab. Doing this brings up the Row Categories dialog box, where you will begin to design the table format.

4. The upper-right corner of the dialog box asks the question, "Which database fields contain the values you want as Row headings?" Below that, the Crosstab ReportWizard displays the names of the fields in your database. Select Product to indicate that you want each of the product lines to occupy a row in the summary.

5. Click the Add button. Product is now listed under Row Categories at the left of the dialog box.

6. Click the Next button to go on to the next screen, labeled Column Categories.

7. Double-click Date to add the field as a column category. (You want each of the three months to occupy one column in the table.)

8. You're not done with the column category. You still have to tell Excel which time interval you want it to use, so click the Options button. Doing this brings up the following dialog box:

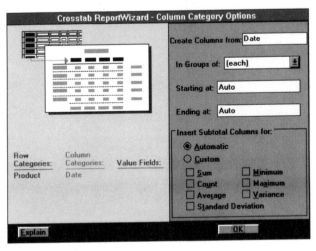

9. Open the In Groups Of list and click the Months option to group the data by month.

10. Click OK. Click the Next button when the Column Categories screen reappears. Now you see the following dialog box:

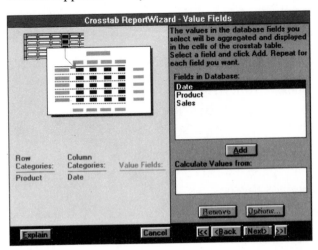

11. In this screen you select the field containing the values to be shown in the table. Double-click Sales, and then click the Next button.

12. In the Final screen you can choose to create the report or to set some additional options. For this example, click the Create It button to create the report.

Excel calculates the results and puts them in a new worksheet, as shown in Figure 10-19.

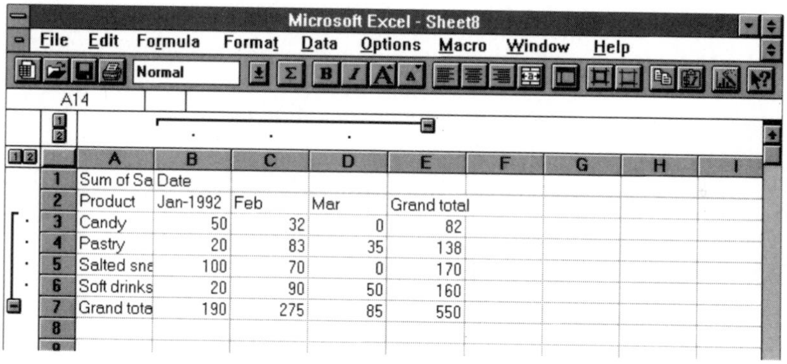

FIGURE 10-19. *The crosstab report of the Junk Food Distributors data.*

Notice that the Crosstab ReportWizard used your choices to put the row and column descriptions in the proper places. It also correctly added 1992 to the January column description.

Recalculating a Crosstab Table

The crosstab table you just created contains numeric values from the database. If you change the database, you can also recalculate the report. Follow these steps:

1. Move to the worksheet containing the transactions and change the *15* in cell C3 to *25*.

2. Move back to the worksheet containing the crosstab report.

3. Choose the Crosstab command from the Data menu.

4. Click the Recalculate Current Crosstab button.

The crosstab report quickly reflects the change to candy sales in the database.

Obviously, the more you learn about database concepts, the more you will get out of the Crosstab ReportWizard. In particular, understanding tables and the different ways you can choose to organize their contents is key to getting the information in the proper form. Practice visualizing the variety of ways in which you can "slice" your database, and you'll find that Excel can function much like a relational database program.

CONCLUSION

If there's a theme to this chapter, it's *value added*. Here, you learned to use Excel's screen and toolbar options to customize and streamline your run-of-the-mill spreadsheet work. You also saw that outlining, views, and reports help summarize and preserve the value of your handiwork for use by others. Finally, you observed how the Scenario Manager can transform Excel into an experimental laboratory of sorts in which you can test various assumptions, and you learned about the ease with which the Crosstab ReportWizard can tabulate, arrange, and summarize database data.

In many ways this chapter is the book's capstone. But you still haven't seen all that Excel has to offer. Limitations of both space and scope preclude covering the Solver, the What-If Manager, the Analysis Tools add-in, the Slide Show add-in, and many other power features. If you want to sample the best that Microsoft Excel has to offer, keep striving to learn more.

In the next and final chapter, you'll learn how to record and run macros to automate Excel tasks.

Chapter 11

Creating Macros

Now that you're used to Microsoft Excel, you're probably starting to depend on it in your daily work. You might have noticed that you're using certain commands over and over again, and you might also be spending a great deal of time entering and formatting data. That's where *macros* come in: They can save time and reduce errors by automating routine worksheet tasks. In this chapter, you'll learn how to record and run simple macros.

RECORDING AND RUNNING MACROS

Microsoft Excel offers an easy way to get started with macros. By using the *macro recorder*, you can create a macro simply by typing and carrying out commands. After you finish recording, you can run, or "play back," the macro and have it perform the recorded actions.

Turning On the Macro Recorder

Let's start work with the macro recorder by recording a very simple formatting macro. Follow the steps outlined below.

1. Open a new, blank worksheet and maximize the window. Cell A1 should be selected.

2. Choose the Record command from the Macro menu. You see the dialog box shown on the next page.

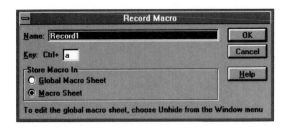

3. The Name text box is where you replace the default name *Record1* with a name that will later remind you of what the macro does. The macro you're about to record will apply a pattern to the current selection in the worksheet, so for this example, type the name *Pattern*.

4. The Key text box is where you specify a shortcut key that you can use later (in conjunction with the Ctrl key) to run the macro. In this case, type a lowercase *p* for *Pattern*. It's simple and is probably the easiest key to remember.

 Excel recognizes capitalization in macro shortcut keys, so even though you assigned p *to this macro, you can still use* P *for another macro.*

5. In the Store Macro In area of the dialog box, you can choose to store the macro in the Global macro sheet (which will be explained shortly) or you can accept the default, Macro Sheet. Click OK, or press Enter, to accept the default and turn on the macro recorder.

When the dialog box disappears, things seem to be back to normal. Behind the scenes, however, Excel has opened a macro sheet—an Excel document that resembles a worksheet but is used only for storing macros.

Recording Macros

From the moment you click OK or press Enter to carry out the Record command, Microsoft Excel translates the commands you choose into its own *macro language*, and it records the commands in the macro sheet. The *Recording* message in the status bar at the bottom of your screen alerts you to the fact that your keystrokes and mouse actions are being recorded. As Excel records your actions, it also carries them out in the worksheet.

280

To record the commands for the *Pattern* macro, follow these steps:

1. Choose the Patterns command from the Format menu. The Patterns dialog box appears.

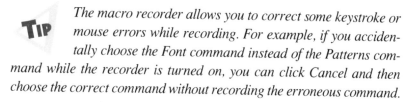

The macro recorder allows you to correct some keystroke or mouse errors while recording. For example, if you accidentally choose the Font command instead of the Patterns command while the recorder is turned on, you can click Cancel and then choose the correct command without recording the erroneous command.

2. Display the Pattern drop-down list shown below by clicking the arrow to the right of the box. (Don't worry if your screen doesn't show all the patterns you see here.)

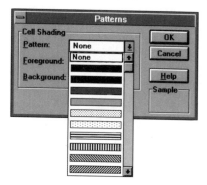

3. Counting the solid dark bar as the first pattern, select the fourth pattern from the top.

4. Display the Foreground drop-down list and select yellow as the foreground color. (If you do not have a color monitor, choose the sixth color from the top.)

5. Click OK, or press Enter, to carry out the Patterns command.

6. Choose the Stop Recorder command on the Macro menu to turn off the macro recorder. (When you started the macro recorder, Excel changed the Record command to Stop Recorder.)

Your worksheet now looks like the one in Figure 11-1 on the next page. Excel has applied the new pattern to cell A1. On a color monitor, cell A1 is pale yellow. On a monochrome monitor, it is shaded.

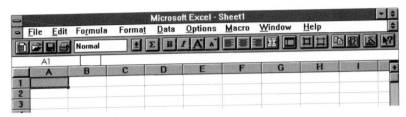

FIGURE 11-1. *The worksheet after the* Pattern *macro is created.*

Running Macros

To use the *Pattern* macro in another location in your worksheet, follow the steps below:

1. Select the range C3:F6.

2. Choose the Run command from the Macro menu. The following dialog box appears:

3. The Run list box displays the names of all the macros in the currently open macro sheets. Select the *Pattern* macro.

4. Click OK or press Enter; click outside the selected range.

Your worksheet now looks like the one in Figure 11-2.

FIGURE 11-2. *The worksheet after the* Pattern *macro is run with the range C3:F6 selected.*

282

Now run the *Pattern* macro again, a different way.

1. Select the range B2:B8.

2. Press Ctrl-p, the shortcut key combination you assigned when you recorded the macro.

Microsoft Excel applies the pattern and color to the selected range.

Using the Macro and Stop Recording Toolbars

The Macro toolbar and the Stop Recording toolbar offer a faster way to record and run macros. Follow these steps:

1. Point to any location on the Standard toolbar and click the right mouse button.

2. Click Macro on the shortcut menu that appears. Excel displays the Macro toolbar shown below.

3. Point to any location on the Macro toolbar and click the right mouse button.

4. Click the Toolbars command on the shortcut menu that appears. Now, Excel displays a Toolbars dialog box.

5. Double-click *Stop Recording* in the Show Toolbars list box. The Stop Recording toolbar shown below appears on the screen.

6. Drag both the Macro and Stop Recording toolbars up to the toolbar dock, below the Standard toolbar.

Creating a Macro that Enters Column Headings

Creating the *Pattern* macro was a simple way to practice some basic macro techniques, but now let's try something that may be more useful in your day-to-day work.

Suppose you work in the accounting department of a chain of retail stores. You have to prepare schedules that summarize financial results by month, and you want to automate the process of entering the month names at the top of the columns. Follow the steps below.

1. Open a new, blank worksheet.

2. Select cell B1, and enter *1/1/93*.

3. Click the Record Macro tool shown below. (This tool is the second from the right on the Macro toolbar.)

The Record Macro dialog box appears.

4. Type *Topdates* in the Name text box.

5. Type lowercase *d* (for *date*) in the Key text box.

6. Click OK, or press Enter.

Now you're ready to record the macro. Follow these steps:

1. Select the range B1:M1.

2. Choose the Series command from the Data menu.

3. Double-click the Month option in the Date Unit group.

4. Choose the Number command from the Format menu.

5. Double-click the *mmm-yy* format.

6. Click the Stop Recording tool on the Stop Recording toolbar.

Your worksheet now looks like the one in Figure 11-3.

	A	B	C	D	E	F	G	H	I
1		Jan-93	Feb-93	Mar-93	Apr-93	May-93	Jun-93	Jul-93	Aug-93
2									
3									

FIGURE 11-3. *The worksheet after the* Topdates *macro is created.*

Your *Topdates* macro is set up to affect cells B1:M1 only, so before you test the shortcut key for the macro, you'll have to clear away the existing cell contents.

1. Select the range B1:M1 if it is not already selected.

2. Choose the Clear command from the Edit menu. Select the All option to delete the headings and formats, and click OK or press Enter to carry out the command.

Now use the shortcut key as follows:

1. Select cell B1 and enter *7/92* as the start date for the new series.

2. Run the macro by pressing Ctrl-d.

Your worksheet now looks like the one in Figure 11-4.

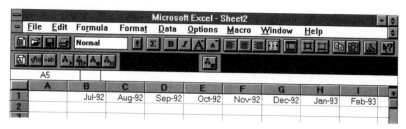

FIGURE 11-4. *The worksheet after the* Topdates *macro is run with the starting date 7/92.*

HOW MACRO SHEETS WORK

To get the most out of Microsoft Excel macros, you need to understand their structure and mechanics, so let's move on to examine the unique qualities of macro sheets.

Macro Sheets vs. Worksheets

Although they have an entirely different function, macro sheets generally resemble worksheets. Macro sheets have the same row-and-column structure as worksheets, and most menu commands operate as they do in worksheets.

But there are differences. Macro-sheet columns are wider than their worksheet counterparts, because the Formulas option in the Display dialog box is selected by default for macro sheets, and this option automatically produces wider columns. If you turn off the Formulas option, the macro-sheet column widths return to normal worksheet dimensions.

Another key difference between macro sheets and worksheets lies in the functions you can use. To view the functions available for use in macros,

1. Choose Macro1 from the Windows menu to display your macro sheet.

2. Now choose the Paste Function command from the Formula menu. A dialog box lists the available functions, just as it does when you choose Paste Function while working with a worksheet. But there's a difference.

3. Scroll to the end of the Function Category list box. Notice that it includes a great many categories, such as Customizing and Macro Control, that are not available in worksheets. Many of the Excel macro functions perform macro operations that have no command equivalents.

4. Press Esc now to remove the Paste Function dialog box from the screen.

If you write your own macros (a topic not covered in this book) you can use the macro functions to pass values from one operation to another and to control the sequence in which operations are carried out.

Microsoft Excel's Macro Language

Now that you've seen how to record and run macros, it's time to take a look at the "language" Excel uses to describe the commands you record.

The macro sheet should be displayed now. To examine the macros you created earlier,

■ Widen column B so that you can see all the text in the column.

Your screen now looks like the one in Figure 11-5.

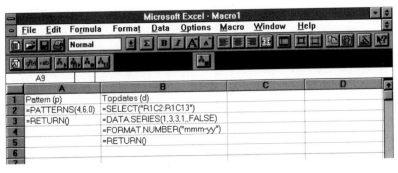

FIGURE 11-5. *The* Pattern *and* Topdates *macros as they appear in the* Macro1 *macro sheet.*

Macro functions are the building blocks of the Microsoft Excel macro language. Look first at your *Pattern* macro. Cell A1 shows the name and shortcut key you assigned to the macro. Below that are representations of the macro commands themselves. The first command you chose after turning on the macro recorder was the Patterns command. This action generated the PATTERNS function in cell A2 of the macro sheet. Notice that the PATTERNS function has three arguments. These arguments correspond to the three list boxes in the Cell Shading area of the Patterns dialog box. In Figure 11-5, the values 4, 6, and 0 indicate the option you chose from each list box when you recorded the macro: pattern 4, foreground color 6, and background color 0.

The PATTERNS function is an example of the way Excel macros represent commands that use dialog boxes. You don't have to worry about which number goes with which dialog box option when you record macros. However, when your recorded macros don't work as they should, you will probably have to learn more about specific macro functions. If you need more details, see the Microsoft Excel documentation.

Now look at the first function in the *Topdates* macro. The argument (R1C2:R1C13) uses what's known as *R1C1* (*R* for row, *C* for column) notation instead of the A1 notation you've seen throughout this book. When you record a macro, Microsoft Excel uses R1C1 notation to specify cell references.

MANAGING MACROS

You can run any macro in any open macro sheet from within any Microsoft Excel document. However, a macro sheet must be open in order for you to run any of its macros. As you add macros to your personal collection, you need to plan ahead so that you can find the macros you want when you need them.

Storing Global Macros

One way to ensure that a macro is always available is to store it as a *global macro*. You do this by selecting the Global Macro Sheet option in the Record Macro dialog box. After you record your macro, Excel saves it in a macro sheet titled *GLOBAL.XLM*, which is itself stored in a special startup directory on your hard disk. Excel always checks this startup directory at the beginning of a session and opens any documents it finds there, so the global macro sheet is automatically opened when you start Excel, and your global macros (the ones you use the most) are always available. Excel hides the global macro sheet by default, but you can unhide it by choosing the Unhide command from the Window menu, and then clicking the filename *GLOBAL.XLM*.

Storing Macros in New Macro Sheets

The first time in an Excel session that you record a macro using the Macro Sheet option, Microsoft Excel opens a new macro sheet and names it Macro1, as it did when you recorded the *Pattern* macro. After you record that first macro in the session, Excel might store subsequent macros in many different locations, depending on what you do after recording the first macro.

As you saw in Figure 11-5, Excel put the second macro you recorded, *Top-dates*, in column B of Macro1. If you were to continue recording, subsequent macros would go into column C, then column D, and so on.

You can, however, work with two or more macro sheets open. In that case, Excel records each new macro in the macro sheet that contains the most recently recorded macro.

Storing Macros in a Predetermined Location

Sometimes you need to override Excel's automatic macro storage system by using a *recorder range*. To specify where you want Microsoft Excel to store a recorded macro, follow these steps:

1. Open the macro sheet you want to use. For this example, click the New Macro Sheet tool (the one at the left edge of the Macro toolbar).

2. Select the first cell of the range where you want to record the macro. For this example, choose a cell such as B5.

3. Choose the Set Recorder command from the Macro menu.

4. Switch to your worksheet and click the Record Macro tool.

5. Name and record a simple macro, such as one that uses the Border command on the Format menu to add a double-underline bottom border to the selected cell.

6. Click the Stop Recording tool.

7. Switch back to the macro sheet.

Excel has recorded the macro in the recorder range you specified.

Table 11-1 summarizes the effects of the Set Recorder command when you use it in conjunction with the Store Macro In options in the Record Macro dialog box.

Store Macro In Option	Recorder Range	Where Macro Will Be Stored
Global Macro Sheet	Set	GLOBAL.XLM
Global Macro Sheet	Not Set	GLOBAL.XLM
Macro Sheet	Set	Recorder range
Macro Sheet	Not Set	If no macro has been recorded in the current Excel session, in a new macro sheet; otherwise, in the macro sheet in which the last previous macro was recorded

TABLE 11-1. *Where Excel macros are stored in different circumstances.*

Editing Macros

If you change your mind about some of the details in a macro after you've recorded it, you don't have to start over. You can simply edit the macro in the macro sheet. Before you look at an editing example,

1. Eliminate your experimental Macro2 sheet by choosing Close from the File menu and clicking No when Excel asks if you want to save the changes.

2. Display the Macro1 sheet.

3. Select column A and choose Delete from the Edit menu to delete the column from the macro sheet. This removes the *Pattern* macro and leaves *Topdates* in the new column A.

4. Finally, name and save the macro sheet by choosing the Save As command from the File menu and giving the file the name *DATES*.

Suppose you now decide that you want all the date headings created by the *Topdates* macro to be centered. You want to insert this formatting command at the end of the macro, but recording the entire macro again would duplicate work you've already done. To add the command without rerecording the entire macro, follow these steps:

1. Select cell A5, which should contain =*RETURN()*.

2. Choose the Insert command from the Edit menu.

3. Select the Shift Cells Down option if it is not already selected and click OK or press Enter.

4. Enter the following function in the new cell A5:

```
=ALIGNMENT(3)
```

The ALIGNMENT function is like the Alignment command on the Format menu, and the value 3 corresponds to the Center option. Your macro sheet now looks like the one in Figure 11-6.

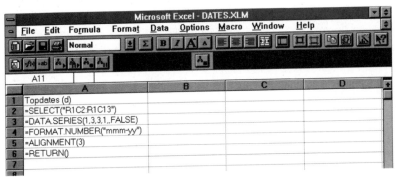

FIGURE 11-6. *The* Topdates *macro with the ALIGNMENT function added.*

To try out your revised macro,

1. Switch to your last worksheet and clear the formulas and formats from the first row.

2. Enter 1/1/93 in cell B1.

3. Run the macro by pressing Ctrl-d.

The result should be a series of centered dates in cells B1:M1. If your macro didn't work, compare it with the one in Figure 11-6 to see if you made any typographical errors.

CONCLUSION

This chapter has introduced you to some macro basics. You've taken some all-important first steps, but for advanced instruction, you should turn to the Microsoft Excel documentation or a book like *Running Microsoft Excel* (Microsoft Press). You should also stay alert for magazine articles on the subject. Remember, there's a lot more power in Excel than you've learned so far. Make the most of it.

Section IV

Appendixes

In this section, you'll find help on installing Microsoft Excel on your computer. The section also includes a useful index to toolbars and tools described elsewhere in the book, and it gives you some helpful hints on migrating from Lotus 1-2-3 to Excel.

Appendix A

Installing Microsoft Excel

This appendix briefly reviews the procedure for installing Microsoft Excel. Before installing Excel, you must first install Microsoft Windows version 3.0 or later. If Windows is not yet installed, consult your Microsoft Windows documentation for details.

When you install Excel, it proposes setting itself up in a directory named *EXCEL* on your primary (or only) hard disk drive. If you want to install on a different drive or in a different directory, it's best to make your choices ahead of time. Follow these steps to install Excel:

1. Start Microsoft Windows.

2. Choose the Run command from the Program Manager's File menu. The following dialog box (or one similar to it if you are using Windows version 3.0) appears:

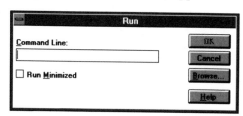

3. If you are installing from drive A, type the following in the Command Line text box:

```
a:setup
```

Naturally, if you are installing from another floppy disk drive, you should substitute the appropriate drive letter.

4. Insert Microsoft Excel Disk 1 in the designated drive, and press Enter.

5. In the dialog box that appears, type your name and (optionally) an organization name, and then press Enter. Confirm (or correct) your entries, and then click Continue or press Enter.

6. The following dialog box appears:

Press Enter to select the default C:\EXCEL directory, or enter a different drive, pathname, or both and click Continue or press Enter.

7. If the setup program detects an earlier version of Excel on the directory, it displays a dialog box that allows you to replace the prior version or enter a new pathname. If the setup program does not find the directory on your hard disk, it asks you to confirm that you want to create the new directory. Choose the desired option.

8. A dialog box now offers you the choice of a Complete, Custom, or Minimum installation.

   (If you are running Windows on a network, a fourth option called Network Installation might appear. Network installation procedures are beyond the scope of this book. See your network administrator or consult the Microsoft Excel documentation for more information on this topic.)

9. If you choose a Complete or a Minimum installation, Setup will immediately begin copying files to your hard disk. If you choose a Custom Installation, however, Setup displays a dialog box like the one on the next page.

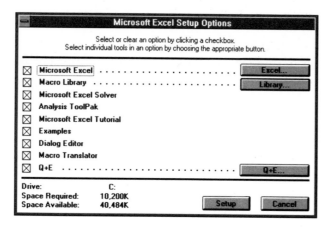

In this dialog box, you can choose which components of the Microsoft Excel program you want to install on your computer. For more information on your options, refer to the Microsoft Excel documentation.

10. After you choose your setup options and click Setup, Excel displays a dialog box asking if you want it to change your AUTOEXEC.BAT file. Click the appropriate button.

11. Excel then asks if you want to turn on its special Lotus 1-2-3 help features. If you are migrating from Lotus 1-2-3 to Excel, click Yes in the initial dialog box, and then click Enable in the second dialog box. See Appendix C, "Making the Transition from Lotus 1-2-3," for more information.

From this point on, the Setup program displays a dialog box that advises you of the progress of the installation. At appropriate points, Setup instructs you to insert specific Excel program disks. When Setup has finished, it displays a message telling you installation is complete. Click OK to close the message box.

You can then double-click the Microsoft Excel 4.0 icon in the Microsoft Excel 4.0 group (created during the installation process) to start Excel. The first time you start Excel, you'll be greeted by a short preview of Excel's new features. You can continue or exit this preview, as you choose.

INSTALLING ADD-IN MACROS

Excel comes with several add-in macros that create additional commands and functions. When the macros are installed, these add-in commands and functions are available from the Excel menus and work as if they were part of the Excel program itself.

Six of the add-in macros—Add-in Manager, Crosstabs, Report Manager, Scenario Manager, Solver, and View Manager—are automatically installed unless you choose to remove them during a Custom installation. A seventh add-in macro—Analysis ToolPak—is installed if you choose the Complete installation or you choose to include it in the Custom installation. The Scenario Manager, Crosstabs, and View Manager macros are described in Chapter 10.

Excel also includes many other add-in macros, which are installed if you use the Complete installation or include them during the Custom installation. See the chapter on customization in Book 2 of the *Microsoft Excel User's Guide* for information on including add-in macros in Excel's standard working set of add-ins.

Appendix B

Toolbar Reference

This appendix lists all the worksheet tools described in this book, along with equivalent menu commands, explanatory comments, and references to earlier chapters. The Chart toolbar, not included here, is described in Chapter 6, "Creating Charts Quickly."

Tool Name	Command Equivalent	Comments	Chapters
STANDARD TOOLBAR			
New Worksheet	File New (Worksheet option)		1
Open File	File Open		1
Save File	File Save		1, 9
Print	File Print	Bypasses Print dialog box	1, 5
Style box	Format Style	Also on the Formatting toolbar	1, 4
AutoSum	[No command equivalent]	Enters a SUM function and arguments	1, 2
Bold	Format Font (Bold font style)	Also on the Formatting toolbar	1, 4

(continued)

297

Tool Name	Command Equivalent	Comments	Chapters
I Italic	Format Font (Italic font style)	Also on the Formatting toolbar	1, 4
Increase Font Size	[No command equivalent]	Increases font size to the next larger size	1, 4
Decrease Font Size	[No command equivalent]	Decreases font size to the next smaller size	1, 4
Left Align	Format Alignment (Left option)	Aligns selected text or object to the left	1, 4
Center Align	Format Alignment (Center option)	Centers selected text or object	1, 4
Right Align	Format Alignment (Right option)	Aligns selected text or object to the right	1, 4
Center Across Columns	Format Alignment (Center Across Selection option)	Centers text horizontally across selected columns	1
AutoFormat	Format Autoformat	Formats tabular worksheet data	1, 4
Outline Border	Format Border (Outline option)	Adds an outline border around selection	1, 4
Bottom Border	Format Border (Bottom option)	Adds a border at the lower edge of each selected cell	1, 4, 9
Copy	Edit Copy		1, 3, 4
Paste Formats	Edit Paste Special (Formats option)		1, 4

(continued)

Tool Name	Command Equivalent	Comments	Chapters
ChartWizard	[No command equivalent]	Starts the ChartWizard	1, 6
Help	Help menu		1

FORMATTING TOOLBAR

MS Sans Serif ↓			
Font Name box	Format Font		4
10 ↓			
Font Size box	Format Font		4
$ Currency Style	Format Style (Currency style)		4
% Percent Style	Format Style (Percent style)		4

UTILITY TOOLBAR

Undo	Edit Undo		1
Zoom In	Window Zoom (increase magnifications)	Click repeatedly to zoom in	10
Zoom Out	Window Zoom (decrease magnifications)	Click repeatedly to zoom out	10
Sort Ascending	Data Sort (Ascending option)		8
Sort Descending	Data Sort (Descending option)		8

(continued)

299

Tool Name	Command Equivalent	Comments	Chapters
Promote	[No command equivalent]	Moves up to the next outline level	10
Demote	[No command equivalent]	Moves down to the next lower outline level	10
Show Outline Symbols	Options Display (Outline Symbols option)		10
Select Visible Cells	Formula Select Special (Visible Cells Only option)		10
Text Box	[No command equivalent]	Also on the Chart toolbar	4, 7
Set Print Area	Options Set Print Area		5
CUSTOM TOOLBAR			
Text Color	[No command equivalent]	Changes text color to the next color in the color palette	10
MACRO TOOLBAR			
Record Macro	Macro Record	Starts the macro recorder	11
New Macro Sheet	File New (Macro Sheet option)		11
STOP RECORDING TOOLBAR			
Stop Recording	Macro Stop Recorder	Stops the macro recorder	11

Appendix C

Making the Transition from Lotus 1-2-3

If you are an experienced Lotus 1-2-3 user, this appendix will help you switch to Microsoft Excel version 4. You'll be pleased to know that you can use all your 1-2-3 data files in Microsoft Excel worksheets. In addition, Excel provides an online cross-reference of commands, as well as numerous other aids to ease the transition from Lotus 1-2-3 to Excel.

This appendix covers only a few of the highlights of the manual titled *Switching to Microsoft Excel from Lotus 1-2-3*, which is included with Excel. This appendix is not by any means a substitute for that excellent manual. It's more of an overview of what's available.

WORKING WITH LOTUS 1-2-3 DATA FILES

Open a Lotus 1-2-3 data file in Microsoft Excel just as you would an Excel file. Choose the Open command from the File menu and select the correct drive and directory. At this point do either of the following:

- Click the down arrow to the right of the List Files Of Type box and select Lotus 1-2-3 Files from the list that appears. Select the file you want from the list that appears.

- Type the full name (including extension) of the Lotus 1-2-3 file you want to import, and click OK or press Enter.

Data, formulas, and macros in 1-2-3 files come into Excel completely and accurately, with very rare exceptions. Excel even brings in WYSIWYG formatting information contained in FMT and FM3 files. If you open a WK3 3-D file, Excel imports it as a workbook file. See the manual for more details.

Saving Lotus 1-2-3 Files in Excel Format

Unless you anticipate needing to export the Lotus 1-2-3 file back into Lotus 1-2-3, you should convert the file to a Microsoft Excel document as follows:

1. Choose the Save As command from the File menu.

2. Type a new filename, if you want, in the File Name box.

3. Click the down arrow to the right of the Save File As Type list box to display a list of file types, as shown in Figure C-1.

4. Select the Normal option.

5. Click OK or press Enter to save the file.

Excel applies its file format and filename extension to the data file. If Excel encounters a problem converting a cell formula, it attaches a note to the cell in the converted worksheet.

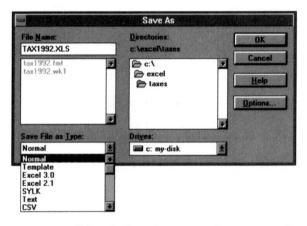

FIGURE C-1. *Using the Save As command to convert a Lotus 1-2-3 data file to a Microsoft Excel document.*

Saving Excel Files in Lotus 1-2-3 Format

If you have to export an Excel-format file back to Lotus 1-2-3, you can save the file in any of the Lotus 1-2-3 formats (*WKS, WK1,* or *WK3*).

1. Choose the Save As command from the File menu.

2. Type a new filename if necessary; specify the drive and directory (again, if necessary).

3. Select the desired format from the Save File As Type list box, and click OK or press Enter.

Because Microsoft Excel has options and features not found in Lotus 1-2-3, some formatting and other attributes are lost when you save a file in Lotus 1-2-3 format. For example, embedded graphics and outlining don't carry over to Lotus 1-2-3 data files.

When the worksheet being converted contains functions not offered by Lotus 1-2-3, Microsoft Excel displays a message identifying the problem cells so that you can correct the problem in Lotus 1-2-3.

LOTUS 1-2-3 COMMAND EQUIVALENTS

When you need to know how to execute a familiar Lotus 1-2-3 command in Microsoft Excel, the answer is always close at hand.

- If you enabled Help for Lotus 1-2-3 when you installed Excel, you need only press the slash (/) key. (See Appendix A, "Installing Microsoft Excel," for more details.)

- If you did not enable Lotus Help, choose Lotus 1-2-3 from the Help menu.

In either case, Excel displays the dialog box shown in Figure C-2.

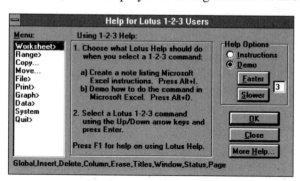

FIGURE C-2. *The Help For Lotus 1-2-3 Users dialog box.*

To use Help For Lotus 1-2-3 Users, do the following:

- Select the appropriate Lotus 1-2-3 menu from the Menu list box, and move through the menus as you would if you were using Lotus 1-2-3. You can press Esc to move back to previous menu levels, just as you can in Lotus 1-2-3.

Instructions on replicating the selected command in Microsoft Excel appear in the text box labeled To Perform Command In Microsoft Excel in the middle of the dialog box. Figure C-3 shows the Help instructions for the Lotus 1-2-3 Range Protect command.

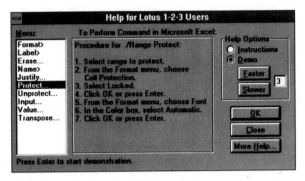

FIGURE C-3. *The Excel Help instructions for the Lotus 1-2-3 Range Protect command.*

You can display the instructions in the worksheet itself by selecting the Instructions option in the Help Options group, and then clicking OK or pressing Enter.

Alternatively, you can ask Excel Help to demonstrate how to carry out the equivalent Excel command.

■ Select the Demo option in the Help Options group, and then press Enter.

Excel will prompt you for the information needed to carry out the command. Once you provide the required information and click OK or press Enter, Excel then demonstrates the steps for performing that operation on your worksheet.

If you want to investigate the equivalent Excel command further before carrying it out, click the More Help button in the Help For Lotus 1-2-3 Users dialog box. Excel then starts its own Help and displays the relevant list of choices or the help text related to the selected entry in the Menu section of the Lotus 1-2-3 Help dialog box.

LOTUS 1-2-3 FUNCTION EQUIVALENTS

To find the Excel equivalent of a specific Lotus 1-2-3 function, do the following:

1. Choose Contents from the Help menu.

2. Select the Switching From Lotus 1-2-3 topic at the end of the Microsoft Excel Help Contents list.

3. Select the Functions topic to display explanatory text followed by a list of Lotus 1-2-3 functions indexed to their closest Microsoft Excel equivalents, as shown in Figure C-4.

4. For additional information about any Microsoft Excel function, click the function name (or select the name with the arrow keys and press Enter).

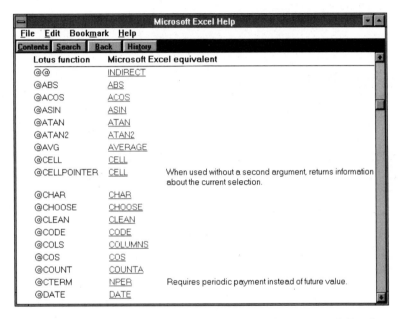

FIGURE C-4. *Lotus 1-2-3 functions and their equivalent Microsoft Excel functions, displayed in an Excel Help window.*

Index

Numbers in italics refer to illustrations.

Special Characters

! (exclamation point), 227
' (quotation mark), 29
(pound sign)
   in cells, 101
   in number formats, 106
$ (dollar sign), 29, 85–87, 106
% (percent sign), 29, 44, 45
( ) (parentheses), 29, 46, 47
* (asterisk) as multiplication operator,
   44, 45
* (asterisk) as wildcard, 211
+ (plus sign), 29, 44, 45, 58
, (comma), 29
– (minus sign), 29, 44, 45, 58
. (period), 29
/ (division operator), 44, 45
; (semicolon), 107
< (less-than operator), 56, 211
<= (less-than-or-equal-to operator), 56,
   212
<> (not-equal-to operator), 56, 212
= (equal sign) in formulas, 44
= (equal-to operator), 56, 211
> (greater-than operator), 56, 211
>= (greater-than-or-equal-to operator),
   56, 212
? (question mark), 211
^ (caret), 44, 45
0 (zero) in number formats, 106

A

absolute cell referencing, 85–87
active cell, 10, 13
"adding machine" mode, 245–46
add-in macros, installing, 296
addition operator (+), 44, 45
addresses
   absolute, 85–87

addresses *continued*
   fixed, 85–87
   mixed, 86–87
   overview, 9, 46–47
   relative, 85–87
Add Scenario dialog box, 269
Add View dialog box, 257
alert messages, 55
Alignment command, 113, 114, 115
Alignment dialog box, 113, 114
Alt-F1 key combination, 154–55
Alt key, 14
AND criteria, 212–13
application Control menu, 6, 20
application window, 6
area charts, 159–60
Area Chart tool, 160
arguments, function, 47, 50
Arrange command, 226, 231, 234
Arrange Windows dialog box, 226, 234
arrow keys. *See* direction keys
arrows, *168, 169,* 175
ASCII files, 36
assigning names, 68–70
asterisk (*)
   as multiplication operator, 44, 45
   as wildcard, 211
attached text in charts, *168, 169*
Attach Text dialog box, 170–71
AutoFormat command, 126
AutoFormat dialog box, 126
AutoFormat tool, 126, 298
automatic recalculation, 90, 91
AutoSum tool, 48, 52, 297
axes, *168, 169,* 172–74, 186
Axis Scale dialog box, 173, 186
axis titles, 170–71

B

Backspace key, 28
bar charts, 158–59

ABOUT THE AUTHOR

Ralph Soucie has been a contributing editor to *PC World* magazine for four years and writes the magazine's monthly "Excel Shortcut" column. He has also contributed heavily to recent bestselling books on Windows and Word for Windows.

Ralph is a partner in CFO Consultants in Tualatin, Oregon. He helps businesses of all sizes to manage the transition to Microsoft Excel and other Windows programs; use Excel to analyze information from large databases; and design management reporting systems for use by multilocation companies.

The manuscript for this book was prepared and submitted to Microsoft Press in electronic form. Text files were processed and formatted using Microsoft Word.

Principal editorial compositor: Debbie Kem
Principal proofreader/copy editor: Kathleen Atkins
Principal typographer: Lisa Iversen
Interior text designer: Kim Eggleston
Principal illustrator: Lisa Sandburg
Cover designer: Lani Lindell
Cover color separator: Color Control

Text composition by Microsoft Press in Times Roman with display type in Kabel Bold, using the Magna composition system and the Linotronic 300 laser imagesetter.

Printed on recycled paper stock.

46

The Books of Choice
for Microsoft® Excel Users

RUNNING MICROSOFT® EXCEL 4, 3rd ed.
The Cobb Group

Once you've mastered the fundamentals of Microsoft Excel, you'll want to delve deeper into this versatile spreadsheet. Look no further than RUNNING MICROSOFT EXCEL 4, 3rd edition. It's packed with step-by-step instructions, superb examples, and dozens of screen illustrations. The easy-to-follow tutorial style will help you quickly learn both the basics and most advanced features of Microsoft Excel, including

- customizing your own toolbars
- using the AutoFormat command to apply built-in formats
- creating charts more easily than ever using the ChartWizard
- using Lotus 1-2-3 commands and macros automatically, with Microsoft Excel's improved support features
- loading macros automatically at the start of every Microsoft Excel session
- using the new Analysis ToolPack to perform distribution analysis and statistical tests

RUNNING MICROSOFT EXCEL 4—complete answers to all your spreadsheet, database, and charting questions.
896 pages, softcover $29.95 ($39.95 Canada)

MICROSOFT® EXCEL MACROS STEP BY STEP
For Windows™ and the Macintosh®
Version 4
Steve Wexler and Julianne Sharer

Whether you're a novice programmer, a power user, a Lotus 1-2-3 convert, or a professional programmer, MICROSOFT EXCEL MACROS STEP BY STEP will show you how to use macros efficiently and effectively. The proven step-by-step method used in this book combines self-paced lessons and disk-based practice files. Each lesson includes clear objectives, step-by-step instructions, and useful tips. Learn how to

- record, write, run, and debug macros
- build custom tools and toolbars
- create and control custom dialog boxes, including dynamic dialog boxes
- control the flow of your program with conditional branching, repeating loops, and subroutine macros

In addition to practice files and useful tools, both disks include a full-featured client-tracking, invoicing, and mailing-list management application. Covers version 4 for Windows and the Macintosh.
**250 pages, softcover
with one 720KB 3.5-inch PC disk and
one 800KB 3.5-inch Macintosh disk
$34.95 ($47.95 Canada)**

Microsoft Press books are available wherever quality computer books are sold. Or call 1-800-MSPRESS for ordering information or placing credit card orders. Please refer to BBK when placing your order. Prices subject to change.*

*In Canada, contact Macmillan Canada, Attn: Microsoft Press Dept., 164 Commander Blvd., Agincourt, Ontario, Canada M1S 3C7, or call (416) 293-8141.
In the U.K., contact Microsoft Press, 27 Wrights Lane, London W8 5TZ.

FIRST WORD PROBLEMS

Time & Money

········· by ·········

Natalie Lacroix-White
Brenda H. Hammond

NEW YORK • TORONTO • LONDON • AUCKLAND • SYDNEY
MEXICO CITY • NEW DELHI • HONG KONG • BUENOS AIRES

SCHOLASTIC
Teaching
Resources

We would like to acknowledge our families and friends,
whose patience and encouragement have sustained us.

For Connor
—NLW

To my mother, Ruth Johnson Hines
—BH

Cover design by James Sarfati
Cover and interior artwork by James Graham Hale and Patricia J. Wynne
Interior design by Sydney Wright

ISBN: 0-439-43465-3
Copyright © 2003 by Natalie Lacroix-White and Brenda H. Hammond

All rights reserved. Published by Scholastic Inc.
Printed in the U.S.A.

3 4 5 6 7 8 9 10   40   09 08 07 06 05

Contents

Introduction

Several years ago we began using riddle-style math word problems to engage our young students in thinking about the mathematical concepts we introduced to them. We collaborated on writing some word problems and experimented in Natalie's classroom. To test the versatility of the problems with different groups of students, Brenda sampled some problems in other classrooms. The word problems were well received and a great success!

If the children in your class are anything like ours, they will love the word problems in this book. They'll be eager to solve new problems, excited about writing their own originals, and disappointed when word problems are not a part of the day's plan. Our students enjoy reading classmates' problems, particularly when word problems are displayed on a classroom wall. Students enjoy writing word problem "books" to share with family and friends. One child even included a word problem in a spontaneous letter she was writing to a pen pal.

As you look through this book, you may think, initially, that some of the math word problems are too difficult for the children you teach. In that case, begin with the easier ones and introduce new concepts as they come up. You may be pleasantly surprised at how well your students develop problem-solving skills.

—*Natalie Lacroix-White*
—*Brenda H. Hammond*